Naga Movement

Longest Surviving Insurgency in Asia

Attention Authors

'We Convert Fighters into Writers'. That has been the motto of Manas Publications, since more than four decades. Our message to the world is that India can win the battle, not only by the bullet but also by the pen. There is no dearth of intellectuals in our country, but their knowledge is confined to them only. No sincere effort has been made by any other publisher to channelise their knowledge in national interest. That is why the talent of a large number of intellectuals, remains latent. An author transforms his knowledge, into a manuscript, and it is our job to spread his/her knowledge by converting it into a beautiful book.

For over four decades, Manas has been motivating the intellectuals by publishing their manuscripts and would like to publish your manuscript too. If you or your colleagues have any manuscript, ready for publication or are working on it, kindly contact us with detailed synopsis and the list of contents. We would transform your work, into a valuable publication. If you wish, we can also suggest you, the suitable subjects for writing books, related to your area of expertise. Manas is known for its publishing quality and commitments. We take utmost care in production and give wide publicity to the book, as well as its author, through our national and international distribution network.

Naga Movement

Longest Surviving Insurgency in Asia

Colonel (Dr) MP Sen

Manas Publications
(We Convert Fighters into Writers)
New Delhi-110002 (INDIA)

MANAS PUBLICATIONS

(We Convert Fighters into Writers)

(Publishers, Distributors, Importers & Exporters)
4402/5-A, Ansari Road (Opp. HDFC Bank)
Darya Ganj, New Delhi-110 002 (India)
Off. 23260783, 23265523, Res. 23842660
Fax: 011-23272766
E-mail: manaspublications@gmail.com
manaspub6@gmail.com
Website: www.manaspublications.in

ISBN 978-81-7049-542-0
₹ 995/-

Designed at Innovative Processors

Printed in India at
R.K. Print Service, Delhi and
Published by Mrs Suman Lata for
Manas Publications, 4402/5-A, Ansari Road (Opp. HDFC Bank),
Darya Ganj, New Delhi-110 002 (INDIA)

Preface

Prelude: THIS BOOK is actually an outcome of a discussion with Dr. AJ Majumdar, my Supervisor, that took place in the Department of International Relations and Conflict Studies, Jadavpur University, Kolkata (India), just prior to my posting to Nagaland in March 2002. An enormous challenge that involved in this endeavour, I could never imagine at that time, that too I had a rare privilege to attend a lecture on the Naga Issues from a battle hardened General of Indian Army in Indian Military Academy in 1986 and subsequent experiences shared by my ex-colleagues who had at least one stint in Nagaland. Thus knew it well that this was one of the most difficult insurgency operations that Indian Army had undertaken ever. The reality struck me as soon as I landed in Dimapur airport with my family. An eerie calm that prevailed in the air, the reception that was organised for us by the reception team (soldiers in civvies – means civil clothes), move to garrison in a non-military car with guns kept inside, *de-facto* spoke volumes. As this was my fourth stint in insurgency ridden area, I could smell the difference in the operational philosophy of the Army deployed in Nagaland and elsewhere.

Means of Information

During my two years stay in Nagaland, I got ample opportunity to interact with the people across the board and that helped me greatly to complete the project. During that period, I got ample opportunity to understand – the Naga people, their culture, root cause of the problem and most importantly what they have been fighting for? I met with people from all the sections viz. the undergrounds, politicians, students, teachers, journalists, scholars, common Nagas, Non-Nagas, Security Forces and the Army that gave me an opportunity to understand the problem in a more holistic manner. In addition, I travelled the entire area which is ridden with ethnic conflicts (viz. states like, Assam, Meghalaya, Mizoram and Manipur) extensively and that was vital to understand the nuances of the *modus operandi* of the undergrounds and the counter-insurgency operations by the security forces. I am fortunate enough to say that I was never suspected as an intelligence operative by the undergrounds which many of the non Nagas had confronted with and some had lost their lives. During my stay only, an officer (Captain) was killed in March, 2003 by the undergrounds due to suspicion. His mutilated body was thrown near the National Highway-39. Reasons were not known for such gruesome killing. I do consider myself to have qualified to some extent to state that the Naga Movement has been through the crucial juncture and can change the course either way depending upon the maturity with which it is handled.

Objectives

This study is aimed to explore the reasons and genesis for perhaps the longest surviving insurgency movement in Asia, i.e. the Ethno-Political Movement of the Nagas for independence. Another objective is to carry out an in-depth analysis capable to answer questions like whether or not, there exists a solution to the problem? What will be the future if an agreement is duly signed between the Government and a particular faction? Will there be peace and how that can be achieved? Finally, I have concluded with recommendations to bring the conflict to an end.

Topics Highlighted

I have examined the dynamics of Ethno-Political Movements in theoretical as well as real perspective in general and for the Nagas in particular. The ethnicity, unique history and culture have a great role in fuelling aspirations of the Nagas to be an independent people and that is why the movement is continuing. The role played by the leadership and actions taken to address the issue (both the undergrounds and mainstream Indian politicians) through successive generations has been dealt in greater details. What is the present status of the movement with respect to the ceasefire followed by **'Framework Agreement'** by NSCN(IM) and role of the present generation leadership of various all other Naga factions, civil society, church and politicians ? What are the implications of Inter factional rivalry (all Naga groups) and its direct impact on the management of the conflict which has delayed the eventual solution of 'peace'?

A Descriptive-analytical Approach

So far as the Research methodology is concerned, the study has been primarily based on descriptive–analytical approach on the subject. Substantial amount of information was gathered from primary sources and scholarly journals on related subjects. These were books, papers, magazines, internet, various archives data, circulation of underground factions and captured documents. The information gathered through theoretical study was corroborated by field research. Many aspects were ascertained and verified through interactions and interviews with the Naga, Non-Naga people, scholars, journalists, politicians, NGOs, central and state government officials and the undergrounds.

Management of the Conflict

Since, resolution of conflict is preceded by management of the conflict, the statesmanship lies in the art of its management by the concerned authorities. Though resolution is the ultimate aim, the greater time is consumed in containment of the conflict, creating conducive situations for negotiations, environment management and midwifery of an acceptable solution. Hence, management of the conflict during this period holds more importance than the resolution itself. In case, the resolution does not meet the genuine aspirations of the people, it will set the ground again on fire and the future generations will get sucked into a bigger conflict and outcome cannot be imagined at this time. Therefore, I have looked into the problem in a holistic manner, through the prism of pragmatism and conciously, made an effort to suggest some formulations for resolution of the conflict. *Since this conflict is entangled in the throes of hurdles, there is greater need for the authorities to tread the thorny path, more cautiously.* The recommendations have been drawn up based on the popular sentiments and the practicality of the state-craft. Now it is up to the concerned authorities and the civil societies to examine the proposals. If the recommended formulations could be one of those potential solutions to resolve the conflict, aim of this book will be more than achieved.

Salient Features of this Book

The book has been divided into number of chapters and sections within the chapters for better assimilation. The **first chapter** briefly refers to the literature on ethnic conflicts focused specially on South Asia. The **second chapter, 'The Naga People: A Backgrounder'**, has been devoted to describe the history of the Nagas with respect to the migration to settlement in the present habitat and their transition to modern era. The root cause of the problem coupled with inept handling at the beginning that drew the Nagas into violence and insurgency has been dealt in the **third chapter** namely **'The Naga Imbroglio'**. The **fourth chapter: 'The Naga National Council: Insurgency and Violence'**, has been dedicated carrying out an indepth analysis with respect to the role played by the Naga National Council (NNC) leadership and failure to address the problem with due care by the political leaders of that time. The actions taken by the authorities and civil society to bring a lasting peace to the Naga Hills in the 1960s and the outcome thereof, have been discussed in the **fifth chapter** namely **'An Era of Peace Initiatives'**. The disastrous fallout of the Shillong

Accord which again brought the Naga Hills under the grip of insurgency and violence, military actions and ceasefire for 19 long years and signing of **'Framework Agreement'** has been discussed in the **sixth chapter**. The seventh chapter, **'The Naga Movement: External Factors and Human Rights'**, is dedicated to study the role of external agencies, foreign actors and practical aspects of human rights along with brief account of human rights violations in this conflict. At last in the eighth chapter, **'Delhi's Dilemma: Compulsion and Complexities'**, the political limitations vis-à-vis demands of insurgent groups have been discussed. Finally, an endeavour has been made to suggest some remedies for peaceful resolution based on the entire study in the **'Conclusion'**.

What's Future View?

As the poor conflict management and resolution leads to catastrophe, it would be prudent to take note of these small little endeavours and learn the lessons from the history, lest we are condemned to repeat the mistakes. Case of Yugoslavia can be projected as the case of poor conflict management and its resolution. The pain of any nationalist Yugoslav can be felt in the concluding remarks of Lampe in his book (**Yugoslavia as History'**, *Cambridge University Press, 1996, p.356*)

> "What ended in Bosnia-Hercegovina in 1992 was the long search for a Yugoslav identity, in the very republic whose ethnic diversity made it a microcosm of what any Yugoslavia had to be, however, the idea behind it was abused. Now, after seventy two years two Yugoslavias created two world wars and their survivors, another war has incinerated even the identity. Perhaps the saddest of the present survivors are those for whom, the ashes still aglow. For they were Yugoslavs, and once, or twice, they had a country."

Colonel (Dr.) M.P. Sen

Acknowledgements

The research was conducted under the auspices of the Department of International Relations and Conflict Studies, Jadavpur University, Kolkata, India. It awarded me Ph.D in the year 2009. I would like convey my sincere gratitude and thanks to Dr. Anindya Jyoti Majumdar, my Supervisor, whose idea, initiative and pains got this project through, from the conception to the final presentation of this Book. My sincere thanks to some of the Naga scholars viz. Dr. Aosenba from Kohima, Dr. Longchar (Principal, Salt Christian College, Dimapur), Jakhugha Sema, Lecturer, Science College, Dimapur, Dr. Khate of Kohima village, Capt (Retd.) Hekiye Sema, senior BJP leader Dimapur for their contribution in terms of collection of material specially from the undergrounds and helping me in understanding the problem in a better manner. I would like to thank Colonel Ved Prakash and his entire library staff, Colonel(s) YPS Wadhwa and Nawab Singh and Shivaji of Military Intelligence, Lt Colonel(s) P Paul and Goswami, PRO, Kohima and Imphal respectively. I am grateful to Lalbabu (my driver) who worked indirectly and even accompanied me in risky forays of interviews with the undergrounds, and my assistant MJ Meitei, who has grown up in the insurgency ridden atmosphere of Manipur, kept on managing my study strewn and littered during his stay with me for five years.

I would like to thank all the staff of Libraries of HQ, Eastern Command, Fort William, Kolkata, Nagaland University, Kohima, MJP Rohilkhand University, Bareilly, Raj Bhawan

(Shillong and Kohima) and Delhi University for their help and cooperation during the course of research and completion of the book.

I would be failing in my duties, if I fail to mention the names of my friends Raju TR (PA) and Anil Kumar who typed the manuscripts numerous times. There are many from whom, I have received help and their names do not figure here, I feel indebted to them as their names could not be included for the limitation of space.

Lastly I would like to thank Geeta, my wife, daughters Ayesha and Monisha, Krishna Joshi, sister-in-law, my brothers and sisters for their unflinching support, without which the book could not have been completed.

Contents

Major Abbreviations

FGN/NFG	Federal Government of Nagas/Nagar Federal Government
NNC	Naga National Council
NPC	Naga Peoples Convention/Peace Council
NSCN	National Socialist Council of Nagaland/Nagalim
(IM/K/U/)	Issac-Muivah/Khaplang/Unification/
(KK/R)	Khole Kitovi/Reformation
NPMHR	Naga Peoples Movement for Human Rights
NMA	Naga Mothers Association
NSCA	Naga Senior Citizens Association
NSF	Naga Students Federation
TMPO	Tuensang Mon Peoples Organisation
NEFA	North East Frontier Agency
RGN	Revolutionary Government of Nagaland
NBCC	Nagaland Baptist Church Council
CNBC	Council of Nagaland Baptist Churches
NVHRG	Naga Vigil Human Rights Group
UNPO	Unrepresented Nations and Peoples Organisation
ULFA	United Liberation Front of Assam
CFMG	Cease Fire Monitoring Group
CFSB	Cease Fire Supervisory Board.
LIC	Low Intensity Conflict
CI Ops	Counter Insurgency Operations

1

Ethno-Political Conflicts: A Theoretical Perspective

Section-I

Defining Ethno-Political Conflicts

Conflict is both natural to human existence and part of the evolution process of any society. The people have their own independent views on all matters which may or may not concern them. These views are rooted in their psyche, level of understanding, education and experiences in life. Since each individual has his own perception, beliefs and value system, thus individual view on any subject may differ from others. When these differences are vocal, intense and at times imposing on others; it leads to a conflict. The human societies are developed as part of evolution and interlinked in some way or the other, at the same time they are divided on the lines of race, culture, colour, religious faiths, economy and even geographical entities. With these divisions, they interact at personal or at group level, and thus, contradictory situations/ views may appear in a natural way. Such views of one group or that of an individual may be imposing over the weaker partner, group or a society or clashing with the interests and thus these, manifest in socio-political or any other dimensions and may lead to a conflict. Since conflict is intrinsic nature to human existence, discourse on the subject appears to be appropriate for a better perspective.

The social scientists and political scholars define conflict as a 'natural and very typical phenomenon in every type of human or beliefs of any society (collectively or individually) relationships, at every level from interpersonal to global, has very significant common characteristics and dynamics and therefore, it makes sense to examine them together and comparatively'.[1] The pattern and behaviour of conflict depends on socio-cultural, ethno-politico-cum-religious or politico-economic structure of the society. Not necessarily the conflicts are merely a clash of conflicting views among individuals but also of social, political or even group interests, that influence the dynamics of conflict. The conflict wherein group interests of any community divided on race, culture, religion, language or even geography are tempered with, it can be subtitled as ethnic conflict, especially when appears between two groups (majority and minority racially, culturally or linguistically) tends to be a long drawn affair. It is not easy to conclude definitively that whether or not the ethnic conflicts are part or a sub set of larger political conflicts along clan, caste, creed, religion or party (political) lines experienced by any developing society.[2]

The ethnicity based conflicts in multi-cultural, multi-racial society, have a tendency to use force to subdue the dissent and majority group; display disdain to accept the views or demands of minority groups if not completely rejecting it *en masse*. As there are arrays of theories trying to explain as to why the conflicts are ethnic in nature and attempts to explain the reasons for ethnic mobilization due to which large number of conflicts (guerilla war/insurgency) were born and raging all over the globe. Similarly, there are also large number of

---

[1] D Yagcioglu, 'A Brief Introduction to Conflict Analysis and Resolution', Institute of Conflict Analysis & Resolution,George Mason University, http://www.geocities.com/ Athens/8945/ sycho.html.

[2] Atul Kohli, 'Can Democracies Accommodate Ethnic Nationalism? Rise and Decline of Self Determination Movements in India', *Journal of Asian Studies*, Vol 56, No.2, May 1997, pp.342-343.

theories for conflict resolution, most of them cannot be templated either to generally define or to understand the nature of any given conflict and suggest a set remedy for conflict resolution.

Ethnicity and Nationalism

The reason for current academic interest in ethnicity based nationalism within India and elsewhere which is a matter of great concern for peace and does not seem to be getting resolved and thus, such phenomena have become impossible to ignore. In early twentieth century, many social scientists held the view that ethnicity based nationalism would decrease in importance and eventually vanish as a result of modernisation, industrialization, globalization of economies and growing individualism. But this never came about; on the contrary, they have grown in numbers around the world. Thus, recourse to the medley of meanings to what is 'ethnicity, ethnic conflict, insurgency and conflict resolution' etc becomes imperative.

The word 'ethnic' or 'ethnicity' has been a very recent phenomenon in terms of usage which is derived from a Greek word called 'ethnikos' meaning thereby a race or large groups of people having common traits and customs or groups 'in an exotic primitive culture'.[3] The term ethnic or ethnicity were defined probably for the first time and became part of the colloquial social sciences dictionary somewhere in early 1960s. Modern day understanding of ethnicity is social traits of an ethnic group; a social group that shares a common and distinctive culture, religion, language, or the like e.g. Representatives of several ethnicities (Arab or Indian etc.) were present. However, Webster's Encyclopedia defines ethnicity in the following manner:

> "People's own sense of cultural identity; a social term that overlaps with such concepts as race, nation, class, origin."

---

[3] Urmila Phadnis, *'Ethnicity and Nation-Building in South-Asia'*, Sage Publications, New Delhi, 1989, p.13.

Social scientist T.H. Erikson opines that the concepts such as 'ethnic group', 'ethnicity' and 'ethnic conflict' all of which belong together with 'nationality' and 'cultural identity',[4] however, others believed 'tribal' communities as synonymous with ethnic groups and used it as a substitute for the minority people. Many scholars specially European scholars put forward their logic that ethnic group encompasses not only small communities but also those with large communities be it from developed and evolved societies or countries (like in Europe) or those who practice their age old traditions and primitive ways of living and called 'backwards' (from third world countries).[5]

One of social scientists namely-**Calvin** says that 'there are many ways to identify ethnic groups in comparative and historical contexts. Ethnic groups have been identified by the **birth place of the individual** or the group, regional area of parental birth or origins and generations in the destination country. Other, more subjective measures include **language usage, religious affiliation, ethnic self identification and ancestry.** Ethnicity is almost always some combination of self identification and a label imposed by others. As a side effect of political mobilization, economic development, social integration and cultural changes; the boundaries defining some ethnic origins have become blurr.... The increasing fluidity of boundaries among ethnic groups and the varying definitions of ethnicity make it more difficult to compare the same group historically and among communities'.[6] Efforts have also been made to explain the phenomena of ethnicity as a crisis in 'cultural identity', by some scholars but **Erkki Servanan** opines that cultural identity is a much wider concept and national identity can be based on ethnic bonds. He wrote:

---

[4] For views of T.H Erikson, *See* Erkki Sevanen, 'The Study of Cultural Identity: Development and Background of a Multi-Disciplinary Field of Research', in Jari Kupiainen et al (ed) *'Cultural Identity in Transition'* Atlantic Publishers, New Delhi, 2004, p.33.

[5] Phadnis, op.cit, pp.13-14.

[6] Calvin Goldscheider, *'Population, Ethnicity and Nation Building'*, West View Press, Colorado, USA,1995, p.3.

> "Cultural identity is a wider phenomenon than ethnic and national identity, which are sub species of it. The concept of ethnicity usually refers to a group or community whose members believe that they descend from the same common origin. This type of belief is not necessarily based on facts, with the consequence that it is often difficult to prove it. For this reason, one could label it as myth. Nevertheless it can provide members of an ethnic community with a firm collective identity, their own ethnic identity. National identity, in turn can be based on ethnic bonds, but this is not always the case".[7]

There are other schools of thoughts wherein they define ethnic group or ethnicity in terms of social denominations. The Objectivists (fully secular and absolutist, they are neither liberal nor conservative nor anywhere in between, rejects mysticism or scepticism) lay special emphasis on the socio-cultural identities such as race, language, descent etc constituting the basic framework of formation of ethnic groups. The Subjectivists (those who talk subjectivism or conceptualized subjectivity, which considers human being as subjects (with feelings and behavioural traits rather than objects) maintain that the self and group feeling, identity distinctiveness and its recognition by others are the reasons of ethnicity. However, the Syncretists (those who does reconciliation or fusion of differing systems of beliefs) feel that there is a linkage between the former view points and their complementarities which facilitates understanding of the process of evolution and growth of an ethnic group, characterised by continuity, adaptation and change. Thus, an ethnic group can be defined 'as a historically formed aggregate of people having a real or imaginary association with a specified territory, a shared cluster of beliefs and values connecting its distinctiveness in relation to similar groups and recognized as such by others'.[8]

It has also been argued that ethnic communities did exist from the time immemorial and certainly not a recent phenomenon, however, there have been changes in the

---

[7] Erkki Sevanen, op.cit, p.35.

[8] Phadnis, op.cit, p.14.

ethnicity and its character with time which is part of the process of evolution. There is ample evidence in existence wherein ethnic identities have shown flexibility and accommodation of new groups coexisting since ages within the same geographical boundaries even when there are marked differences in certain tenets of ethnicity such as language, social customs and even racial differences(like in the case of Nagas). In other words, ethnic group formation involves socio-politico cum cultural osmosis, fusion and fission process as part of the social evolution. Moreover, in a different situation and context ethnic identity can be 'imagined' or even deliberately 'created' to suit the interest of the group/(s). It has also been observed that a group has inclination to change its ethnic identity when there is profit or socio-political gain whether tangible or intangible, immediate or futuristic.[9]

There are some social scientists like **Charles F Keys** who looks at the ethnic identity as similar to a 'gyroscope' which changes form, content and boundaries with time and changed circumstances.[10] The pressure of ethnic groups and identity *per se* are not the sole reason for conflict but it is the politicisation of the society and/or mobilisation of ethnic groups by politically motivated leadership, do create 'ethno-political' conflict. In some cases, identity crisis* gives rise to the conflict but more often than not; it is economy driven rather than any other social denomination specially in the developing countries. Ethnicity is also defined as an aspect of social relationship between two groups who consider themselves as distinct from member of the other groups with whom they have a minimum of regular

---

[9] Benedict Anderson, *'Imagined Countries: Reflection on the Origin and Spiral of Nationalisation'*, Verso, London, 1983, pp.35-36.

[10] Charles F Keys, 'Ethnic Mobilisation in World Politics: The Primordial Perspective', in JF Stack Jr (ed) *'The Primordial Challenge: Ethnicity in the Contemporary World'*, Green Wood Press, 1986, p.4.

* Movement for separate Bangladesh out of Pakistan started due to identity crisis in 1952, initially manifested in mass agitation over the issue of national language Urdu which was imposed over the majority (Bengalis-Hindu and Muslims) by politically superior group of West Pakistani elite. Also case of Assam (India) agitation against ethnic Bengalis falls in the same category of 'identity crisis'

interaction.[11] This also is often conceived as a device or tool and forms the basis for group mobilization through select use of ethnic symbols for socio cultural and politico-economic purpose. In other words, ethnicity appears to be an instrument to resolve the insecurities which are inherent in the process of development or may be the part of the evolution of social system within a defined socio-political structure such as state and more often than not, these are used to satisfy politico-social ambition of an individual (say politician) or even a group. Thus, the dynamics and influence or the interface between the state and the groups become important.

Many multi-racial, multi-cultural states have experienced this tendency of small groups to pursue its goals and interests where they felt threatened or insecure. This insecurity feeling has been found more acute, specially in the newly born independent nation states governed on the principles of democracy as the opportunities never existed earlier before.[12] There are different approaches to explain ethnicity and ethno political conflict which are based on the ethnic feeling (perceived or actual) to the ethnic group in the modern era of globalization and digital economy. **Erkki** observed:

> "In the present day of globalizing economy, nation-states have no effective means of controlling digital flows of capitals, currencies, investments and information, with the result that their ability to regulate economic activities has declined. This in turn, has strengthened trans-national as well as local and regional units at the expense of traditional nation-states, whose officials and members have regarded it as a crisis."[13]

Ethno-Political Conflicts: Why?

Ethno political conflicts are generally an outcome of social dynamics and interplay of politico-economy driven agenda, fuelled by psychological and symbolic factors. The

---

[11] T.H. Erickson, *'Ethnicity and Nationalism: Anthropological Perspective'*, Pluto Press, London, 1993, p.12.

[12] Atul Kohli, op.cit, pp.326-338.

[13] Erkki Sevanen, op.cit, pp 53-54.

Primordialists (those who believe that ethnic groups and nationalities exist because there are traditions of belief and action towards primordial objects such as biological factors and especially territorial location) assume that ethnicity is based on social identities connected to them from beginning which keeps an individual tied to a region, kin, clan, religion, descent and social organizations. Therefore, states, political parties, state machinery, political structure and bureaucracies manifest these pre-existing ethnic cleavages and identities which lead to conflict. 'Instrumentalists' and 'Modernists' assume ethnicity as 'plastic and malleable instrument for other ends, usually those of political elites'.[14] However, the 'Post-Modern' social scientists see the ethnicity as 'cultural artifacts, constructs of cultural engineers or chefs who tailor pre-existing mythologies, symbols and history for their own ends'[15] and such line of thinking exaggerates the roles of elites to mobilize and manipulate the masses to their advantage.

The 'manipulation' of 'pre-existing' ethnic 'factors' which are predominately sectarian in its nature, changing canvas of development and modernization leads it to heightened sense of ethnic consciousness. These factors also have given boost to the secularist politicians who 'mobilise the voters' to gain an advantageous position so that their bargaining power increases manifold specially on ethnic or regional issues. Since the democratic systems are population oriented, political parties with small following, tagged as regional party, who cannot influence the decision making systems or make an impact on the national political system without mobilising the ethnic interests to a much higher degree and then extrapolate the benefits through political or economic concessions, which is seen abundantly in a state run by coalition.

Marxism and Ethnicity

The Marxism, which is more of an extreme philanthropic theory rejects ethnicity or any theory of human endeavour based

[14] AD Smith, *'The Ethnic Revival'*, Cambridge University Press, 1981, p.446.
[15] ibid, pp.446-447.

on belongingness to kinship, religion, culture, race or 'blood and soil' as a basis for organisation of state power. Actually, it opposes the concept of Primordial beliefs and on the other hand it sanctifies equality in power and wealth distribution. It believes that as long as power is distributed unequally outside the sphere of law, it contributes to reproduction of inequality; thus conflict. In addition, the Marxist and Neo-Marxist groups suggest that the ethnic conflict is the outcome of conflicts related to ethnic identity, which is defined as 'false consciousness' of the members of the class based society and its manipulation by political leadership with vested interests. In fact, wherever and whenever the state policy is to subordinate any particular ethnic group(s) then it is bound to culminate into a conflict e.g. Sri Lankan Civil War is a case in point.

In modern era, the political divides of modernity appears to transcend the socialist projects that Marx envisioned. But it is not clear that Marx's analysis of conflict and resolution can easily inform or accommodate protests associated with ethnicity, race and gender etc. There is no doubt that Marx had a deep and sincere interest in eliminating unnecessary human sufferings, emancipation of individuals and societies from both capitalist exploitation and political oppression.[16]

Contributor of Ethnicity

In sum, ethnicity has a latent political desire of the group for an effective participation in the politico-economic process of a country. In fact, it is the politics which is concerned about the authoritative allocation of valued goods or resources.[17] It is basically sharing of the resources or 'relative deprivation' which may or may not be true but the fear of unseen and unknown resource deprivation may lead to a dissent. In case, there exists a persistence of gap between 'value expectations' and 'value capabilities' vis-à-vis a group to another group, in the share of politico-economic power gives

[16] Antonio Robert J.(ed), '*Marx and Modernity: Key Readings and Commentary*', Blackwill Publishing, Malden, MA, USA, 2003, pp.110-125.

[17] David Easton, ***'A System of Primitive Life'***, John Wiley & Son, 1965, p.75.

rise to dissent which is nothing but neo-political conflict. In other words, ethnicity is a mobilization of a group of people based on certain social identities which is looking for political power. In fact, 'the ethnic identity once built up by a community is not necessarily a tangible aspect. Its cognizance is there but the intensity and degree to which it is manifested, maneuvered and utilized is situational'.[18] Finally, we may conclude by saying that the feeling of ethnic or sub-national togetherness still provides a basic framework for state building or at least, for movement seeking to establish their own political unit.

Thus the question arises as to how group-ethnicity manages or mobilizes itself for an effective participation in the socio-political process in a given polity or a system. This takes us to the question of ethnic mobilization. There are mainly four reasons or dimensions which causes ethnic group formation so to have an identity for themselves in pursuit of political ends. These are: (i) urbanization, (ii) increased scales of organization, (iii) the expansion of secondary and tertiary sectors of the economy and (iv) the national organizations. These factors have expanded the appropriation for the ethnic mobilization on a scale hitherto-fore never experienced in any societies.[19]

Besides these dimensions ethnicity possesses objective markers e.g. race, kinship, religion, language, customary mode of livelihood and geographical congruity or regionalization thus, it allows space for political mobilization. In addition, in a transitional society, where demography plays bigger role in political power structure, ethnic mobilization is high, more so in a society where a single ethnic group dominates the rest.[20] **Yagcioglu** strongly articulates psychological theories that are

---

[18] SHM Rizvi and Shivani Roy, *Ethnic Diversities in India* (earlier published as 'In Search of Roots'), BR Publishing Corporation, New Delhi, 2003, p.44.

[19] JF Stack, *'The Primordial Challenge: Ethnicity and Contemporary World'*, Green Wood Press, Londan 1986, p.5.

[20] Ekkart Zimmerman, 'Ethnic Mobilisation and Conflict: A Perennial Theme?', in Gunther Bachler(ed), *'Federalism Against Ethnicity'*, Verlogg Ruggers, Zurich,1997, p.74.

used to explain these conflicts in which culturally minority population is mobilized against the majority. Due to the identity crisis or fear of being swamped by the culture of the majority population, minorities become extremely conscious and sensitive.

Assam and Tibet: Examples of the Present and Future Conflicts

Thus, relations between ethno-cultural minorities in non-homogeneous societies all over the world have almost always been uneasy and often conflictual. 'More so, such conflicts have often been characterised as 'intractable' and 'deep-rooted' due to their psychological dimension which prevailed over the political and economical ones.[21] Conflict in the North Eastern state of Assam (India) is a classic case supporting Yagcioglu's 'Psychological' theory. The conflict basically started due to the fear of cultural extinction of Assamese in their home land by ever increasing population migrating from a neighbouring country, Bangladesh. It appears Tibet may experience similar phenomenon wherein Hans (Chinese mainland people) are made to settle in a big way and local Tibetans are weary of this development as they are being suppressed in socio-politico cum economic spheres of life. Socio-political mobilization of the existing cleavages will lead to a long term conflict wherein multinational forces are likely to get embroiled in intermediate future.

Social Mobilization: Pointer to Future Conflicts

But **Ekkart Zimmermann** has argued contrarily and opines that it is the mobilization of differences that causes ethnic conflicts and not due to cultural identities. Zimmermann articulated that ethnic mobilization encompasses as concentration of resources, such as people, skills, money,

[21] Dimostenis Yagcioglu, 'Psychological Explanations of Conflicts between Ethno cultural Minorities and Majorities', www.geocities.com/Athens/8945/Sycho.html.

belief, system, commitment and time (availability), media access in favour of an ethnic group. Zimmermann bases his argument on the 'Social Mobilization' model of Karl Deutsch. Social mobilization by means of communication, urbansation and ghettoisation or dwelling in different class based clusters lead to assimilation and integration or conflict depending on the phase in the mobilization cycle. Conflict is more likely in these societies which are heterogeneous and undergoing 'mobilization', **Mumbai, Delhi (India)** and **Cape town, Johannesburg** are classic examples of this theory.[22]

Economy Driven Conflicts: In the Making

Another theory on ethnic mobilization is purely based on the economy. 'Widening markets', globalization of business and changing 'Cost Benefit Analysis' (CBA) such as resource rich nations have a propensity to buy the product or services from the world market at cheaper prices than they get the same from local or regional market. IT hubs/Call Centers in all metro cities of India is an example of the same process which may lead to conflict in those countries that are losing out on employment. At least mobilization of public opinion during elections has been seen in USA against outsourcing of jobs even during latest elections of 2016. This fall out is visible after the change in H1B Visa regulations and the local population can be mobilized against the ethnic Indians residing in USA. The same can be seen after Britain's Exit (BREXIT) and no more Europian Union (EU) citizens will be welcomed in UK. Though, there is no open conflict at this moment, but under currents can be felt in respective national parliaments in EU. This is a possible flash point for conflict which is purely economy driven involving two or more nationalities.

Unequal Distribution of Wealth: A Strong Cause

That's not only limited to two or more nations but there is a possibility that within a nation-state of unequal distribution of

---

[22] Ekkart Zimmermann, op.cit, p.74.

wealth (comparatively less poor) may lead to conflict, this factor may not be true in rich nation-states wherein people are affluent (degree may vary). While refering to a situation in Congo, **Emmanuel Walterstein** observed that 'inevitably some region will be richer (less poor) than others and if the ethnic claim to power combines with relative wealth, the case for secession is strong',[23] which appears to be true in case of Sudan and South Sudan which ultimately led to secession.

In the case of ethnic mobilization in India, the scenario is almost the same. Though, there are states who are rich in terms of resources, but in the economic graph they lie on the lowest ebb, hence, local population are being mobilized by the regional parties for political gains in electoral politics. The same could be seen in the form of Naxalite Movement in various forms of **armed struggle** (e.g. mobilization based on local issues in India) or **full blown insurgency**. Thus, political mobilization of ethnicity will have a long term impact in the life of nation-states, more so in case of the developing countries. According to **Zimmerman,** ethnic mobilization leads to ethnic conflict or competition and these are likely to occur under the following circumstances:

(i) If the population undergoing modernisation is heterogeneous.
(ii) If ethnic competition is involved.
(iii) If an ideological apparatus of interpretation has been developed for these 'imagined' communities.
(iv) If the world market tolerates running one's own policy.[24]

But the problem with the above postulations is that one can easily anticipate or predict where ethnic conflict can erupt and thus, provides a lead to its possible manipulation. In this connection **Sydney Tarrow's** framework is quite interesting. His argument is that 'political opportunities widen in the context where there is elite dissent' which in turn leads to

---

[23] For views of Emmanuel Walterstein, See Phadnis, op.cit, p.49.

[24] Zimmermann, op.cit, p.78.

reduction of state repression against heterogeneous groups. 'When the political system opens up, new coalitions are likely to be formed and ethnic entrepreneurs become active'.[25] Based on above assumption **Tarrow** opined that in the post cold war era, possibility of proliferation of small states is very high, which proved to be true when Balkanization of USSR into 15 ethnically/nationality based states and also of erstwhile Yugoslavia took place and UK may be heading towards the same if political dissent is not addressed in time.

Rationale of Mobilization

The mobilization of ethnic groups are for greater participation in political, economic process of the nation and to have a greater say in national decision making in their favour thus can be easily politicised, creating an acute problem for the multi-racial multi-cultural states. It is the sign of increasing ethnic consciousness following the greater contact due to improvement in transportation and communication facilities, involvement of media (local, national and international) and literacy or print capitalism in any heterogeneous society. Post independence, India has practised the concept of 'welfare state' which revolutionized the people's expectation. In a democratic setup like India, collective identities and collective group behaviour has become an effective mechanism for demand articulation and aggregation, therefore, ethnicity is a handy tool to claim for not only 'equality of opportunity' but for 'equality of result'. Moreover, the tendency of the state for controlling its resources leads to intense competition to grab a bigger share which in turn politicizes the numerous cleavages and thus, a stage was prepared for conflict and that these cleavages were/are being exploited by political class in the name local/regional development.[26]

---

[25] For views of Sydney Tarrow, See Zimmerman, p.78.

[26] Atul Kohli, op.cit, p.327.

Section-II

Ethno-Political Conflicts: Low Intensity Conflicts

Ethnicity has proved to be more resilient and powerful force subsuming even communism wherein the ideology of global brotherhood and equality of resources have taken backseat under the pressure of regional identity and resource management. 'The failure of communist regimes to subordinate ethnicity to clan identities is a manifestation of the endurance of ethnicity'.[27] In other words, it can be said that ethnic conflict is a natural outcome of interactions and related dynamics in any heterogeneous and multicultural society but then there would have been innumerable cases of conflict in these societies, which has not happened. Thus, the identity and group formation appears to be quite flexible and notion of exclusion-inclusion i.e. ethnic boundaries is quite malleable. In fact, identification of politically active ethnic entities known as 'ethno political' groups are based on two criteria: (i) people who are subjected to discriminatory treatment because of any reason, be it cultural, ethnic or religious and (ii) when people or ethnic groups are politically mobilized to promote or defend their common interests. Several present-day states in Central, East and Southeast Europe also have their own ethnic and sub-national minorities. Most of these states were already previously multicultural units, but before the 1990's, ethnic and sub-national contrasts usually remained latent mainly for the reason that they were dominated by the powerful socialist parties and backed by the government of the Imperial Soviet Union or the central government of Socialist Federal Republic of Yugoslavia.

During post Cold War Era, 'ethno Political' conflicts have intensified all over the globe and in 1995, there were 268 groups with a total approximate population of one billion; 18

---

[27] Dr. Aosenba Jamir, *'The Naga Resistance Movement: Prospect of Peace and Armed Conflict'*, Regency Publication. New Delhi, 2001, p.12.

percent of world's total populations have intensified 'ethno-political' demands. In South-East, East and South Asia (total of 19 countries) alone, 15 percent of the total population of the region are involved in 'ethno-political' conflicts[28] with disastrous consequences in terms of life and property creating approximately 23 million internationally recognised refugees and 27 million internally displaced. Erikson has calculated that approximately there are 35-37 major armed conflicts in the world today based on sub-national juxtapositions.

The dynamics of ethno-political conflicts have been varied in term of their manifestation. Not only the spectrum of armed conflicts that have manifested is wide all over the world but the tactics adopted by them are different depending on numerous factors e.g. quality of weapon, training, terrain, population support, external help and response of the government. It is a known fact that fighting with government or regular forces by rebels has been the battle of 'wits' vs 'strength'. Hence, more often than not, they adopt the tactics of fighting guerilla war against the 'might of the state'. They may be different in concept and *modus operandi*, but remain within the ambit of conflicts which is shorter than war in its scope and dimension. Since the intensity of these conflicts is lower than an all out war, are defined as Low Intensity Conflicts (LIC) and categorized as Sub Conventional War (SCW). Thus, there is a requirement to understand 'insurgency and art of its management', review some of the aspects of management of the insurgency or Low Intensity Conflict and seek conflict resolution is felt essential at this stage.

Insurgency/Low Intensity Conflicts: An Analysis

Col Yogender Singh while articulating the approach to tackle the insurgency movements in India defines the insurgency as 'an extreme form of civil strife. It is a revolt against perceived or existing disparities in the country and may be fuelled

---

[28] Ted Gur, 'Why Do Minorities Rebel', in Gunther Bachler(ed), *'Federalism Against Ethnicity, Institutional, Legal and Democratic Instrument to Prevent Violent Minority Conflicts'*, Zurich, Verlog Rugger, 1997, p.5.

by outside support. However, its basic causes are always internal and mainly created and sustained by existing politico-administrative environment'.[29]

The so-called **Low Intensity Conflicts** are certainly new phenomenon and involved poor nations but affected the influential and rich states as well. **John F Kennedy,** (then the President of the USA) defined it as a new challenge to the nation-states way back in 1962. He articulated LIC as a new type of war in the following manner:

> "This is another type of war in its intensity, ancient in its origin, war by guerrillas, subversives, insurgents, assassins, war by ambush instead of combat, by infiltration, instead of aggression, seeking victory by eroding and exhausting the enemy, warfare uniquely adopted to what has been strangely called wars of liberation, to undermine the efforts of new and poor countries to maintain the freedom that they have finally achieved. It preys on economic unrest and ethnic conflicts. It requires understanding by those situations where we must counter it, and there are kind of challenges that will appear before us in the next decades if freedom is to be saved. It's a whole new kind of strategy, a new and wholly different kind of military training."[30]

Kennedian vision of future (world of today) appears to be more true and convincing than ever. To counter these threats, application of force is restricted to prevent unwarranted casualties on the general population. But these constraints and dilemma are faced by the nation states and democratically elected governments but on the other hand insurgents may or may not have the same psychological dilemma. Thus, 'politico-military confrontation between established authority and group of people with or without external assistance below the conventional war but above the routine peaceful contests or competitions with a view to achieve their (political or economic)

---

[29] Yogender Singh, 'Conduct of Counter Insurgency Campaign: An Alternative Model' *Combat Journal*, Army War College, MHOW, India, Vol 3, No-2, September 2002, p.70.

[30] *Manual on 'Low Intensity Conflict'* Defence Service Staff College, Wellington, India. Vol 1, Part 1, 1998, p.2.

ends. It is waged by a number of means employing political, economic, social, cultural, psychological, informational and military institutions'.[31]

It has been observed that insurgency is an ongoing low cost option to wage a war by the motivated ethno-political groups against the established governments or the state.

These conflicts have a prolonged life wherein armed forces get embroiled to quell the dissent. **Carl von Clausewitz** in his masterpiece ***Von Kriege*** (On War) has 'elaborated on what he considered as the Trinity of modern conflicts i.e, the state, its people and their armed forces. Modern nations developed the Trinitarian structures of governments, people and their armed forces to fight the external threat of societies with similar organisations.

However, with the present day proliferation of low-intensity conflicts and their poorly defined zones of conduct, the governments and their armed forces are now more often than ever before pitted against their own people. And as the legitimacy of government is being undermined by secessionism, Clausewitz's Trinity now stands severely divided within itself'.[32]

Conflicts in South-East and South Asia

These 'ethno-political' conflicts have shown complex trends and patterns. In South East/South Asia, most of the ethno-political conflicts can be categorized as low intensity conflicts. Observers opine that the phenomenon of low-intensity conflicts occur mostly in the third world, occurring primarily in those nations which are in the process of modernization with a plethora of political, social and economic problems but same is not always true. The conflict in Middle-East Asia that has engulfed Iraq, Syria, Turkey and Yemen etc are the live examples of ethnic/sectarian conflict of so called oil rich

---

[31] Manual on LIC,op.cit. p.2.

[32] M Maroof Raza. *'Low Intensity Conflicts : The New Dimensions to India's Military Commitments'*, Kartikeya Publication, Meerut, India, 1995. p.5.

nations except Yemen. **Sam Sarkesian** defines these conflicts (which manifested in East/South East/South Asia) in the following manner:

> "They tend to be asymmetrical, for the revolutionary and the guerillas the struggle is a total one as compared to the governments and its forces, for whom it is limited; Such conflicts are ambiguous making it hard to differentiate a friend from a foe; They are fought unconventionally using political and psychological means and methods, and low intensity conflicts often develop into protracted war of attrition."[33]

However, **Martin von Creveld's** observation about these conflicts manifestation as, not only do they tend to unfold in the less developed parts of the world, but very rarely do they involve regular armies on both sides. Often it is a question of regulars on one side fighting guerillas, terrorists and even civilians including women and children on the other. And the high technology weapons, which are amassed with such pride by most modern armies, may not guarantee success in such future wars,[34] appears to be true and at places not so trained rag-tag and poorly trained guerrillas have turned the table over the professional armies that are better equipped and trained.

South Asia: Ethnic Turmoil

The South Asia as a region has been in this turmoil since early 1950s because of 'shared, historical, cultural and economic features and which, in foreign affairs, have behaved as inter-related parts'.[35] Among all the members of South Asian nations, one aspect is common that almost all these nations were British colonies for more than a century which were treated as inter-related units for administration. Accordingly they exhibit a degree of inter-relatedness. Moreover, another unique feature

---

[33] For views of Sam Sarkesian, See Raza p.56.

[34] For views of **Martin von Creveld**, 'On Future War', Brasseys, London, 1991, see Raza p.56.

[35] **P.S. Ghosh**, *'Co-operation and Conflict in South-Asia'*, Manohar Publications, New Delhi, 1989, p.7.

in South Asia is that everything in this region is affected by 'Indo-centric' contiguity. Moreover, these countries are in the same geographical region, cultural and political heritage stems from common though variegated, ancient and medieval roots.[36] Unfortunately a major transformation that had taken place during the colonial rule and its indelible impact were left as legacy over the non-elites. A major change under the British colonial rule relates to irreversible changes in peoples' image of their collective selves and conditions of identity such as one is being Muslim or Hindu 'acquired a new unconventional dimensions'.[37] Not only that in the social spheres, under the colonial administration, the region experienced demographic constellation never experienced earlier and introduced 'codification' of traditional social norms. The objective was to 'divide and rule', make ruling easier and to some extent development and progress of the society which, in turn created indigenous elites as a fallout. But during post decolonization period, these factors have left a disquieting trend, moreso, once the state power was transferred to the indigenous elites, disequilibrium along-with dis-location and problem of legitimacy within the new states took place.

The introduction of democratic system of governance conferred on masses opportunity for participation in the political process with powers to rule, elect and reject political parties.

However, the representative government could not fulfill all the aspirations and expectations of the people. Therefore, collective behaviours with respect to ethnicity, caste, religion or a combination of cultural markers became the rallying point for political mobilization seeking legitimate group entitlement.

As a corollary, equal opportunities and access to education, occupation, material resources, income, privileges, title and offices, power, prestige, material goods or quest for group

---

[36] **Istiaq Ahmed**, *'State, Nation and Ethnicity in Contemporary South Asia'*, Pinter, London, 1996, p.15.

[37] **Sudipta Kaviraj**, 'Crisis of the Nation-State in India: *'Political Studies'*, New Delhi, Vol. XLII, 1994, p.117.

equalization became the center of the foci.[38] In such a context, interface between state and society, the role of the central leadership vis-à-vis the state, its perception, policies and strategies in respect of ethnic groups is crucial in analyzing ethnic relationship. Alongwith this, the dynamics of demand-divergence of ethnic groups dictates the nature of the ethnic conflict.

Lastly, external powers also played a dominant role in the entire gamut of ethno-political conflicts wherein the said power have its own geo-political interests to support the splinter groups and mobilize them in order to achieve its geo-political goals in the region. It has been observed that home grown unrests/insurgencies died down when these support channels dried up due to changed geo-political realities.

Management of Ethnic Conflicts: Long Drawn Affair

Since the conflicts have been on the rise with economic growth, socio- politico-economic changes and perceived inequalities, putting additional burden on the exchequer and drain on the meager resources, the conflict management and its final resolution is extremely important. It is said that successful conflict management with apt political negotiation supported by socio-economic and political packages, leads to conflict resolution. In other words, **conflict management** covers all the aspects which are to be undertaken (i) to win over the ethnic groups and (ii) mobilize its opinion in the reverse direction coupled with negotiation, either by choice of ethnic leaders or otherwise forced by armed action of the state, and strike a 'package deal' to de-escalate a conflict. Though, de-escalation can also be effected by use of force and capitulation but these methods have seldom succeeded in the past. 'They do not resolve the conflict, anyway, the conflict remains; it just loses its intensity',[39] but it resurrects as and when it gets an

---

[38] **Stanley Jambiah**, Ethnic Conflict in the World Today, '*American Ethnologist*', Vol 16, No 2, May 1989. p.345.

[39] Dimostenis Yagcioglu, op.cit, p.1.

opportunity. It is easy to resolve a conflict stemming from a clash of economic interests but extremely difficult to deal with a conflict which emanates from a clash of ideologies or values, which are no doubt; really deep-rooted and intractable from the cognitive domain. The success of conflict resolution depends greatly upon the methodology adopted while formulating the strategy of its management.

In fact, no ethno-political conflict could be resolved if the problem has been addressed in politico-economic or politico-military dimension in silos in the management stage. Though, the conflict could be brought under check but complete extinction of the same would remain a dream. **Colonel Yogender** asserts that Indian Government has been dealing with all ethno-political conflicts as a 'Law and Order' problem and concentrated all the efforts towards the 'Management of violence',[40] and thus, has been fighting the menace for decades, although some degree of success in terms of its 'containment' cannot be denied or overruled. This has ensured an eerie peace, over decades but problems remain simmering at sub-cutaneous level, which needs to be addressed.

In fact, conflict resolution is more of addressing the cognitive domain of the individual leaders of the ethnic group wherein the negotiator attempts to allay the fear which is deep seated in the minds of the leaders or in other words it is called 'Perception Management'. It requires a balanced approach, positive attitude and above all, matching chemistry between the negotiators to solve a problem amicably. It may extremely be frustrating, long drawn and time consuming effort but it is worth the pain.

Pakistan: A Classic Case of Identity Crisis

All the ethno-political conflicts in South Asia have been very complex and most of them were aimed at secession. The ethno-political conflicts in Pakistan present a complex pattern as it was created on the principles of two nation theory based on

---

[40] Yogender Singh, op.cit, p.70.

religious denominations. However, even after seven decades, a common Islamic identity has failed to integrate all the ethnic groups (Balochs, Pathans, Pakhtoons distinctly remain separate), although such traces of ethnic incompatibility, notwithstanding subscription to a common religious platform, was detected from the beginning. In the aftermath of the announcement of Urdu as the official language, there was a strong protest from the Bengalis of East Pakistan. Later on, Bangladesh emerged as the fallout of extremely sensitive ethno-political conflict. The socio-economic exploitation of ethnic Bengalis (Muslims and Hindus combined), inequality in sharing political power by the West Pakistani elites (again Muslims) were the reasons for creating a political upsurge and a partition of the state.

Sindhi-Mohajirs Vs Punjabis: Clash for Dominance

The 'Language Riot' of Karachi in 1972, following announcement of Sindhi as second official language in the Sindh province is also an illustration of ethnic incompatibility. Not only that, the then Chief Minister of Sindh province **Mumtaz Ali Bhutto** (first cousin of ZA Bhutto) also demanded preferential job quotas for Sindhis in Sindh province. During the 'Language Riot', the Mohajirs, who are concentrated mostly in Karachi, raised the demand for separation of Karachi from Sindh.[41] Subsequently, large scale refugee influx of Pathans following Soviet invasion in Afghanistan and immigration of Punjabi Muslims significantly has eroded the economic prowess of *Mohajirs**. Nevertheless, the *Mohajirs*, with roughly ten percent of the country's total population, control one-third of Pakistan's financial and industrial assets. *Mohajirs* have a stronghold over country's powerful and elite bureaucracy. The dynamics of ethno-political conflicts compelled ethnic Sindhis

---

[41] **Ishtiaq Ahmed**, op.cit, p.194.

* *Mohajir*: Muslims who migrated from present day India to join Pakistan, new nation carved out of India in 1947, also spelled as Muhajir or Mahajir, an Arabic term.

to form 'Sindhi Awami Tehrik' as a counter to the *Mohajirs*, whom the Sindhis identify as the usurper and responsible for their economic and political deprivation. On the other hand, the over representation of Punjabis in all affairs of the state, more so in the ruling army is also an important factor for breeding ethno-political conflict in Pakistan (for instance, the Punjabis are over represented in the state Armed Forces; with a population of roughly 50 percent of Pakistan's population, Punjabis constitute 85 percent of Pakistan's Army) which is a heartburn for all other ethnic groups in Pakistan.

Scenario of Baluchistan

Baluchistan, another province based on ethnic group identity constitutes 44% of Pakistan's total geographical area with merely 7% of total population, but Baluchi separatism has been simmering since the days of independence of India. The roots of Baluchi 'ethno-political' problem are interlinked to the Treaty of Accession in 1947. Their demand ranges from autonomy, confederation, secession to irredentism (demanding restoration of their territory as a separate nation which formerly belonged to them).[42] Not only Baluchis are fighting for autonomy but other ethnic groups such as Baltistanis, Mirpuris are also fighting for their ethnic rights within or out of Pakistan.

Bangladesh: Conflict between Buddhists and Muslims

Bangladesh, though is the outcome of ethno-political conflict between two wings of Pakistani Muslims (linguistically and culturally different), have been facing the conflict between the tribal population of Bangladesh (mostly Buddhists) and the ruling Bengalis (Muslims) in the state, as the government did very little to address the genuine fears of tribals. These tribal population is roughly one percent of the total population of Bangladesh, mostly concentrated in the Chittagong Hill

[42] **Phadnis**, op.cit, pp.174-190, Also Ishtiaq Ahmed, pp.185-186.

Tracts, the tri-junction of India, Bangladesh and Myanmar. They always wanted to be part of India but the Radcliff Award knotted their destiny against their wishes to join erstwhile East Pakistan, later Bangladesh.

The Buddhist Chakmas, since then had been fighting for a just solution against the ever increasing pressure from Muslim population grabbing the land with overt support of the government and the military.[43] The problem had dislocated 1,00,000 people who took refuge in Indian North Eastern states. The conflict was purely based on ethnic mobilization of Muslims against the Chakmas and inadequate compensation to ousted people due to Kaptai Dam in 1956. The large scale influx of the Muslims in the CHT tilted the demographic balance against the Chakmas, moreover, there was no concerted efforts in terms of their development led to ethno political conflict under the leadership of Larma brothers.

The Shanti Bahini or the armed wing of the Parbottya Chattagram Jana Sanghati (PCJSS) with an estimated cadre of 8000 to 10,000 had been waging a war of separation in Bangaldesh till an honourable settlement was brokered by Hasina Government[44] in 1997. However, ousted population (approximately 60,000) due to the Kaptai Dam still remains as refugees in North Eastern States of India.

Many of these people have accepted the reality and settled in India with citizenship but many are still 'stateless' people and the same can be exploited for ethnic mobilization in India in future.

Sri Lanka: Sinhala-Tamil Ethno-Political Conflict

In Sri Lanka, Sinhala Tamil 'ethno-political' conflict had been the bloodiest and most complex due to various factors such as racial, religious diasporas and erosion in the socio-political power structure. The problem with the introduction of

---

[43] **Sanjay Hazarika**, *'Strangers of the Mist'*, Viking, New Delhi 1994, pp.285-290.

[44] **Ishtiaq Ahmed**, op.cit, pp.220-238.

majoritarian principle of representative democracy in the post-independence period made Sinhalese population too powerful and reduced the Tamils as minority partner without any say in the affairs of the country. Thus, in post-independence era institution of preferential quotas for Sinhalese in educational, professional and other occupations pushed the Tamils in a socio-economic disequilibrium which fuelled ethnic discontent and thus allowed its mobilization. It was apparent with the kind of preferential staffing in the higher state services, in lucrative and white collar profession, the majority Sinhalese are disproportionately represented to the detriment of the Tamils. The centre-state-policy also exacerbated the Sri Lankan Tamils' demand from autonomy to secession.[45]

Following the mass exodus of Sri Lankan Tamil refugees, India intervened in the affairs of Sri Lanka which had revived the bogey of India's hegemony in South Asia. This also alleged that India has been instigating the Tamils on the similar lines as was done prior to creation of Bangladesh from Pakistan. Even after the Accord was signed in 1987 between Indian Prime Minister Rajiv Gandhi and Sri Lankan President JR Jayawardene, the ethnopolitical conflict could not be resolved and Indian Army had to be called off without cessation of hostilities.[46] Thus, an all out guerilla war by Tamil separatist led by the LTTE (Liberation Tigers of Tamil Eelam) continued to disturb the Sri Lankan society at large. For more than two decades, all efforts had failed to bear any fruit. Later Sri Lankan Government had to use all the might under its command to neutralize the top leadership of LTTE and crush the militancy, but it crossed the conventional limits of fighting an insurgency movement for which Sri Lankan Government's conduct has been under scanner of the world community because of serious human rights violation and thus, it falls under the ambit of war crimes.

---

[45] **Phadnis**, pp.190-206; Also Ishtiaq Ahmed, pp.236-269.

[46] https://en.wikipedia.org/wiki/Sri_Lankan_Civil_War

Section–III

Ethno-Political Conflicts in India

It is very difficult to club all the conflicts in a single group, given the divergence of opinion and flexibility of the cultural tenets specially how to basket ethnic groups in India. As a result, the question of what constitute an ethnic group remains as unclear in India as it does in so many multi-ethnic societies where ethnicity itself has been in a state of flux. By employing various socio-cultural denominations, i.e., race, religion, tribe, language, 'imagination' or belief, the societies can be identified for the group affinity. There are thousands of groups in India, at times there is congruence of a set of cultural identities and in another a different set.[47] Sometimes, various groups try to 'create' an ethnic community by aggregating number of tribes e.g. the Nagas in North Eastern India.

It has also been seen, that to earn political mileage some of the ethnic groups have shown flexibility to accommodate some of the tribals in their own fold even if they differ in many aspects. Whatever be the type of conflict and its nature, "India has over half a million conflict induced Internally Displaced Persons (IDPs) – 2,00,000 Adivasis, Bodos, Muslims, Dimasas and Karbis in Assam; 2,62,000 Kashmiri Pandits from J & K, 35,000 Brus, Reangs from Mizoram and about 50,000 displaced persons in Tripura.[48] Out of these many have accepted the changed reality and pursuing their lives so far, with a hope that they will be rehabilitated in their land some day!

Looking at the ethno-political movements as a political process, most of the movements typically follow the shape of an inverse 'U' curve whereby the state and various groups discuss to bargain for their relative power balances in their respective as well as national affairs.[49] In such a context,

---

[47] Phadnis, pp. 196-208.

[48] **Suhas Chakma**, 'The Orphans of Conflict', *Times of India*, November 28, 2005.

[49] **Atul Kohli**, op.cit, p.326.

mobilized ethnic-groups confront the central authorities initially on a high pitch followed by negotiation and then there is lull followed by repression or co-operation of leaders and mutual accommodation is reached. This depends on how the leadership on both the sides made their strategy for negotiation and keep some allowance for accommodating each other's sensitivities. More often than not, the settlement of any ethno-political conflict depends on the negotiators chemistry, political directions of authorities and future ambition of both the sides and a 'will' to resolve the issue.

Kashmir: Dangerous Cocktail of Geo-Political Strategy and Islam

The Kashmiris, residents of only five districts (Muslims) in the valley of Kashmir, have been mobilized by Pakistan in the name of Islamic solidarity for its geo-strategic aim of annexing Jammu and Kashmir state since 1947 and fought four wars wherein Pakistan was cut to size in 1971. This 'ethno-political' movement of the Kashmiri Muslims is a unique case where religion, strategic consideration and external party involvement are making it an intractable issue and it may lead to disastrous consequences as both are nuclear powers and a possible skirmish can not be ruled out because of Pakistan's poor control over it's military and state run terror machinery unleashing death and destruction on India for more than two decades. The Kashmiri's case does not fit into the inverse 'U' curve hypothesis. The movement has escalated since late 1980s and as of now the final settlement is far from resolution despite brisk business of Confidence Building Measures (CBMs) intermittently by both the Governments of India and Pakistan which gets mired by Pakistan state policy on Kashmir and influence of Pakistan Army in its foreign affairs every now and then. It may also be noted that the other parties of conflict e.g. Mujaheedins, controlled and directed by Pakistan and common people of both sides of Line of Control (LoC) have been kept out of negotiations, which causes dissent and at times suspicion about the whole affair. There has been a proxy named Hurriyat

Conference, funded and supported by Pakistan which works as conduit of Pakistani establishment and keeps fuelling dissent through their propaganda and under arm tactics. However, these so called pro-Pakistani Hurriyat leaders are bunch of opportunists and keeps on enjoying Indian largesse as well as terror funding from Pakistan. Though, duality in their conduct and actions are highly deplorable but dichotomy and apparent compulsion of Indian government to keep them in good humour is seldom understood. However the present Indian government has started taking stern action against the terrorists trying to enter into Indian territory and the pro-Pakistani separatist leaders based in India.

Movements in North East India: A Cultural Microcosm

Various political movements have mushroomed in the North Eastern India since independence. Culturally as well as racially, Hills districts of erstwhile Assam (North East India) are different from the rest of India. Internally also it is divided along cultural, racial and other social lines. The canvas is so vast and colourful that no two ethno-political conflicts are same in nature except the reason for insurgency. *Modus operandi* and tactics differ too. The cultural dissimilarities as well as deep rooted sense of deprivation and dissemination (real and attitudinal) have posed a diverse pattern of demand articulation and aggregation.

Incessant waves of migration, which can not be traced correctly to the colonial era, have played no less a role than physical isolation of many tribes in the ethno-political dynamics of the region and can be seen it's manifestation in the nature of 'ethno-political' demands. The migration of population specially neighbouring country East Pakistan or now Bangladesh in modern times has given rise to ethnic dissent in all the North Eastern states as well as other states of India. This is an open secret that majority of Indian cheap labour (manual) have come from Bangladesh and more or less they have settled in India with the help of political patronage and use of corrupt system.

Assamese Movement: Cultural and Identity Crisis

The Assamese movement began as a protest against the domination of these Bengalis (mostly migrated from East Pakistan/Bangladesh) over the socio-economic and cultural canvas of Assam in such a way that Assamese feel reduced in their own homeland.[50] The threat, not only in cultural dimensions but the economic dominance of affluent Bengalis supported by the sheer number of **unlawful immigrant workers** and labourers from Bangladesh, has taken the local Assamese populace by surprise and they fear **socio-cultural extinction.** The reasons for migration of Bengalis to Assam since early 1930's till date is vividly described by **Sanjay Hazarika** in the *'Strangers of the Mist'* and *'Rites to Passage'**. The problem is real and it was initiated about a century ago by partisan politicians. The Assamese initially demanded for the rights of 'sons of the soil', but later the agitation turned into a secessionist movement. Assam's case is perceived as an internal colonialism of Indian heartland to a large extent, not in the ethnic terms *per se* but in the structural characteristics of capitalism in operation in India.[51] For instance, Assam used to produce 60 percent of India's crude oil production but received less than 4 percent in its value in the form of royalties. The case is no different from other mineral rich states like Jharkhand, Chattisgarh and Orissa but physical alienation, distance from centre (New Delhi) and ethno-cultural threat made Assam to mobilize its people whereas other states demanded redrawing of state boundaries within India e.g. Jharkhand, Chattishgarh and Uttaranchal (now Uttarakhand).

Even within Assam, the Bodo movement which began as demand for equitable representation following the creation of State of Nagaland from Assam had gone beyond control.

---

[50] S. Bhatnagar and P. Kumar, *'Regional Political Parties in India'*: Ess Ess, New Delhi, 1988, p.53.

* Sanjay Hazarika, *Strangers of the Mist*, Viking Penguin, New Delhi, 1994, and *Rites to Passage*, Penguin, New Delhi, 2000.

[51] S.K. Das, *'ULFA: A Political Analysis'*, Ajanta, Delhi 1994, p.29.

The Bodos, the northern plains tribe of Assam, demanded autonomy within Assam's political structure and even had been voicing for separation from the Indian Union which later was changed for creation of a separate Bodo state within India. It appeared that this issue had been amicably settled through negotiations by addressing the genuine concerns of the ethnic Bodos, but of late ethnic killings and bomb blasts in Bodo dominated areas specially Kokrajhar township in August 2016 points contrarily to the claim of complete resolution of the conflict.

Gorkhaland Movement: North Bengal

The demand for Gorkhaland under the umbrella organization Gorkha National Liberation Front (GNLF) had taken a disastrous turn of events. The basic reason for the uprising was migration of people from neighbouring states of Bihar, East Bengal, Nepal etc which started in 18th century and continued even after independence of Bangladesh, tilting the demographic balance of the area resulting into heavy pressure on land and other resources. The discontent among the Gorkhas in these areas over the issues of neglect and socio economic deprivation and their consequent demand for autonomy was addressed in time by forming an autonomous administrative body (Darjeeling Gorkha Hill Council - DGHC) in August 1988. However, the extreme elements of GNLF and Gorkha Janamukti Morcha (GJM) along with Kamtapuri Liberation Organization (KLO) and Maoist groups, ethnic mobilization of this area can turn the situation volatile which may need attention of the authorities.

Mizo Insurgency

Insurgency in Mizoram was one of the bloodiest insurgencies in the north east. The ethno-political conflict began just prior to independence wherein initial demand for autonomy became the demand for outright secession. The lack of development by the government and imposition of Assamese as official language created much of the discontent. There was major famine during 1959-61 and failure of the government to address the grievances of the people gave rise to the birth of Mizo National Front (MNF). The political process, greater autonomy and military operations coupled with development compelled the MNF to accept the offer of negotiation and Mizo Accord was signed in June 1986. The Accord ended the hostilities with surrender of undergrounds, statehood to Mizoram and ushered the era of peace.

The Naga Movement

The Naga Movement has been an intractable issue just prior to Independence of India. This is the longest surviving insurgency in entire Asia. The Nagas have been demanding a sovereign state for all the Naga tribes (Greater Nagaland). To meet the demands and allay the fears with respect to their culture and rights to land, statehood within the union of India was granted to the Nagas but the problem could not be solved. The state of present Nagaland was created by carving out Naga inhabited areas of Assam in 1963, but the demand for a free sovereign Nagaland and spirit of the independence has not diminished till date. Armed groups continue to fight for the cause of Naga independence. There was a lull in the activities of the Nagas fighting for independent Nagaland after the Shillong Accord in 1975. The optimism generated in both the parties to the conflict was short lived. Heavily armed separatist groups Nationalist Socialist Council of Nagaland (NSCN) resurfaced again in 1980s. Later, NSCN has also bifurcated into two factions NSCN (Issac-Muivah) group and NSCN (Khaplang) group, who are engaged in bitter clashes amongst themselves as well as with the common enemy, India (as they perceive). Efforts of the Government of India were multipronged viz, military operations suitably clubbed with development and initiation of dialogue has brought the armed conflict to the state of ceasefire in 1997 and now a '**Framework Agreement**' with the IM group. The truce between the Army and both the NSCN (IM) groups has been effective but Khaplang group is up against the Agreement. They have attacked Army in recent past in 2015 and still trying to draw attention as they feel that they have been side-lined as representative of the ethnic Nagas. In addition, there are other groups e.g. NSCN (KK), NSCN(Reformation), NNC and over ground groups are also stakeholders whose opinion will be important for ensuring durable peace and final settlement of the conflict.

Political Mobilization of Ethnicity in Nagaland

So far as the Naga movement is concerned, it has emerged as a classical ethnopolitical conflict in which political mobilization of ethnicity has taken place. This conflict falls within well defined parameters of Primordialist Theory, wherein social denominations such as race, region, kin, clan, descent etc keeps an individual or a society tied to its social identity for which they are fighting. The pre-existing ethnic cleavages and isolated existence from pre historic times are some of the factors for the conflict. The Naga insurgency *per se* has not remained limited to fight against the central authorities of India or the non Nagas but also opponents within the Naga society. The conflict has remained unsolved till date as the demand of the outfits could not be met which could satisfy their ethnic aspirations. The conflict resolution of longest surviving insurgency movement in Asia would depend upon the willingness of both the parties and other stakeholders', political acumen to address the issues with greater sensitivity, so that honourable and lasting solution is arrived at. The sooner it is resolved, better will be the future of the society.

2

The Naga People: A Backgrounder

Ethno-Political Conflicts in India

Most of the insurgency movements in India can generally be classified as ethno-political conflicts based on deep-rooted sub-nationalistic feelings. There are large number of tribes with (i) unique lifestyle (ii) culture (iii) language, social governance, (iv) customs and (v) traditions which are of great importance to their lives, simultaneously strong apathy for others, specially people from other tribes or races. This has been one of the motivating factor for fighting for separate homeland, however feasibility, sustainability as an independent nation in today's world requires serious introspection. Thus, all insurgency movements in North Eastern India, specially Naga insurgency can be considered as emanated from strong race consciousness and independent living as isolated groups since centuries. Before we set out to study and analyse the reasons of genesis of the insurgency in detail, it is imperative that we should have an overview of the Nagas as a people (i) who the Nagas are? (ii) Does culture and ethnicity have any linkage with the insurgency movement? (iii) Is there any other factor which could be attributed to this longest surviving insurgency? With this backdrop, we shall make an endeavour to study the Nagas as a tribe from the pre-historic days to the modern era and try to find the intrinsic link between ethnicity and the movement.

Section-I

The Nagas : A Historical Perspective

The **'Nagas'**, a group of tribes of Indo-Mongoloid origin, very proud and fiercely race-conscious people among many tribes that inhabit in the enormous tracts between the two main watersheds in South Asia i.e. (i) Irrawady and (ii) Brahmaputra. The **'Nagas'**, being one of the distinct communities in the Northeast India divided, in many tribes and sub-tribes who are spread in the present state of Nagaland, on the ridge lines of Manipur, North Cachhar, the Mikir Hills, Lakhimpur, Sibsagar and Nowgaon districts of Assam, Tirap and Changlang districts of Arunachal Pradesh and Somra Tracts and adjacent areas in North Western parts of Myanmar. It is claimed that they remained confined within their limited geographical boundaries from the days unknown to themselves and supposedly were never subjugated by the outside world, at least for couple of centuries which forms the part of recorded history.

It is true that until the British established some form of control over the **Naga Hills** (areas inhabited by the **Nagas**) in early 1900s, almost nothing was known about the **Naga** people to the present world.[52] Broadly, there is an academic consensus that the **Nagas** are 'a conglomeration of a number of distinct tribes and sub tribes belonging to the **Mongoloid** racial group that share a set of physical and cultural traits'.[53] The common cultural traits or characteristics among the **Naga** tribes are approximately 14 in number (as per **W.C. Smith,** a British anthropologist) out of which head-hunting, Morungs (village dormitories for the unmarried male folks), sexual promiscuity and the slash and burn method of cultivation, known as

---

[52] A Mackenzie, *History of the Relations of the Government with the Hill Tribes of the North Eastern Frontier of Bengal'*, Calcutta, 1884, pp.102-105.

[53] Ram Narayan Kumar and Laxmi Murthy, *Four Years after Ceasefire Agreement,* Civil Society Initiatives on the Naga Peace Process, New Delhi, 2002, p.12.

Jhum is very prominent. 'While it is debatable whether these characteristics even actually defined the Naga identity. It is certain that they do not apply in the modern context'.[54] However, in today's context Udayon Mishra's suggestion seems to be more relevant and nearer to the reality wherein he suggests that, 'a deep attachment (among themselves) and rejection of outside domination characterize the modern Naga identity'.[55]

Who Are the Nagas?

There had always been an apparent confusion regarding the question that who are the **'Nagas'** or which all tribes are the **Naga tribes**? The Encyclopedia Britannica attempts to define the Nagas as a conglomeration of 20 main tribes with numerous sub tribes. However, there had been various claims and counter claims regarding the number of tribes that are **Nagas.** As per **Lt Gen S. K. Pillai** (Retd), former Inspector General of Assam Rifles, Nagas are constituted of broadly 35 tribes, but **Prakash Singh,** former Director General of Police of Assam, refer them to be of 14 major tribes.[56] Whereas **B. G. Verghese** believes that the **Nagas** consist of 32 tribes 'five of them in Burma and remainder scattered within Nagaland (16), Manipur (7), Tirap in Arunachal (3) and the North Cachar and Karbi Anglong districts of Assam (1)'.[57] But there had been social intermixing of some of the tribes in the past and thus, new tribal groups have been originated totaling it up to 40 tribes and sub-tribes.

The Nagas: Conglomeration of Tribes

Of late, it has been observed that **Naga** political groups claim

54 Sushil K. Pillay, 'Anatomy of an Insurgency'. *Faultline,* Vol 3, The Institute for Conflict Management, New Delhi, November,1999, pp.40-43.

55 Udayon Mishra, 'The Periphery Strikes Back ', Indian Institute of Advanced Studies Shimla, 2000, pp. 16-17, quoted in Kumar and Murthy, op. cit. p.12.

56 Kumar and Murthy, op.cit, p.13.

57 B.G. Verghsese, *India's Northeast Resurgent*, Konark Publishers, New Delhi, 1996, p.83.

many tribes within the definition of **Naga tribes'** e.g. National Socialist Council of **Nagalim** (Issac - **Muivah**) claims 43 and the **Naga** National Council (NNC) claims that about 84 tribes constitute the **Nagas,** because of their own political ambitions which are intricately related to the land and other resources. Notwithstanding, major groups among the **Nagas** are – **Ao, Angami, Chakhesang** (earlier known as Eastern Angamis and supposedly intermixed group of **Chokri, Kheza** and **Sangtam**), **Konyaks, Khianmungian, Lotha, Mao, Maram, Maring, Sema, Rengma, Chang, Zeliangrong** (another group formed out of **Zemi, Liangmai** and **Rongmei**), **Phom, Dimasa, Yimchunger, Thangal, Tangkhul, Kom, Chiru, Anal, Moyong, Mongsang, Laimgang, Nocte, Tangsa, Wancho, Singpho, Khampti, Hemi, Htngram, Rangpah, Para, Kalyo Kengyu** etc.[58]

These 'Nagas', though known or classified as Indo-Mongoloid stock, speak Tibeto-Burman dialect but differ in terms of language, culture, social practices, political systems and customary laws in such a way that it is difficult to classify them as one single homogeneous social group, despite striking similarities in some of the social practices. They may be genetically same lot but they are as alien to each other as they claim to be different from Indian race (be it Indo-Aryan or Dravidian race). Each tribe has its own language or dialect and even the dialects within the same tribe are impossible to understand. They have to depend upon another language, i.e. Nagamese, which is pidgin of broken Assamese, Hindi and even Manipuri. Not only they differ in language but also in social customs and political administration within their tribal community which is more or less village based, for instance, Konyaks, Sema and Tangkhuls follow the autocratic way of ruling by the village headman, generally known as *'gaonburah'*, whereas Aos have a kind of republican system with councils and Angamis have 'pure democracy' wherein consensus is the norm for arriving at a decision. Thus, the Nagas can be divided socially into two groups for the autocratic and

---

[58] Charles Chasie, *The Naga Imbroglio,* Standard Publishers, Kohima, 1999, p.15.

democratic administration viz. kilted, that pursue democratic norms, known as Tenyimia and non-kilted group that 'follow a combination of tribal and a pseudo-feudal system of sorts, although of the former are more visible and widely practised'.[59] Thus, it remains to be established that how and when these tribes and sub-tribes have been grouped together and defined as a single (social or political) entity. They were identified as one group of people, probably because of lack of knowledge about their language and customs which is due to the impregnable character of the groups. It may also be possible that these people inhabited in the so-called rugged terrain with disdain to intermingle with other groups or people from plains, remained secluded in its primitive communes for centuries together. Thus, outsiders, without having adequate knowledge, grouped them to form a single entity i.e. 'The Naga'.

The Origin of Word "Naga": Mystery Unresolved

The word 'Naga' itself is alien to the people for whom it is used to define. There are couples of school of thoughts that attempt to explain the origin of the Nagas. Suniti Kumar Chatterjee, supported by many other scholars, believes that the 'Nagas' are the descendents of *Kiratas* of the Vedic period. The Nagas were known to the Hindu world as a group of people with yellow skin whose original home was in the lower Himalayan slopes and in the mountains of the East, particularly in Assam and they were spread all over the plains of Bengal upto the sea.[60] Though, many of the scholars do not believe in this theory but it may be true, specially in the light of the last sentence i.e. they were spread upto the coastal lines of Bay of Bengal, otherwise the fascination of Nagas for conch shells and *Kowries* can not be explained for the people who are secluded in the landlocked hilly regions covered with thick Jungles for thousands of years.

---

[59] Charles Chasie, p.16.

[60] Suniti Kumar Chatterjee, 'Kirata-Jana-Kirti : The Indo Mongoloids. Their Contribution to the History and Culture of India'. *The Journal of Royal Asiatic Society of Bengal*, Vol XVI, No. 2 (1950), pp.26-38.

Also the ancient Sanskrit literatures explain that the *Kiratas* were/are the people with golden bright skin with expertise in warlike exercises and lived in hills, in contrast to the so called pre-Aryan race with dark skin. G.P. Singh does not agree with the proposition of Chatterjee's assessment on *Kiratas*. He Said:

> "...All Indo-Mongoloids of north-eastern and other parts of India have been misunderstood by him (Suniti Chatterjee) as *Kiratas*. He has associated the *Kiratas* with Tibeto-Burman family and Sino-Tibetan speaking tribes, who are supposed to have come from north western China and spread in different parts of the Himalayan and Sub-Himalayan regions in the early centuries of the Christian era.... Apart from it, he is the first scholar who correctly used the term *Kiratas* for some of their remnants in the North East India. It is undeniable, that all the tribes discussed in his works are not *Kiratas*, but, however some of them are definitely associated to them..."[61]

Chatterjee's proposition appears to be partly true as in the Mahabharta period, the legendry Arjuna (third brother of the ***Pandavas***) had visited ***Kirata*** areas which were located North and East of ***'Prag Jyotishpur'*** (present day of Assam, India). It is plausible to guess that *Kiratas* are none other than the Nagas and certainly not the Manipuris or other tribes because in **Mahabharta,** kingdom of Manipur is recognized as a separate state, however, the demarcation of boundaries remained unascertained. Thus, it can be said that the abode of the *Kiratas* was the present state of Nagaland and hilly areas of Manipur.

Place of Origin of Nagas: Another Mystery

Another question which arises in this context is that from where these people came or since when did they permanently inhabit in the present land? According to some linguists and anthropologists, the Nagas belong to Tibeto-Burman family which is a sub family of Tibeto-Chinese race. **Aosenba Jamir,** a **Naga** scholar, opines that they had been wanderers for some

---

[61] G.P. Singh, *The Kiratas in Ancient India*, Gian Publishing House, New Delhi, 1990, pp.10-11.

time till they settled in the present habitat. He reasons out that as per the comparative philology 'the **Nagas** were among those who came down through Tibet to the Brahmaputra valley and the valleys of the Chindwin, Irrawady, Salwin, Mekong etc. but were forced out by successive Tibeto-Chinese invaders and driven in to the mountains, where they eventually settled down'.[62] The views of **Suniti Kumar Chatterjee** are further strengthened by the belief of various **Naga** scholars, such as Rev. **V.K. Nuh**. He opines:

> "...that the **Naga** culture was a group of related cultures who, after mastery of the sea, spread out in a similar fashion to Europe at later time. Traces of their culture are almost always at or near the sea coast and when the Naga culture is found further inland it can be linked to an area near the sea coast. The Naga people were both an aquatic and a hydraulic civilization."[63]

Aosenba has also tried to establish the link of **Naga** origin to Malay Archipelago through the latest historical evidences wherein he suggested that 'the Nagas consisted of many races of which most populous was probably the **Malay.** These people are known by experts today as Austronesians or Nuasanto ... meaning people of the Island homeland'.[64] The theory proposed by Suniti Kumar Chatterjee appears to be very near to the truth but fails to satisfy certain other questions related to the origin of the Nagas, as there is no evidence to suggest as to what happened to those *kiratas* and journey to the modern times, whose trace could be found subsequently only during Ahom period i.e. 1228 A.D. and there after. It may be noted that Indian History is silent about the period of post epic war Mahabharta (1000 BCE and beyond)* as to how the ***kirata***

---

[62] For Aosenba's views, see George A. Grierson, *'Linguistic Survey of India'*, Vol I, Part I, Tibeto Burman Family, Calcutta,1842 p.42.

[63] Rev V.K Nuh, *The Naga Chronicle* (ed by Wetshokhrolo Lasuh), Regency Publication, New Delhi, 2002, p.9.

[64] George A. Grierson, op.cit, p.11

* Chandan Priyadarshi, *Ancient India: What is the scientific date of Mahabharata war?*, countered through logic by Sunil Sheoran. https://www.quora.com/ (in the same blog).

civilization progressed and developed through the times till they came in contact of Ahoms in 13th century. It may be possible that they may have migrated from Tibet or Mongolia and settled in the present habitat through Burma in different time segments in the history. As per this theory, they certainly should have settled much before the Mahabharata period in the present land, more than 3000 years.

The theory of migration is acceptable to a great extent but routes of migration has been lost in the haze for there could be no proof or written document living for such a long time, only could be traced with the help of the oral traditions of folklores and folktales. These stories which lived through the times have been 'indispensable to the reconstruction of the historical events of the **Nagas** as much as in the case of other people across the world'.[65] However, some of the **Naga** scholars do subscribe to this school of thought but they relate the history of **Nagas** to be approximately 2000 years old, much lesser than what appears to, if theory of ***Kiratas*** of Mahabharta is taken into account. **Kaka D. Iralu** opines:

> "the **Naga** ancestors who belonged to the **Sino-Mongoloid** race came from South-East and East Asia to the present land of **Nagas.** Their entry points to the present land were through Himalayan region and the Burmese corridors, whether in historical record or oral tradition passed on from one generation to the other through word of mouth ... The fact is that the **Naga** ancestors like many other nations in the world, migrated at some specific time in history (around CE 1) from more populated region of this Asian continent."[66]

Contact with Ahoms and Manipuri Kingdoms

It is believed that Ahoms were the first who came in contact with the **Nagas** in the modern times e.g. 13th century. The

---

65 V.K. Nuh, op.cit, p.14.

66 Kaka D. Iralu, A reply in the context of Naga Political History and Economic Background presented in seminar on 'Constraints to Development in Nagaland', March 14-15, 2002, Kohima, quoted in '*White Paper on Naga Integration*', compiled by Naga Hoho.

traces of the **Naga** history could be found in the write-ups of **Claudius Ptolemy** (2nd century) the Greek philosopher and historian in 150 C.E. where Nagas have been referred to as ***Nagalagoi*** (the realm of the naked), (*Geographic*, Volume VII (II), I-18). The presence of **Naga** people has been established through 7th century to till about 10th century through the Royal Chronicles of Manipuri Kingdom (***Cheithron Kumbaba***).[67] Their presence in the present land has been confirmed in Ahom Royal Chronicle in the 13th century as well. This living document of Ahoms from the earliest times till the end of **Ahom** rule, speaks that **Nagas** were present with them since eternity. The Ahom Royal Chronicle, known as *Ahom Buranji* is required to be interpreted correctly as it talks of the *early man and woman*, probably the period appears to be beginning of their existence in this part of the globe (**Ahoms** migrated from Laos in the early 13th century). In any case, **Ahoms** had passed through **Naga Hills** *en route* to the present habitat in Assam and certainly they would have faced opposition from the **Nagas.** Since it mentions of a **Naga** slave, due to familiarity of the word **Naga,** it appears that **Ahoms** had been socially interacting them in the past.[68]

Though, there are other versions of origin of **Nagas** but neither substantiated by logic nor supported by documentary analysis. Most prevalent theory is that the **Nagas** moved to the present habitat from North Western China between the upper waters of **Yangtse-Kiang** and **Hoang-Ho** rivers. It will be fair to assume that the oral traditions also would have undergone change with the time to such an extent that there is hardly any information of value and thus no worthwhile historical facts can be derived from those. **Visier Sanyu,** a Naga scholar and Visiting Fellow of La Trobe University, Melbourne, Australia; does not agree to the historical accounts that are commonly believed about the **Nagas** specially written by Indian (**Non-Naga**) scholars. He feels that, 'the Indian scholars are more a

---

[67] Naga Hoho, *White Paper on Naga Integration*, pp.3-4.

[68] GC Barua (Ed and Translated). *Ahom Buranji*, Spectrum Publications, Guwahati, Reprinted Edition, 1985, p.24.

case of misinformation or lack of source material rather than a malicious interpretation'.[69] Despite conflicting views, there is no doubt that the **'Nagas'** are living in the tri-junction of India, China and Myanmar since about more than thousand years. While admitting the fact that **Nagas** have moved from Tibet or Western China, certain pertinent questions remained unanswered i.e. how, why, from where and through which route **Nagas** migrated to the Naga Hills?

M. Horam, a renowned Naga Scholar, believes that '**Nagas** must have wandered about before they found their permanent abode, from their myths and legends one gathers that there is a dim relationship with the natives of Borneo in that the two tie a common traditional way of headhunting; with the Philippines and Formosa (Taiwan) through the common system of terrace cultivation; and with the Indonesians, as both use the loin loom for weaving cloth'.[70] This observation may be true but not sound enough for the reason that the tribes of Borneo, Taiwan and Indonesia have only one thing in common in each of the cases. Also if they belonged to the same origin, what happened to the other habits, customs and traditions? What about the route of migration? M. Alemchiba, who himself is an Ao Naga, proposed that the **Nagas** originally moved from Sinkiang province in China. He said:

> "The original stock starting from the centre of dispersion in Sinkiang province first moved Westerly and upon reaching the headwaters of Irrawady and Chindwin rivers, bifurcated into several directions, ultimately leading to Tibet, to Assam, to the hill ranges between Assam and Burma. That branch which came to the hill ranges moved further west and entered Naga Hills. Another wave from South East Islands taking a North-Westerly direction and entered Naga Hills using Burma as a corridor".[71]

---

[69] Visier Sanyu, 'A Reflection on Naga Historical Research', *Naga Journal of Indigenous Affairs*, Dec-May 2002, Vol-I, pp.48-49.

[70] M Horam, '*Naga Polity*', Delhi, 1975, p.28.

[71] M Alemchiba Ao, '*A Brief Historical Account of Nagaland*', Kohima, 1970, p.19.

Another view has been expressed by **Visier Sanyu** who has referred the Burma Census Report of 1911 based on which, he proposes that the **Nagas** came from the region of Western China, between the sources of **Yangtse-Kiang** and **Hoang-Ho** Rivers due to the successive invasion of Tibeto-Burman people.

As per the above propositions, the **Nagas** came from two regions i.e. one from the Sinkiang Province of China and the other one is the South Eastern Islands (not very specific) but may be from Phillipines, Borneo/Brunei or from Indonesian islands. **M. Horam** concluded that these moves were in various waves and from various places of origin. He believes that the Nagas came to the present habitat in four waves and Konyaks probably were the first group which came first. They originated from Tibet and Nepal and entered via Arunachal Pradesh (erstwhile NEFA) as some of these tribes i.e. Noctes and Akas have similarities with the Konyaks and probably can be assumed to belong to the same family. The Second wave came from Indo-China Peninsula consisted of Mon-Khmer group and inhabited in the South of the Naga Hills. The third wave of immigration was probably from the Yunan province of South-China across the valley of Irrawady and that group probably comprised of the tribes like Tais, Shans and Ahoms. During the movement some of these groups established themselves as 'small independent kingdoms in what is now Laos, Northern Thailand, the Shan State of the present Union of Burma, and the upper reaches of the Brahmaputra (Dihang) valley of Assam'.[72] This move of third wave is believed to have taken place sometimes in the first millennium of the Christian era. Allice Taylor proposed that the most recent wave that came to the Hills were the move of Chin-Kuki (Chin tribes of Burma) to the Lushai Hills (Mizoram) which is as late as 1918 and settled in the Churachandpur district of Manipur. Some of

---

[72] *Burma Census Report of 1911*, p.252 (quoted by Visier Sanyu in 'A History of Nagas and Nagaland', Commonwealth Publishers, New Delhi, 1996, p.12).

the Kuki groups moved in the Naga Hills and settled in stray and small splinter groups.[73]

The move in waves as suggested is based on the fact that all the Nagas are more or less different not only in their language but physical features, customs and traditions, but factually they are different people settled in this part of India since long, probably prior to the Mahabharata period. Due to the social osmosis, some of the traditions and culture have been trans-migrated from one group to other group because of intermixing of tribes through social exchanges such as marriages and coexistence in the limited geographical expanse for prolonged period.

Different versions regarding routes of migration: Though, there are few other versions regarding the routes through which movement of the Nagas could have taken place. **Charles Chasie** feels that the Nagas reached to their present location through three eastern routes and all these routes pass through Burma (now Myanmar). This theory gets strengthened from the fact that most of the Nagas believe that 'their spirits would go back east again after death and whenever a person dies; care is taken so that the head lies pointing towards the east. But, where did they come from before reaching Myanmar? Certainly, everything points (to the) north'.[74]

The theory of migration in waves leads to another assumption that the word 'Nagas' *per se,* which today represents one group of people, is probably a mis-nomer. In fact, Nagas are not only a collection of different tribes and sub-tribes of different stock but also belong to different sub linguistic family. Thousands of years of co-existence in the present habitat could not force them to intermingle in such a way that they could form one cohesive social entity, proves the point. However, it is also true that during this intervening period, Nagas would have lost their originality during the

---

[73] For view of Allice Taylor, 'South East Asia', 1972, p.83, see M. Horam, *'Thirty years of Naga Insurgency'*, Cosmo Pub. Delhi, 1988.

[74] Charles Chasie, op.cit. p.18.

process of evolution but they were able to maintain their own separate distinctive tribal identities till date.

So far as the origin of the Nagas is concerned, the scholars depend upon oral sources of information such as folktales, legends, some of the customs and traditions. Various authors have presented their version of stories regarding the single origin for a particular tribe or group of tribes. But they differ in presentation of the story too and methodology of their splitting in various groups. Since the traditions and folklores also would have undergone numerous changes with the time, hence, it is very difficult to arrive at a satisfactory conclusion.

H. M. Bareh has given detailed accounts of **Angami Nagas**. He believes that they belonged to the Kezami village of Khezakenoma. As per the folktale, a couple had three sons and they had a fight for the priority right over a stone slab (still exists till date) for thrashing paddy as it used to multiply many folds in the process in which a spirit lived. Bitter quarrel amongst the sons compelled the couple to set the stone slab on fire and burst it, thereby freeed the spirit. These three warring sons (even four sons story is heard) later became the ancestors of Angami, Sema and Lotha tribes. Incidentally Ashikho-Daili Mao also traces the same story and place of origin for tribes like Chakhesang, Sema, Rengma and Lotha. Similarly, 'the **Ao Nagas'** believe that their first **Naga** came out of stones (Longterok) and later on spread over to the other **Naga** areas'.[75] He asserts whatever be the source, it does not seem to be very convincing because they are based on superstitious and religious beliefs. So far as the **Ao Nagas** are concerned, there are two schools of thoughts regarding two major phratries* found in the tribe, i.e. the Jungli and the Mongsen, both the schools differ sharply.[76] **P. Longchar** asserts that "according to the tradition of the Jungli phratry the **Ao Nagas** originated from the Longterok, the littoral meaning of which is 'six

[75] Ashikho-Daili Mao, *'Nagas: Problems and Politics'*, Ashish Publishing House, Delhi, 1992, p.11.

* *Phratries*: 'Bhratries' in Sanskrit means brethren also in Hindi, Bengali & Assamese.

[76] Purtongzuk Longchar, *'Historical Development of Ao Nagas'*, 2002, p.43.

progenitors' who came out of six stones at a place called the Longterok, that lay on the top of a spur on the right bank of the Dikhu (River) opposite of Mokukchung village in the Ao region."[77]

Visier Sanyu and **Horam** have written about the legends which trace their history from the local god at Mekhroma (Maikhel in Manipur). 'There are also a few Angami villages which trace their origin to the Tangkhul country called Piwhema as their original abode.'[78] Another legend in which some of the clans who point very definitely to the snows of the Himalayas seen far to the North – West as the home of their ancestors; giving support to the belief that some of the tribes have indeed migrated from Tibet or Nepal and entered the NEFA region before moving to the present abode. Thus, it appears that the Nagas cannot be a single lot anthropologically or even genealogically, but the people who inhabited in the land that lies between the two prominent watersheds of South East Asia i.e. Irrawady in the East and Brahmaputra in the West. The information available is scanty, incomplete and till these are corroborated with historical or anthropological findings; mystery would remain shrouded.

Origin of the Word Naga

Many scholars have made serious efforts to find out the origin of the word 'Naga'. Probably it has been given by the outsiders who were even distantly not related to Nagas, as none of the dialects of any of the tribes has a word or syllable similar or even nearer to the phonetic sound of 'Naga'. Most plausible explanation seems to have been derived from Sanskrit ***'Nagna'*** i.e the naked or Hindi ***'Nanga'*** (in both cases 'n' is half silent) became 'Naga' if we go by **Haimendorf's** own account that farther in the hills, young and old alike went about completely naked, for they still lived in the good old times. There the **Konyaks** were still the '**Naked Nagas**'.[79]

---

[77] ibid, p.44.

[78] M Horam, 'Thirty years of Naga Insurgency', op. cit. p.6.

[79] C.F. Haimendort, op.cit, p.31. AD Mao, op cit, p.31.

As per **B.B. Ghosh**, basis of Sanskrit or Hindustani for the origin of word 'Naga' can be ruled out because the people from heartland of India did not come in contact for a prolonged period. Contrary to the above, there is another school of thought, which claims that the name has been in use since the Mahabharta period. As Arjuna was married to Ulupi, daughter of the legendry *Nagaraja* (king of the Nagas) and the residence is generally identified with Hanima in the South West of Nagaland. Thus, the subjects of Nagaraja are called Nagas. Similar opinion has been expressed by Kiran Shankar Maitra who says that the word 'Naga' is derived from 'Nag' (*Pannag*)'.[80] **Maitra** has cited the same incident of the Mahabharata regarding marriage of Arjuna with Ulupi, who (Arjuna) also married to Chitrangada, princess of Manipur; both were from different races and Kingdoms. He further writes:

> "Both Nagaland and Manipur are neighbouring states and it is to be noted that while the Princess of one land had introduced herself as the 'daughter of Snake-king', the other was an emancipated girl, well trained in horse-riding, warfare etc."[81]

There are other stories regarding the origins such as it has been derived from the name of '**Naga Sadhus**' of India, who remain naked or even from the Assamese word '***Noga***'. As the Assamese pronounce Bengali 'A' as 'O' thus, it may be possible that '*Noga*' or '**Naga**' name has been given by the Assamese people who came in contact with the Nagas in the thirteenth century during Ahom period. 'Though this view cannot explain all the pros and cons and extension of the generic term to all the people to whom it is applied now, it satisfies most of the requirements as to the origin of the word.... It has to be noted that originally the word '***Noga***' or for that sake '**Naga**' used to be applied to the naked people of the hills. ... Gradually the name was applied to a greater number of

[80] Kiran Shankar Maitra, '*The Nagas Rebel and Insurgency in the North East*', Vikas Publishing House, New Delhi, 1998, p.6.

[81] K S Maitra,op.cit, p.6.

people and ultimately it has become a generic term for many tribes'.[82]

But majority of **Naga** scholars do not accept the view which has any relation to the Indian mythology. It appears that the view subscribed by the Naga scholars who tend to find the link of home culture in the far off places such as Malaya or even farther, is a reflection to ward off the relationship with the Hindu mythological stories. While trying to establish their link with far off places they fail to realize that such a generic name could not have been imported by the people while they traversed through the ages and forgotten forever. Today none of the tribes do have any word which is similar to the word 'Naga' or a phonetic sound in their diverse canvas of languages of all the tribes. Thus, theory behind the linkage/import of the name does not appeal to many, rather what appears to be logical is that it has come from *'Noga'* or *'Nagna'* in its present state.

The Nagas: Descendents of the Kiratas?

Certainly, the 'Nagas' had been in the present habitat since the Mahabharta period and have been mentioned as the *'Kiratas'*. May be all the tribes were referred as *Kiratas* which also included Nagas. Some of the scholars felt that theory of Suniti Kumar Chatterjee is merely a conjecture. But if the following *shloka* from the Mahabharata is analysed in its correct perspective, the existence of the Nagas in the present habitat can be correlated alongwith Chins who are presently habitating in upper reaches of Myanmar:[83]

स किरातैश्व चीनैश्व वृतः प्राग्ज्योतिषो भवत!
अन्यैश्व बहुभियोध्यै सागरानुपवसिभिः!!

(षड् विंश्योध्यायः, दिग्विजयपर्व, प्रथम खण्ड, महाभारत, श्रीमंमहर्षि वेद व्यास प्रगीत)

---

[82] B.B. Ghosh, op.cit, pp.18-19.

[83] Shri Ved Vyas, *'The Mahabharata'*, First Part, 26th Chapter, Digvijay Parva, 9th Shloka, Geeta Press, Gorakhpur, p.743.

Which means the king of *Prag Jyotishpur* (Assam) was surrounded by many brave warriors from *Kiratas*, Chins and various Islands in support, when the latter was challenged by Arjuna. If the King of Assam had **Kiratas** and Chins as soldiers in his army, obviously the people referred as **Kiratas** are none other than Nagas as Manipur has been clearly cited as another kingdom in the same epic. Huen Tsang, the famous Chinese pilgrim who visited India between 629 AD-645 AD, visited Assam around 645 AD, wrote 'The East of this Country is bounded by a line of hills so that there is no great threat to the Kingdom. The frontiers are contagious to the barbarian of the South West China.'[84] Based on the foregoing, it can be assumed that most probably the **Kiratas** were none but the **Nagas.** Another saying goes that the kingdom of *Dimasas* was at Dimapur where the ruins are still present. The locals of Dimapur believe that the name of Dimapur came from its original 'Hidimbapur' after the name of 'Hidimba', wife of the legendary *Pandavas*, 'Bhim'*. The claim can be challenged by the fact that there is a Hidimba Temple in Manali (Himachal Pradesh, India) too and the locals claim the same genuinely. It appears that during the epic period of Mahabharata (3000 BE) the bordering area of Nagaland (presently Disputed Area Belt (DAB) were occupied by the **Nagas** (Katcha Nagas) who identify themselves as *Dimasas*. Thus trace of the **Naga** civilization can be found in the area from that time.

Conflict with the Ahoms

It is believed that the Ahoms were the first to come into the contact of **Nagas,** but it was also the Meteis of Manipur who would have come in contact with them. These are recorded in the Royal Chronicles of Manipuri kings in *'Cheithron*

[84] V.K. Nuh and Wetshokhrolo Lasuh, *'Naga Chronicle'*, Regency Publication, New Delhi, 2002, p.15, *'White Paper on Naga Integration'*, Naga Hoho, 2002, p.3.

* Bhim was the second brother of the Pandavas of the Mahabharta epic and he had a son from Hidimba named as Ghatautkatch.

Kumbaba'.[85] As well as *Ahom Buranji*, Royal Chronicles of Ahom Kings. These chronicles do affirm that **Naga** slaves were present with the Ahoms but from which period, it could not be ascertained. Since the Manipuri Kings were ambitious, they would have tried to bring the **Nagas** under their control and the **Nagas** must have resisted and ultimately were defeated. A.D. Mao writes:

> "As a consequence the Ahoms compelled these subdued Naga tribes to pay tributes in the form of Mithuns (a kind of Buffalo) and other commodities as a token of their allegiance to the Ahom Kings. In return the Ahoms granted the Nagas exemption from rent over the lands and the areas meant for fishing purposes."[86]

Though **Nagas** were made subservient to the Ahoms, but they were free in running their own internal affairs, which the Ahom Kings never probably interfered with, which appears to be true in sharp contrast to the acclaimed invincibility of **Nagas** by the **Naga** scholars.

Also there is no evidence to suggest that all the Naga tribes, specially the people in deep jungles, were subdued by the Ahoms but the Nagas in bordering areas of plains of Assam were brought under control of Ahom kings by the end of 17th century. Subsequently, they would have also challenged the authority of the Ahom kings, when later became weak. Probably, by the end of 18th century the Angamis were organized well to provide the security to other groups (under the control of Ahoms) and thus they began raids upon the plains of Assam, a reverse process of seeking power. In modern times, Angamis started contacting Kachhari Dimasas in Dimapur, the capital of Dimasas. The clash was inevitable. 'The relationship soon took on the nature of intermittent periods of war and peace, and both were influenced by each other's military tactics and other affairs as well'.[87] It is believed that love-hate relationship

---

[85] E.N. Ram Mohan, 'The Naga Insurgency' (Pt-I) *USI Journal*, Jul-Sep 2003, p.390.

[86] A.D Mao, op.cit, p.14.

[87] Visier Sanyu, op.cit, p.33.

between the Ahoms and Nagas continued for couple of centuries and even inter-tribe marriages were also solemnised.

'Traditions of the Konyak Nagas tell of an Ahom king who, fleeing from his enemies into the hills, found refuge in the village of Tanhai. He married the daughter of the Chief, and even today the people of Tanhai point to the stone which served the exiled king as a seat'.[88] Kumar and Murthy also agree to this kind of arrangement. The Nagas received some revenue free lands on the borders on the understanding that they would deposit their spears with the local Ahom official called Naga-*Katakis*. These Naga tribes also offered some hill products as their tribute. A special office of *Khamjangia Gohain* was even set up to manage Ahom-Naga relations remained peaceful. By the end of 18th century, Ahoms lapsed into decadence. They settled down in the peasantry to have a more peaceful life in the fertile valley of Brahmaputra. But the Nagas often targeted the plains people from the nearby mountains. 'The taking of a head from the villages of the plains became a convenient habit, and one that was hard to extirpate even after the country was taken over by the British'.[89]

Section–II

Nagas Journey into Modern Era

By the end of 18th century, the British had annexed India from Bengal to Kashmir. The territorial expansion and exploitation of resources of India was at its peak, so to safeguard the Indian peninsula and keep mercantile interest alive the British had to secure India from all sides. Moreover, Burma was a lucrative market for the British commodities for which securing Northeast region along-with open trade route to Burma through **Naga Hills** was necessary.

---

[88] C Von Furer-Haimendorf, *'The Naked Nagas'*, John Murray, London, 1976, p.28.

[89] Haimendorf, op.cit, p.28.

While the British was consolidating power in the heartland of India, the small kingdoms in the Northeast were engaged in bitter rivalries. The Ahoms had lost their erstwhile power, so to ward off the threat from Naga tribes and internal feuds led to the invitation to the Burmese King and send their troops to help the Ahoms. But slowly, the excesses of the Burmese troops themselves in turn, invited the intervention of British who defeated the combined Ahom-Burmese troops. This led to the **'Treaty of Yandabo'** in 1826 and marked entry of the British into Assam and setting up their administration.[90] Through this treaty, the British annexed Arakan, Tenasserim and declared both the Metei Kingdoms to be their protectorates. However, in 1830 'the British returned the valley of Kale-Kabaw to *Bodawpaya* (King of Burma), thus reached a broad understanding on the limits of their and Burmese sphere of influence, with the Naga territory divided between the two sides. The Kabaw valley converges in the Sagaing region now in Myanmar and originally inhabited by the Naga, Kuki and other Chin tribes – to Manipur through Moreh town'.[91]

The Treaty of Yandabo made the British more powerful with additional territories and thus, they needed to open up new routes between Cachhar and Manipur through the **Naga Hills** so that they could administer the area and extend their mercantile interest into Burma. 'The importance of opening up direct communication between Assam and Manipur was at that time much insisted upon and it was in the course of explorations directed to this end we (the British) first came into conflict with Nagas of these hills'.[92]

History of Fierce Fight against the British Expeditions

The Angami tribes first came in contact with the British expedition team led by Captains **Jenkins** and **Pemberton** on 18 January 1832. After bloody and fierce battle due to

[90] Charles Chasie, op.cit, pp.20-21.

[91] Kumar and Murthy, op.cit, pp.16-17.

[92] A Meckenzie, *'The North East Frontier of India'*, Mittal Publications, New Delhi, 2001, p.101.

superiority of fire power of the British, the Angamis gave up. The next expedition was undertaken by Lieutenant Gordon in the months of winter in 1833 and pursued 25 miles east of the route pursued by Captain Jenkins. Lieutenant Gordon was 'accompanied by the late Rajah Gumbheer Singh,* King of Manipur with a force sufficient to overcome all opposition, but a powerful coalition was entered into by all the hill tribes to arrest his progress and ultimate success was entirely owing to his fire arms'.[93] It is pertinent to mention here that these expeditions were aimed to survey the route for development but nothing was done after the expeditions returned to their bases for obvious reasons.

Subsequently, further expeditions were also undertaken to save the Northern Cachar from exaction and raids of Nagas between 1836 and 1847. The British, finally, managed to gain a foothold in Mezoma village and Khonoma still remained indifferent towards the British. In November 1845, 'Captain Butler, Principal Assistant of Nowgong, was deputed to the hills with a force and made a peaceable progress through the country, conciliating the tribes and mapping the topography'.[94] Captain Butler was successful in bringing some token gifts, but these gestures again were not to be construed as acceptance of British as the ruler. Later on, an advance post was established at Mezoma, which led to killing of the Government Agent Daroga Bhogchand. This was retaliated by attacking Khonoma in November 1849. Khonoma was the strongest village which was well fortified and could withstand couple of attacks. Later it was captured, of course, with the covert/overt support of other Naga villages. Every British retreat from Khonoma was celebrated with fresh raids along the borders. Finally in December 1850, 10th expedition was launched to relieve Lieutenant Vincent, returned after capturing Khonoma as they had outstretched their physical and logistics capabilities about which Meckenzie wrote:

---

* Raja Gumbheer Singh, King of Manipur (Meitei tribe).

[93] V Elwin, *'The Nagas in the Nineteenth Century'*, Oxford Press, 1969, p.115.

[94] A Meckenzie, op.cit, p.108.

"with difficulty in capturing a strong Naga fort at Konemah and fighting a bloody battle against great masses of the tribes at Kekremah, the troops were eventually in March 1851 withdrawn from the hills."[95]

Compromise and Policy of No Interference

This was the turning point in the Anglo – Naga relationship; wherein the British realized how difficult it was to maintain an advance post up in the hills and thus, the decision to pull out troops to Dimapur. Friendly clan of Mezoma village was given the option either to fall back to Dimapur or rely solely on their own strength. The decision to pull out from the hills was coupled with the policy decision of non-interference taken by **Lord Dalhousie,** who wrote in the minute:

> "Hereafter we should confine ourselves to our ground, protect it as it can and must be protected, not meddle in the feuds or fights of these savages, encourage trade with them as long as they are peaceful to us and rigidly exclude them from all communication either to all what they have got or to buy ..."[96]

Contrary to the belief, the policy of non-interference did not bring peace and amity, as in the first year after adoption of this policy there were twenty two raids in which 178 persons were killed, wounded or carried away as slaves. So in 1854, an officer was posted in Asalu (in North Cachhar) and a line of frontier posts were established, but they were not of much use and the raids continued to be frequent occurrence. In 1854, 'a Manipuri force invaded Angami Hills and destroyed many villages and then twenty two villages sought British protection but it was not granted on the ground of non interference'.[97]

The British policy of non interference in the **Naga** affairs continued till 1865, the passivity was seen as weakness by the

---

[95] **A Meckenzie**, op.cit, p.112.

[96] **V. Elwin**, *'The Nagas in the Nineteenth Century'*, op. cit. p.163.

[97] B.B. Ghosh, *'History of Nagaland'*, S Chand & Company, New Delhi, 1982, pp.95-96.

Nagas and hence, they (mostly Angamis) increased the ferocity and frequency of the raids compelling the British to carry out a reappraisal of the policy of non-interference. In 1862, Lieutenant Governor **Cecil Beadon** recommended proactive policy to safeguard the British interests but 'nothing decisive was done for over two years or until further raids in March and April 1866 forced upon Government a definite settlement of the question'.[98]

From No Interference to Proactive Policy

As per historian **B.B. Ghosh**, an effort was made to recruit Angami youth into the military police so that it could help preventing raids, but 'it too was ineffectual because it was found that the hillmen could not be induced to remain under discipline for long. Out of 37 Angami recruits the average service period proved to be only eight months'.[99] **Lieutenant Gregory**, the actual proponent of the proactive policy was given a go ahead to use his discretionary powers to deal summarily with the villages concerned in any gross outrage and a rough system of judicial procedure was laid down.

The policy adopted was a show of force to deter the raiders and the British Indian Government but 'gave no sanction to occupy the Naga Hills as the British Bengal Government had desired but merely allowed the establishment of strong central station at Samagooting (Chumukedima) and the officer–in-charge of which was to endeavour to maintain conciliatory intercourse with the **Nagas**'.[100] In 1866, district of **Naga Hills** was formed and Samagooting became the seat of Lieutenant John Gregory, the first Deputy Commissioner (D.C.) of the **Naga Hills** district. The D.C. had the authority to deal with any situation with a rough judicial system. Simultaneously, another decision was taken to restrict the Angami Nagas visiting the plains and they were required to deposit their

[98] V. Elwin, op.cit, p.166.
[99] B.B. Ghosh, op.cit, pp.95-96.
[100] A.D. Mao, op.cit, p.24.

weapons which were generally spears, to the authority at Samagooting and collect it back on the return.[101]

It appears that the British had understood that the territory was with them so far as the treaties with Burma and Manipur were concerned which recognized the Patkai and Burrail ranges of the hills running in a continuous line from the sources of the *Dihing* in the extreme east of Assam to those of the Dhansiri River in the North Cachhar as the boundary but it was futile to take on the Nagas for complete subjugation, better they were left to themselves to run their own affairs, 'but they have never enjoyed or acquired political or territorial independence, and it is clearly open to the British Government in point of right, as it is incumbent on it in good policy, to exercise its sovereign power by giving them the benefit of a settled administration'.[102] It is, in this light can be said that since the time of Burmese and Manipuri Kingdoms which was a recent phenomenon the **Nagas** were left to administer themselves (upto the village level only). Moreover, many of the villages were under the influence of British for trade and security against the **Angami Nagas.**

Protection of Interests

The establishment of the new administrative zone at Samagooting (Chumukedima) under Lieutenant John Gregory, the Government desired that Lt Gregory should 'do his best by tact and good management, supported by a moderate display of physical force, to bring that portion of the hill tract adjacent to the plains into order'.[103] It was important to remember here that main object in having any dealing with the hill people was to protect the low lands. Chumukedima, of course, had a police contingent for protection. While the setting up of new headquarters was in process, the Nagas of Rezepemah raided one of the Mikir villages in the North Cachhar in January 1866,

[101]B.B. Ghosh, op.cit, p.97.

[102]V. Elwin, op.cit, pp.169-170.

[103]A Meckenzie, op.cit, p.120. Also, Elwin, p.17.

hence, it was punished in the month of March 1866 by **Lt. Gregory.** The Razepemah Nagas retaliated again and raided Sergaincha village and butchered 26 Mikirs, and thus it was again punished severely while other villages were not touched to drive home a point in the minds of savages. **Capt Butler,** the successor of **Lt Gregory,** most of the time was busy in sorting out inter tribe feuds and internecine conflicts. In the spring of 1874, Captain **Johnstone** had taken the responsibility of providing protection to two Naga villages on payment of revenue which were under imminent threat from the hostile villages, later extended to third village as well. Meanwhile, British carried out the survey of the some of the areas, obviously not without any resistance.

In the year 1875, Colonel **Keating,** the Chief Commissioner of Assam recommended to shift the Headquarters of Chumukedima to Wokha, in the Lotha Naga areas, being centrally located would create a buffer zone for protection of Sibsagar district. However, government decided to wait for the result of the survey operations. By the end of August 1876, Konemah (Khonoma) and Mozemah (Mezoma) had earned attention because of their raids on the Naga communities living under Manipur. The reports of exaction and raids on Cachari people by Mozemah village in February 1877 invited expedition. **Elwin** Writes:

> "Mozemah refused all reparation and (*hence*) an expedition in force was arranged for the next cold season to settle the Angami question once for all."[104]

British Policy Reviewed

In short, the Naga hostilities at this moment were at its peak and thus, Government of British India had to review its policy of maintaining of peace in the border areas of Assam and Naga Hills. In December 1877, a strong contingent led by Political Officer Carnegy, launched expedition which came under attack while approaching Mozemah village. The village was

[104]V. Elwin, op.cit, p.180.

adequately punished by burning it leaving only few houses. Fines were imposed which were termed as lenient because they were punished enough by inflicting the destruction of the village with its all contents. The fine was Rs. 50 and return of all arms and accoutrements of three constables who had been waylaid, contents of plundered mailbag and surrender of their own arms. On 18th January, the terms imposed upon Mozemah were fully complied with, and, peace being thus formally concluded, the expeditionary force fell back upon Samagooting on the 28th January 1878.[105] The Chiefs of Khonoma and Jotsoma were extended pardon on tendering their submission.

During this period, borders were pushed to accommodate tea gardens. Large tracts of forests were also transferred to Assam. According to one estimate, approximately 41 tea gardens came up during this period in Sibsagar district, along the lilne of embankments Ladoi Garh, Nagabund and Dodharali, which used to be traditional border of the Ahom kingdom. Moreover, large number of hill tracts were taken away to build Assam-Bengal railways.[106] The acquisition of land for development of tea gardens and railways generally remained limited to the foothills of Naga Hills.

Imposition of House Tax and Resentment

In March 1878, Kohima was occupied and made Chief Administrative Centre and Wokha as Sub-Centre. As soon as the British established themselves in Kohima, they levied 'House Tax' of two rupees per family. This tax continues to be the only tax till date, but the rate has marginally increased to rupees five only in more than a century. Levy of house tax of Rs two per annum, was definitely very high by any standards at that time. It was a pity that even after taking over most of Asia

[105]ibid, p.182.

[106]These areas still from the Disputed Area Belt (DAB) in which 11 Tea Gardens and 8 Reserved Forests were requested to be transferred to Nagaland by T. Aliba Imti and T. Sakhrie to the Governor Hydari on 26 June 1947.

as colony, the British continued to indulge in the exaction of taxes in such areas where the indigenous people had to spend all their energies for eking out the barest sustenance.[107] Heavy taxation of poor villagers also brought out implicit hostility especially from Khonoma.

Fall of Damant and Siege of Kohima

Damant, the first Deputy Commissioner, made genuine efforts to prevent inter-tribal massacres, and was successful in enforcement of penalties on those villages which were guilty of raiding in disobedience to his orders.[108] In fact, the Naga's hostile attitude could not be comprehensively understood by **Damant** and launched again another expedition to Khonoma in October 1879. This time, he was warned by Jotsoma villagers that Khonoma meant mischief. It is said that the interpreter begged **Damant** not to go on, and on several occasions he fell on his feet (the Political Officer) and even caught him by the hand, beseeching him not to proceed.[109] Unfortunately, **Damant** did not pay heed to the request of interpreter (called *'dobashi'*) and as the unsuspecting and overconfident Deputy Commissioner approached the village from the fields below, he was shot from the ramparts of Khonoma fortress along with large number of escorts. Emboldened Angamis, due to fall of Damant, led the siege on Kohima, duly supported by neighbouring Jotsoma and Chetnoma Khel of Kohima. The siege was laid on 16 October 1879 which was lifted on 24th October 1879 (for one week). Till then the little strength in the garrison which was reinforced by Hide from Wokha on 19th October 1879 held out. The British retaliated the siege and punished several villages with great ferocity. Normally all the villages were razed to the ground and then burnt. Excerpts from one of the reports:

> "Of the 13 villages hostile to us, Piphimah, Merramah, Sachimah, Sephemah and Puchamah were attacked and destroyed before

---

[107] Visier Sanyu, op.cit, p.99.

[108] V. Elwin, op.cit, p.183.

[109] ibid, p.185.

the attack on Konemah took place...subsequently, the village of Konemah was destroyed and site occupied by our troops, and Jotsoma, which is close by, was captured on 27 November, and a portion of it was burned."[110]

It would be pertinent to mention here that the British had always been overreacting and were extremely harsh in retaliation whenever any of their officers or men specially a Briton was harmed or shot at. **Ramunny** writes:

"If murder of Damant was cruel, unnecessary and treacherous, the overreaction of the British administration was well nigh barbarous. The punishment meted out to all the villages was far beyond what justice demanded."[111]

Execution of Peace Treaty

The aim of the British had only interest at any place and that was business. Absolute power made them haughty and thus, could never accept reverses. To compare, a century later in 1972, an Indian Deputy Commissioner was shot dead by the underground Nagas in Sema area, the Government did not punish the villages, only curfew imposed so that the villagers did not loiter around, while they were combing the jungles for the undergrounds responsible for the murder.[112] Finally, peace was established and both the sides agreed to abide by certain understandings reached on 27 March 1880. An Agreement was done with the British as per Naga customary practices, being unlettered till then. **Longchar** writes about the process of making treaty as under:

"A circle was drawn on the ground and the representatives of the British and the Nagas got into a circle, a cat was brought of which the head was held by the Naga representatives, the British representatives held the body and the cat was sliced from

---

[110] Elwin, op.cit, p.188.

[111] Murkot Rammunny, *'The World of Nagas'*, Northern Book Center, New Delhi, 1993, p.9.

[112] ibid, p.9.

the neck. That was to signify that there would be no fighting between the two parties and whichever party was treacherous to the other it would meet the same fate."[113]

The British were formally accepted as rulers and thus, could establish their base without any further problems. Some of the scholars feel that the British were allowed in the land of Nagas as guest and friend but lose the sight of one singular fact that the Nagas continued to pay 'House Tax', which did signify the British rule over the annexed territory.

The areas such as Mokukchung and Tuensang were not under the British control. Ao country was easily brought under the British umbrella, due to inter tribal feuds. The Chief Commissioner of Assam had sent an expedition to punish village 'Mazung' in December 1888. The expedition was entirely successful. Porteous (Expedition leader) occupied it on 12th January 1889.[114] At the end of the tour of expedition, **Porteous** selected a site near Mokukchung (Mokoktru) for location of new sub-divisional Headquarters and later took over the control of Seromi, Longsa and Ungma villages and thereby brought under the British control. Soon after the completion of expedition British planned further expansion.[115]

Since the days of truce and subjugation of Angamis, the British kept on expanding the hold over other tribes. With the establishment of Mokukchung sub-division, it became much easier to pursue the expeditions and thus extension of the British rule. Those villages who were not under the British protection had been seeking protection from the British which acted as catalyst in the process. By 1905, the boundary was extended upto Dikhu River in the East. The only Naga tract that remained unoccupied and outside the orbit of the British administration were the Tuensang and the Mon district.[116]

---

[113]Purtongzuk Longchar, *'Historical Development of the AO Nagas in Nagaland'*, Print Home, Dimapur, 2002.

[114]Tajenyuba Ao, *'British Occupation of Naga Country'*, Mokukchung, 1993, p.96. (quoted in L.W Shakespear, *'History of Assam Rifles'*, Spectrum Publications Guwahati, 1980, p.168)

[115]ibid.

[116]P. Longchar, op.cit, p.22.

Prevalance of British Rule after 1947

The unadministered areas of Tuensang and Mon were brought under the British rule in 1914 and were named as North East Frontier Tract (NEFT). It is pertinent to mention here that although present Tuensang district officially was brought under administrative control but it remained turbulent for long time. 'Therefore, the present Tuensang district and a greater part of the present Mon district, remained outside the administration for long till 1948'.[117] The business of head hunting and raids were still in vogue even after Independence of India till late 1950s or even early 1960s which remained unreported basically due to absence of media and remoteness of the area where these forays took place in Nagaland-Myanmar border. Moreover, major part of present Mon district was outside of the Naga Hills district.

While the British Government could consolidate administrative powers by 1922 in the majority of the Naga Areas with its Headquarters at Kohima, which was a part of the province of Assam, but the administration of these tribesmen was not only difficult task but also arduous one and different from the administration in the Plains. Thus, the Government of India Act 1919 was passed and the Naga Hills were declared as 'Backward Area'. Subsequently in 1937, the NEFT was made 'Excluded Area and Partially Excluded Area' and was placed under the Government of Assam under the provisions of Govt of India Act 1935. As mentioned above, the majority of the area of Tuensang district was brought under the administration of the Naga Hills only in 1948. In 1951, the remaining areas of the said NEFT together with the Naga Tribal Area of Tuensang were renamed as North East Frontier Agency (NEFA). In 1954, the administrative units were re-constituted with boundaries and renamed. Tuensang came to be known as Tuensang Frontier Division.[118]

---

[117]ibid, p.14

[118]Longchar, op.cit, pp.22-23.

Though, it was logical for the British to keep these tribes isolated and insulated from the outside world. Later some British officials wanted to make the Naga Hill areas a British colony (Crown Colony) after India's independence. Robert Reid, the Governor of Assam had proposed that the Naga Hills, North Eastern Frontier Agency and the Chittagong Hill Tracts (CHT) of East Bengal (Now in Bangladesh) should be retained as the 'Crown Colony'. Probably this seems to be the reason why some Nagas raised the demand of an independent Naga state, a bone of contention ever since India became independent.[119]

Section-III

Present State of the Nagas

On establishment of British administration in Kohima, the first census was carried out in 1891 and the population was 96,037 which grew to 102,402, in 1901 but in this census, a tract of approximately 30,000 people of Mokukchung area was not included.[120] As per Census of 2011, Nagaland has population of 1,978,502, a decrease from figure of 1,990,036 in 2001 out of which male and female are 1,024,649 and 953,853 respectively. The total population growth in this decade was –0.58 percent. The population of Nagaland forms 0.16 percent of India in 2011.

The **Nagas** followed age old tribal tradition of animism till conversion to Christianity. Most of the tribes believe in the existence of a good number of gods and spirits, both benevolent and malevolent. Christianity came to the Naga Hills with baptisation of seven **Nagas** in the year 1872 by Rev E.W.Clark. Subsequently, Baptist Missionary centre was moved to Impur village where it still stands as Ao Baptist Mission centre. Till

[119] A.D. Mao, op.cit, p.31.

[120] **B.C. Allen.** (et al), *'Gazetteer of Bengal and North East India'*, Mittal Publication, 2001, p.417 (In the Census of 1891, Mokukchung Sub Division was not included).

1891, the first ever census, acceptance of Christianity was slow, as B. C. Allen wrote: 'The American Baptist Mission has branches at Kohima and at Impur in the Mokukchung sub-division and practically the whole of the native Christians (579) were members of this sect'.[121] Initially Nagas had hesitation to accept Christianity as their faith but after a lapse of a century, Nagaland has become a Christ country. Though they have been baptized but still celebrate their traditional tribal festivals with equal gusto. The missionaries brought the Western education to the Nagas, despite lack of common language or even a single script developed so far, the literacy rate is almost 98 percent in the state. Today, the Nagas are no more naked and savages but well educated, well dressed and very warm hearted people.

---

[121]B.C. Allen, op.cit, p.471.

3

The Naga Imbroglio

A Brief Recap

The **Nagas** are a conglomeration of tribes and sub-tribes. Their ancestors had come to this part of the earth from different places, at different time intervals, primarily in search of food. They were organized in very small groups, probably settling down briefly at places and use the resources of that local area and again move to a new place (specially west)*, till they reached the plains of Assam. As they were organized in small tribal groups, later would have formed villages and at times they were sub divided in various clans, restricted to Khels within the villages. They never identified themselves beyond their tribal and village limits and were ever willing to behead anyone specially people from other villages or other tribes, should the opportunity so present itself for prey. They lived in this part of the globe since time immemorial during which they would have been known as one group of people named them as 'the Nagas'. The occupation of the British, uniformity in administration, conversion to Christianity and Western education gave the Nagas some kind of identity as one people despite differences that exist, by the end of nineteenth century.

---

* Hekiye Sema, an NNC underground activist from village Naghutomi district-Zuneboto (near Akuluto) later joined the mainstream, said to the author during an interview at Dimapur on 20 November, 2002.

In this chapter, an attempt will be made to understand the genesis of the conflict, latent and simmering discontents, undercurrents within the Naga society which kept the dissidents motivated to continue the fight through generations. Also would like to find out the reason as to why the authorities failed to resolve the conflict for such a long time (since 1947)? Since this being the oldest surving insurgency movement in Asia and thus makes it special for students of the Military Studies and Social Sciences.

Section-I

Pre World War II Scenario and the Naga Club

When modern civilization dawned upon the **Nagas** in the beginning of 20th century, just down the hills, India as a nation was getting politically awakened for freedom and the Indian National Congress had grown as a formidable organization. To neutralise the growth and political clout of the Congress, the British midwifed the birth of the Muslim League in 1906. It may be recalled here that the British had established their administrative Headquarter in Kohima by the end of 1880. By 1905, the boundary was extended upto Dikhu River in the east and thus can be said that the British had consolidated the administration in the Naga Hills, however, Tuensang and Mon areas were out of it which came under its control in 1914. Meanwhile, an organization named 'Naga Club' was formed in 1918 at Kohima and Mokukchung, of course, the initiative and advice came from the British administration. Their intention seems to have been to set in motion some sort of representative body bringing together a number of villages and later an entire tribe.[122]

The members of this club were government officials and few leading *'Gaonburhas'* (the Headmen of the village) of neighbouring villages basically to discuss social and

---

[122]M. Ramunny, *'The World of Nagas'*, Northern Book Centre, New Delhi, 1993, p.13.

administrative problems. This club later opened a co-operative store in Mokukchung, first of its kind in the district.

It is pertinent to note that both the worlds (i.e. Indian mainland including plains of Assam and the hill people) were living in different ages despite their geographical congruity. The Independence movement was sweeping the country but could not reach the Naga Hills due to lack of social interaction, education and they were leading their tribal life far away from the mainstream. In addition, they were intentionally not allowed to interact with the people of plains to keep the savages away from few lucrative and easy heads. In any case, the British would not have liked to change the peaceful atmosphere in the Hills to a turbulent one and invite additional troubles through political unrest which they were experiencing in rest of India. 'The Inner Line Regulation helped the administrators to keep 'undesirable' people (political leaders) out of the area'.[123]

But there is no evidence available to suggest that any one of the leaders (engaged in Independence Movement) made an endeavour to visit this part of the country either, may be due to its remoteness even from the capital of the state of Assam and generate some kind of awareness about the forthcoming freedom of India. This absence of political interaction helped the British administrators to generate a feeling of alienation of Nagas from the affairs of India.

Naga Hills: Under Government of India Act, 1915

The Naga Hills District was under the charge of Lieutenant Governor of Bengal and in 1874 it was included in the Province of Assam, since then its administration was regulated by a number of Acts with a special provision for underdeveloped tracts. Subsequently, the Government of India Act, 1915 empowered the Governor General to declare any territory in India to be a backward tract. This power was extended on a fairly large scale and by 1928, these 'backward tracts', covered an area of 120,000 square miles and contained a population

[123]M. Ramunny, op.cit, p.13.

of over eleven million[124]. Under the provisions of this Act, the Governor General could decide based on his wisdom that which of the laws will be applicable to the Naga Hills. Moreover, expenditure incurred by the government agencies/ administration in these tracts were neither subjected to audit in the legislature or vote nor any question could be asked without the Governor's sanction.

Vastness of *Damin-e-koh*: These so called backward tracts were spread from Burma border to Afghanistan border (known as *damin-e-koh,* still exists) and purely administered by the provincial Governors, in no way should be construed as alien land just because of separate provisions in the law rather an integral part of India. The fact that the Naga areas came under these regulations did not mean that it was separate from other parts of India or that its inhabitants were receiving different treatment that were given to another tribal people. 'In actual fact they were in the same situation as many millions of others',[125] spread across India.

Situation after World War I

At the end of the World War-I due to growing political pressure on the Government, the British decided to send Simon Commission to explore the possible reforms in the political set up and find out the modalities of transfer of dominion status to India. Notwithstanding, it was a sham so far as its intention was concerned, the Government authorities in India were preparing on the proposals, and similarly the Assam Provincial Government had prepared a comprehensive memorandum on the working of the Reformed Government. **Hutton,** the famous D.C. of Kohima, had suggested the withdrawal of Hill Districts of Assam from the contemplated reforms. He wrote:

"... the interest of hill districts will not only be served by having them included in the reforms but they will suffer very serious

[124]V. Elwin, *Nagaland,* Spectrum Publications, Guwahati, Delhi 1977, p.35.
[125]ibid, p.35.

detriment by being tied up to the politically more advanced plains district, while the later are likely to suffer in the future by being joined with people of an irreconcilable culture in an unnatural union which can ultimately only entail discomfort for both parties..."[126]

Hutton's logic was based on the remoteness of the area and lack of communication with the outside world. He established the differences between these people and the population in the plains of Assam on the basis of race and religion which were true. But he failed to take a note of another historical fact that while the people of India differed from each other in various ways despite being racially same stock, at that time the tribal people of North East India themselves were strangers to each other,[127] with serious antipathy towards sub-groups amongst themselves. Hutton's remarks were based on his personal experiences as people were not lettered, very simple and unexposed to the outside world, thus could have been exploited by others. He concluded that:

> "If the hills and plains be linked together under the Reformed Council, the interests of the hills must (Not) be sacrificed, as their population is impecunious, unlettered, rural and much too simple to compete with the plainsmen in legal or political finesse."[128]

Till date, the tribal superiority feeling runs very high and the micro-identities are too deep rooted. The social divisions amongst tribal groups are so wide that achieving consensus on any issue is almost impossible. Moreover, past animosity, deep rooted distrust and apathy drive their social behaviour irrespective of modernity and coexistence which is relatively a recent phenomemnon. The ethnic affinity reins supreme in each of the tribal groups and certain social denominators have not changed their individualistic tribal identity. Hutton was well within the rights in his discretion and thus the recommendations were more than justified. He recommended:

---

[126]'Simon Commission Report', Raj Bhawan Records, Shillong, Meghalaya.

[127]M. Ramunny, op.cit, p.14.

[128]'Simon Commission Report', p.14.

"..The true solution of the question of their administration is the gradual creation of self governing communities, semi-independent in nature secured by treaties on the lines of the Shan states of Burma, for whose external relations alone the Governor of the province would ultimately be responsible. Given self-determination to that extent it would always be open to a functioning hill state to apply for amalgamation if it so desired and could satisfy the other party of advantage in its incorporation."[129]

Though, the **Nagas** are generally simple but 'have a very stern suspicion that something is being done to take away from them their immemorial rights and customs',[130] and this was also felt by **Cadogen,** who visited Kohima with **Mr. Atlee** and informed the British Parliament during discussion on **Simon Commission Report,** which we shall discuss shortly.

Story of a Black King's Rule?

The humane behaviour, compassion and close relationship the District Commissioners such as **J.P. Mills, J.H. Hutton** and Sir **CR Pawsey** helped Nagas forget the past experiences and accept the white man as their friend. But can a Naga be without an enemy? In fact without the concept of an enemy, definition of a Naga would be incomplete. Thus, the void existed due to the absence of inter tribe exaction and raids, Nagas seem to have one enemy which was automatically the people from the plains, some may name them Indian, but to be more accurate for a Naga it could be only a Bengali or Assamese businessman, definitely not without a reason.

This feeling could be gauged that the Nagas had confided in Cadogen, the member of the Simon Commission by saying that '*We hear that a black king was going to come to rule over India. If that is so, for goodness sake... do not let it be a Bengali*'.[131] It was also told that they would prefer to be a subject of the

[129]'Simon Commission Report', p.14.

[130]V. Elwin, op.cit, p.49.

[131]ibid, p.50.

Queen to an unknown black king that too a Bengali. Probably, these were underlying factors which prompted the British to keep these simple people away from the so called devils. Meanwhile, the so called Naga Club which was formed in 1918 had been functioning as a link between the Government and handful of adjacent villages near Kohima and Mokukchung.

Memorandum to the Simon Commission

The members of the statutory Commission under Lord Simon, which included Clement Atlee and Cadogen, arrived in Kohima on 10 January 1929. The 'Naga Club', one and only civic body, presented the so called famous memorandum to the Simon Commission (Refer Appendix 'A'). Before, we discuss the memorandum *per se*, I would like to analyse the constitution of this so-called august assembly of Naga Club. Following were the members, who signed the memorandum:

(i) Nihu, Head Interpreter, (Angami).
(ii) Nisalie, Peshkar, (Angami).
(iii) Nisier, Master, (Angami).
(iv) Khosa, Doctor, (Angami).
(v) Gepo, Interpreter, (Katcha Naga).
(vi) Vipunyu, Potdar, (Angami).
(vii) Goyiepra, Treasurer, (Angami).
(viii) Ruzukhrie, Master, (Angami).
(ix) Dikhrie, Sub-Overseer, (Angami).
(x) Zapuzhulie, Master, (Angami).
(xi) Zepulie, Interpreter, (Angami).
(xii) Katsumo, Interpreter, (Angami).
(xiii) Nuolhoukielie, Clerk, (Angami).
(xiv) Luzevdi, Interpreter, (Sema).
(xv) Apamo, Interpreter, (Lotha).
(xvi) Resilo, Interpreter, (Rengma).
(xvii) Leng-jang, Interpreter, (Kuki).
(xviii) Nikhiriehu, Interpreter, (Angami).
(xix) Maikra. o, Chaprasi, (Angami).
(xx) Levi, Clerk, (Kacha Naga).

If the composition of representation is analysed, it can be easily said that this group was mostly of Angamis (14/20) who assumed the responsibility of all the Nagas. Moreover, it will not be out of place to question the level of expertise or knowledge as none of them were qualified enough to understand provisions of the Simon Commission, constitutional/legal or otherwise. It is also doubtful that they had any kind of sanction from their respective tribal community parliament (Tatar Hoho*) to represent their views for whatever worth they were.

Purpose of Commission: Lack of Understanding

This so called memorandum, supposed to have been vetted by Hutton, appears to be the brainchild of few (so called) educated Nagas to represent all the Nagas living in the administered and unadministered areas as well. It does not seem to be a conspiracy of Angami tribes to represent themselves as a sole speaker, but was it their fellow feeling for other Nagas or cerebral supremacy over the other tribes remains unclear. But certainly contents of the memorandum do reflect that they were poorly informed about the aim of the Commission, as it said:

> "...Now we learn that you have come to India as representatives of the British Government to enquire into the working of the system of Government and the growth of the education and we beg to submit below our view with the prayer that our Hills may be withdrawn from the Reformed Scheme and placed outside the Reforms but directly under the British Government. We never asked for any reforms and we do not wish any reforms..."

It shows that they had no idea about the 'Scheme' and were working in an apprehensive manner, a reaction to offset undue fears. The understanding of the history of Nagas and relationship with the British probably were either not known to them or had been selectively forgotten but certainly they

* Tatar Hoho – the tribal parliament of representatives from all tribes (not elected).

couldn't be totally ignorant. On the other hand, they had fair understanding that there were more tribes whom they never met, never known and had 'No' unity but they asserted themselves to be representative of all as one social entity, if not a nation politically. They said:

> "Our country within the administered area consists of more than eight tribes, quite different from one another with quite different languages which cannot be understood by each other, and there are more tribes outside the administered area which are not known at present. We have no unity among us..."

Question of Power Transfer

It appears that they wanted the power to be transferred to those so called few **Naga club** members, mostly Angamis (previously Angamis provided security to other tribes), while they felt threatened by unseen, unknown hypothetical *'black king'* who were proposed to be ruling them. What seems to be most intriguing fact is that the misgivings expressed in the memorandum were not clarified by any one, neither by the administration nor by the DC, who according to Ruzukhrie only corrected one word,[132] thus, casting a shadow over the behaviour of the British authorities on this issue. Colonel V.K. Anand has said:

> "In this document, the tribesmen betrayed the paradox of realism and make believe. Their feelings about backwardness were genuine but their suspicion, based on ignorance, hearsay and inspired propaganda projecting fears, were unfounded."[133]

The feelings expressed were not only exaggerated but it appears that this kind of document generated or purported by these poorly educated people raises the doubt over the British aim in the tribal areas. It appears that they had serious reservation about the plains people (which was not unfounded

---

[132]M. Ramunny, op.cit, p.15.

[133]V.K. Anand, *'Conflict in Nagaland'*, Chanakya Publications, Delhi 1980, pp.55-56.

either) or was it a ploy to keep it out of India, as the plea was that the British Government should continue to safeguard their rights against all encroachment from other people who were more advanced than them by placing it directly under its own protection.[134] To remain under the British rule was not an anathema but to remain only as part of Assam Province as they were, was an unacceptable proposition that too based on fear of unknown taxes. They were aware of British taxation and fines that were levied since 1832. Anand is critical about the discussion which took place in the British Parliament. He wrote:

> "the conditions prevailing in the Naga Hills that fulfilled all the requirements of an even more promising and hunting ground could not have gone unexploited. With the foreign missionaries acting as midwife, some British political leaders generated the psychological backdrop for the birth of the Naga demand for a separate homeland. During the discussions in the House of Commons preceding the passing of the 'Government of India Act 1935, the Naga issue was discussed at length. Churchill made no bones about his views that the Indians were incompetent even to take over minor administrative duties and, therefore, could not be entrusted with the affairs of the tribesmen. The great leader was not alone in voicing lack of faith in the 'Indian Bodies'. There were many other English men who did great harm to India and the Nagas in particular by making highly inflammatory speeches, thereby strengthening their suspicions and sowing the seed of discontent."[135]

Interest of the Nagas or The British?

It can now be inferred that the outcome of the Simon Commission Report after the deliberations over the issue of Naga Hills was highly biased against the interests of India as well as the Nagas but favourable to the British. As per Elwin, the general opinion during the debates suggested that 'the only chance for those people is to protect them from a civilization

---

[134]Extracted from the Memorandum to the Simon Commission.

[135]V.K. Anand, op.cit. pp.55-56.

which will destroy them and for that purpose, I believe, British Control is the best'.[136] There were apprehensions in the minds of the British that 'if they were taken away from the direct British rule, then land would be alienated, and they would be recruited for the tea plantations and else where'.[137]

If the analysis of the memorandum is carried out as a whole then it is very difficult to make out what they actually had wanted – 'independence or continuation of the British rule'? Based on the apprehensions, they had asked to be left alone in case the British were leaving them at the mercy of the plains people. Some of the scholars (specially, **Angami Nagas** e.g. **Charles Chasie** and others like **Horam, Asoso Yonuo**) feel that the **Nagas** wanted restoration of their independence that the British had snatched from them but the memorandum does not say so. It says:

> "The **Nagas** had simply wished to be left alone in case the British had decided to leave them at the mercy of others. The **Nagas** had mainly prayed for placing their hill district under direct control and protection of the British. Hence, at that time main issue was not independence of the **Naga** Hills District but just a demand for special status for it under British India's protection."[138]

It appears that the kind of importance given to this memorandum by the British proves hidden aim to continue to rule these areas even after Independence of India for geo-political and mercantile considerations. Since the British Government considered the plea of all tribes in India (not only the Nagas) and formulated the special policy because all the tribes were very poor were living in primitive conditions and the areas were most backward, but to avoid calling them as 'Backward Area' (being an unacceptable word to some of the parliament members) named them differently instead. As the Naga Hills was too small entity to make exceptional laws or

---

[136]V. Elwin, op.cit, p.39.

[137]ibid.

[138]H.M. Bareh, '*Encyclopedia of North East India*', Vol–VI (Nagaland), Mittal Publications, Delhi, 2001, p.2.

regulation by the empire. Similar undeveloped tracts were present in this great sub-continent e.g. Chittagong Hill Tracts, Chhotanagpur plateau, tribal areas in Central, Southern and Western India, thus, making special regulation for each of these undeveloped and backward areas was not possible and justifiably all the backward areas were clubbed together including Naga Hills. Cadogen took exception to the word 'Backward', thus instead of 'Backward Tracts', The Commission proposed the establishment of 'Excluded Areas' of which there were two categories 'Excluded and Partially Excluded'. The principle of their selection was partly 'backwardness' more so, administrative convenience.[139] The areas in which the tribals were in an enclave inhabited by a homogeneous and compact tribe, it was classified as 'Excluded Areas' and the area whereas the population was less homogeneous, but was still undeveloped and substantial in number, these were grouped or called as 'Partially Excluded' areas. But by no stretch of imagination, these areas were excluded from the political jurisdiction or administration of India. The 'Excluded' areas were kept excluded from the competence of the provincial and federal legislature and the administration was vested in the Governors acting in their discretion and that of the 'Partially Excluded' areas were kept in the control of the ministers subject to the Governor exercising his individual judgment.[140]

Outcome of Act of 1935

The Government of India Act, 1935 was promulgated and became effective on 01 April 1937. The Nagas appeared to be satisfied as the aim of these provisions was not to keep them excluded from the mainstream but to provide adequate space to keep their tribal customary laws and administration, traditions and culture alive without any influence from the outside world. **Ramunny** says:

---

[139]V. Elwin, op.cit, p.36.

[140]M. Ramunny, op.cit, p.15.

> "This apparently satisfied the Naga leaders, particularly those of the Naga Club who had put up the memorandum to the Simon Commission. In fact, their British advisers told them this was good enough for them."[141]

Thereafter, the club seems to have lost its co-hesiveness as a socio-political group, because of the World War II, which affected the whole of India and few **Nagas** were sent to France as a part of Labour Corps. Some of the villages were busy in their own inter village wars. Pangsha, a village outside the administered areas happens to be one of them which caused havoc and had taken 200 odd heads from the neighbouring villages. In 1939, Pangsha village was punished severely by Major AR Nye, M C 3rd Battalion of the Assam Rifles with CR Pawsey, the D.C. They were punished 'this time by burning Pangsha and Ukha and imposing stiff fines on other villages. A few guns were provided to some endangered villages for their protection against future raids. As far as known, this was the last time that any serious slave trading or head hunting was reported from this area'.[142]

However, it is believed that the last incident of head hunting that took place in the Naga areas was in 1966 but went unrecorded and unreported for the reasons of remoteness of the area and absence of media, may be this came to the light much later when the information had lost it's relevance, a *fait accompli.**

Section-II

The World War II and the Gallant Nagas

The World War broke out and during the fag end of the War; Naga Hills experienced the wrath of the Japanese. It is the

---

[141]ibid., p.16.

[142]Palit Maj Gen DK, *Sentinels of the North East: The Assam Rifles*. Palit and Palit, New Delhi, 1984, pp.95-96.

* Lt General J R Mukherjee, an authority on North East India in an informal chat told this to the author while traveling by road from Dimapur to Kohima on July 26, 2003.

Naga Hills in which Allied Forces gave a serious blow to the Japanese and thus changed the course of the history of the world in general and India in particular. During those trying times, active support of **Naga** is worth mentioning. Field Marshal **Viscount Slim** has paid rich tributes to the valour of **Nagas** in the following manner.

> "... These were gallant **Nagas** whose loyalty, even in the most depressing times of invasion, had never faltered. Despite floggings, torture, execution and the burning of their villages, they refused to aid the Japanese in any way or to betray our troops. Their active help to us was beyond value or praise. Under the leadership of devoted British Political Officers, some of the finest types of the Indian Civil Service, in whom they had complete confidence, they guided our columns, collected information, ambushed enemy patrols, carried our supplies, and brought in our wounded under the heaviest fire and then, being the gentlemen they were, often refused all payment. Many a British and Indian soldier owes his life to the naked, head hunting Naga, and no soldier of Fourteenth Army who met them will ever think of them but with admiration and affection."[143]

Birth of Naga National Council

It is beyond any doubt that they fought the war on the side of the British, who definitely were known to them as benevolent administrator. However, there were few like A Z Phizo and his brother Keviyallay who fought on the side of Japanese and Indian National Army and was arrested. There can be endless discussion on the fate of India and the Nagas, had the Indian National Army led by Subhas Chandra Bose and the Japanese bypassed Kohima and Imphal and dashed for plains of Assam, especially Dimapur where there was no garrison with a railhead. During this war, Deputy Commissioner CR Pawsey not only stayed with the Nagas in jungles, organized them for assisting the Allied Forces.

---

[143]Field Marshal **Sir William Slim**, *'Defeat Into Victory'*, Natraj Publishers, Dehradun, India,1981, pp.334-335.

Soon after the war had ended, India was about to get independence, C.R. Pawsey, who could foresee the events which were to unfold, established an institution in April 1945, which was called the 'Naga Hills District Tribal Council'. The object of this Council was to unite the **Nagas** and to reconstruct the war ravaged Naga Hills. By then the trace of the famous 'Naga Club' was nowhere to be found. The Council was sponsored by Kevichusa Angami (an officer of Assam Civil Service and later Indian Administrative Services) in which Mayang Nokcha, a teacher, was functioning as the President. This organization was pro government and a moderate body till the organization was taken over by T Aliba Imti as President and T Sakhrie as its Secretary. The 'Naga Hills District Tribal Council' was renamed as 'Naga National Council' in June 1946 after the Wokha meeting.

Meanwhile the peaceful Naga Club with new name the Naga National Council (NNC) had suddenly turned hostile and the control of NNC slipped into the hands of some of the ambitious leaders like **Phizo** who was by then released from Jail just prior to Indian independence. On 20 February 1947, NNC demanded that 'an interim government be set up for a period of 10 years at the end of which the **Naga** people be left to choose any form of government'.[144] It is pertinent to mention here that not all the members of NNC were in favour of Phizo's demand of complete independence, but there were moderate people in the council too, specially other tribal groups who 'were for autonomy within India according to mutually agreed formula'.[145] It is important to note here that prior to return of Phizo, the NNC had put forward a memorandum to Pandit Jawaharlal Nehru on 19 June, 1946 asking Naga Hills should be constitutionally included in an autonomous Assam, in a free India, with local autonomy and due safeguards for the **Nagas**.[146]

---

[144] **H.M. Bareh**, *Encyclopedia of North-East India*, Vol-VI, Mittal Publications, New Delhi, 2001.

[145] **M. Ramunny**, op.cit,p.18.

[146] ibid.

The letter was sent by two young and bright students **T. Sakhrie** and **Sashimeren Aier** (Refer Appendix 'B'), who played the role with their own conviction and foresight. In response to the letter written by Sakhrie, Pandit Nehru replied on 01 August 1946. The letter is quite comprehensive and it throws light on the thought process, the Congress President had in his mind. He said:

> "It is obvious that the Naga territory in Eastern Assam is much too small to stand by itself politically or economically. It lies between two huge countries, India and China, and part of it consists of rather backward people who require considerable help. Inevitably, therefore, this Naga territory must form part of India and of Assam with which it has developed such close association ... it is our policy that tribal areas should have as much freedom and autonomy as possible so that they can live their own lives according to their own customs and desires."

NNC's Demand: Interim Government for the Nagas

It is prudent to understand that the NNC leadership was representing only a handful of Naga educated youth, mostly Angamis. The articulation of Nehru had a vision and included all that what NNC were actually demanding. Ironically, they failed to understand the mind of Nehru in relation to the other issues pertaining to the Nagas. Thus, on February 20, 1947, the NNC sent another memorandum, this time addressed to the Viceroy of India for setting up an 'Interim Government' for the Nagaland for a period of ten years with a 'Guardian Power' (The British and India) for defence and emergency support.[147]

However, the term 'Nagaland' does not define areas under its ambit or jurisdiction because at this stage there was no sacrosanct boundary whether it was in the administered area or outside of it. 'This plan was submitted to the last Viceroy of India, Lord Louis Mountbatten, in a memorandum. No reply to this request was received but it was indirectly made known to the Nagas that their views may be expressed to the Advisory

---

[147]M. Ramunny, op.cit, pp.21-22.

Committee on the Aboriginal Tribes of the Constituent Assembly'.[148] Finally, a Sub-committee of the Advisory Committee visited Kohima on 20 May, 1947 wherein the NNC had an opportunity to present their case. This sub-committee had no statutory powers to recommend anything beyond the Constitution of India thus, it remained limited to projection of their demand in June 1947. Though the Naga Council had been clamouring for autonomy, government had very few options available. These were: complete independence, this option was unsustainable because of lack of tribal unity and concept of Naga nationhood, autonomy within Indian Union and lastly to remain under the British as *'Crown Colony'* but that would have been untenable once India attained its sovereignty.

Differences within NNC

Meanwhile, the NNC made one important decision that the British should quit the Naga Hills but they were fighting among themselves to reach a consensus on a decision about which Ramunny writes:

> "According to Sakhrie, one group of Nagas favoured immediate independence. The moderates favoured the continuance of governmental relations with India in some modified form until such time as the Nagas were sufficiently schooled in the art of running a modern state."[149]

But the opinion of majority of Nagas, who were not forming the part of NNC or any other group, was not known. Thus, it would not be fair to assume that whether or not these two views actually represented the minds of the majority, in any case, they were happy in whatever situation they were in their villages unaware of the transactions that took place in Kohima, Shillong or elsewhere. At the most, if any opinion could be taken of these people, they would have said that they wanted to be left alone and would have liked to continue

---

[148]B.B. Ghosh, *'History of Nagaland'*, S Chand & Co, New Delhi, 1982, p.162.
[149]M. Ramunny, op.cit, p.21.

as their forefathers did in the past. But there was another group of people who were in favour of the Naga Hills to be continuously included in an autonomous Assam in free India with local autonomy and due safeguards for the interests of Nagas.[150]

Section-III

Hydari Agreement: Bone of Contention

The proposal of NNC forwarded to the Viceroy was given to the Advisory Committee of the Constituent Assembly to discuss with the NNC leadership. The committee visited Kohima on 29 May, 1947 but nothing concrete could be recommended by them as mandate was limited, only to recommend within the Constitution of India. On the other hand, the NNC made it clear that the Nagas would not accept any alternative to this kind of constitutional arrangement. All the questions of the sub committee to the Naga leaders remained unanswered and the committee assumed the Naga Hills was to constitute an integral part of India.[151] Similar was the view of the outgoing Governor of Assam, Sir Andrew Clow. PF Adams, Secretary to the Governor, in a farewell message 'appealed to them to accept 'autonomy' and not fight for 'independence'.[152] The future of India was decided by the British and partition accepted based on two nation theory. It's one of the biggest tragedies that were played on the soil of this very land and possibly one of the most painful decisions that were imposed on India by the outsiders. A nation whose past had no parallels in the world just before advent of Islamic invaders 1400 years ago, was found to be unfit to decide its own destiny!

---

[150]For views of Nirmal Nibedon, see B.G. Verghese, *India's North East Resurgent*, Konark Publishers, New Delhi, 2002, p.86.

[151]M. Ramunny, op.cit, p.32.

[152]ibid, p.22. (quoted *The Naga Nation* Vol II, No-2, September 1947).

Nine Points Agreement

Coming back to the Nagas, since no tangible result was forthcoming, Sir Akbar Hydari, the then Governor of Assam, visited Kohima from 27 to 29 June 1947. After detailed deliberations, a Nine-Point Agreement was signed, between the Governor of Assam, Sir Akbar Hydari, and the NNC at Kohima. During this meeting and discussions, Western Angami, Eastern Angami, Kukis, Katcha Nagas, Rengmas, Semas, Lothas, Aos, Sangtams and Chang[153] tribes participated.

The class composition, though, covers half of the Naga tribes but with no official mandate of any particular tribe. Konyaks, the majority population of the Nagas and other tribal representatives were not accommodated at all. Moreover, the NNC was the group that comprised of some educated youth generally based in Kohima only. Apparently, the Governor should have discussed with the representative '*Gaonburahs*' of all tribes and, of course, the NNC. Probably, time was too short for these deliberations and the problem was with some of the members of the NNC only, which challenged the authority of the British to transfer the Naga Areas to the Government of India under the 'Independence of India Act 1947'.

The 'Nine Point Agreement' covered the aspects of judiciary, executive, legislative, taxation etc and the period of Agreement. (The Nine Point Agreement is given as Appendix 'C'). The problem cropped up immediately after the signing of the Agreement on the point number 9 of the agreement which reads as:

> "The Governor of Assam as the agent of the Government of Indian Union will have a special responsibility for a period of ten years to ensure the due observance of this agreement, at the end of this period the Naga National Council will be asked whether they require the above agreement to be extended for a further period, or a new agreement regarding the future of the Naga people arrived at."[154]

---

[153]M.Ramunny, op.cit, p.23.

[154]Hydari – NNC Agreement (Nine Point Agreement, Appendix 'C').

Right to Self Determination: The agreement terms clearly stated that if the NNC desired the same agreement be given further extension for further period which was to be decided after ten years and if the NNC felt it to be continued, scrapped or changed for a different agreement which was to be arrived at. But unfortunately, some of the NNC members were dissatisfied with the wording in respect of the period of Agreement. They were probably ignorant of the demand of the NNC made to the Viceroy just a month ago. **The stand of the NNC changed within one month from the concept of ten years of 'Interim Government' under the 'Guardian Power'** hence it was a new development. One segment of the NNC leadership wanted right to self determination and that clause was also included but after ten years of observance to the agreement (as New Agreement).[155] There is no doubt that aspiration of all the groups in the NNC were met in the agreement. But the time required for in house discussion for the NNC to reach a consensus before signing the agreement was not given to them. **There is enough evidence to suggest that the agreement was rushed through on the face of vehement opposition from one faction of the NNC**. The British officers e.g. Sir Charles Pawsey, the Deputy Commissioner and P.F. Adams, Secretary to the Governor of Assam did their best to explain the members of NNC whose knowledge of the English was limited and it met the aspirations of the people for independence. **Ramunny** writes:

> "Appeals, to be given further time, so that they could discuss the point among themselves were refused on the plea of want of time. Seeing the majority of the members of the Council had been persuaded, Sir Charles forced the members to put the issue to vote. The Agreement was approved by a slight majority. The negotiations were brought to a close with the opposition still protesting."[156]

---

[155]SC Jamir, Interview with the Author, 17 August 2003 (complete interview is at Appendix 'D').

[156]M. Ramunny, op.cit, p.23.

The 'Hurried Move'

It is evident that there the opposing group was neither given due importance, possibly they could ill afford to accept their views, nor were they allowed more time for deliberations. Hence, the historical mistake was committed by the Governor and his team to get the agreement signed hurriedly leaving much scope for speculation. The Government representatives, Sir Akbar Hydari and team of administrators are thus to blame for this 'hurried move' which created suspicion among few Naga leaders that proved to be fatal for India as a whole (Nagas included). While reporting to Pandit Nehru, Sir Akbar Hydari did mention that:

> "...there was a small but influential minority of the Naga people who saw in complete independence their only adequate safeguard against possible exploitation, the alienation of their land, and the destruction of their social organization, customary law and usages. This fear, unfounded though it may be, is shared by practically all the Naga people who are aware of their relative backwardness and poverty."[157]

Since, the Agreement was passed by a slender majority, the extremists under Phizo, having failed to cajole, convince and intimidate the doves, declared the Agreement null and void.[158] Later Phizo with his friends met Mohd. Ali Jinnah, the Muslim League supremo and Jaipal Singh, tribal leader from Chhotanagpur Plateau (Bihar) and Mahatma Gandhi on 19 July 1947. Jinnah had possibly committed nothing but said: 'It is a matter entirely for you to decide'[159] and Jaipal Singh had advised the Nagas not to take a hasty decision.

---

[157]NNC, op.cit, p.24.

[158]V.K. Anand, op.cit, p.65.

[159]The Statesman, Delhi, July 20, 1947, p.4 (quoted by P Sema, in '*British Policy and Administration in Nagaland (1881-1947)*' Scholar Publishing, New Delhi 1992, p.156.

Gandhi's Views: Mis-interpreted

In a meeting with Gandhiji, which has been quoted by many, the philosophical oration by Mahatma Gandhi has been mis-interpreted grossly by one and all and specially the extremist group of the NNC. The philosophical remarks of Mahatma Gandhi had been advertised as an approval stamp for Nagas Independence wherein he said:

> "I was independent when the whole of India was under the British heel. Why 16th of August? you can be independent today if you have non-violence in common with me, no one can deprive you of independence...He further added: "Independence, yes. But if you say you will be independent of the whole world, you can't do it. I am independent in my own house. If I become independent of Delhi I will be crushed to atom. I have no stored food. I have to get it from Delhi...you are in Asia. As I can see you all are slaves. I am not. From where do you get your cloth? (Naga: It is foreign cloth). Then you are slave of foreigners. Will you go naked if the foreigners do not give you cloth? ...You can not be left in complete isolation."[160]

The philosophical oration should be read in its correct perspective for its latent intent and thus, in my opinion; Mahatma Gandhi never endorsed the idea of Naga independence. The understanding of Gandhi by scholars (especially Naga scholars) and the NNC have been misplaced in this regard.

Subsequent Efforts

Subsequently, the NNC held a meeting at Mokukchung to ratify the Hydari Agreement. Wherein there was unanimous opinion for changing the clause 9 to allow for right to secede in ten years' time. The extreme 'independence group' seemed to have violently disagreed with moderates and broke away to form the Naga independence group. This group mainly from Khonoma village and Southern and Eastern Angamis

[160] M. Ramunny, op.cit, p.24.

led by Phizo went on to declare independence on 14th August, 1947.[161] This unilateral declaration of independence (UDI) was informed to the UNO and the Government of India but neither responded nor could he form a government to run the so called independent state.

Position on the Day of Independence

By 15 August 1947, the NNC had new President and Secretary as Aliba Imti and Kumbho Angami respectively. The moderates favoured the modification of clause 9 and the new team of NNC submitted a memorandum to the Governor of Assam stating that the NNC had unanimously decided to modify the Para 9 of the Agreement which should be read as follows :

> "The Governor of Assam as the agent of the Government of the Indian Union will have a special responsibility for a period of 10 years to ensure the due observance of this agreement, at the end of this period the Nagas will be free to decide their own future."[162]

This was a deviation from the agreement, but if seen in correct perspective, there was not much change from the actual agreement. Sir **C.R. Pawsey** had recommended that the NNC be allowed to decide their future but will not be allowed to join Burma or Pakistan thus union with India was certain, however loose it may be. But the Governor proposed that at the end of this period the NNC will be free to decide what arrangements should be made for the future administration of Naga Country.[163] Certainly the NNC and the Governor were now not in the same frequency.

Another Memorandum: An Ultimatum

On 04 November, 1947, the NNC shot another memorandum with regard to the clause 9, stating that at the end of ten years,

[161]Ramunny, op.cit, p.26.

[162]ibid.

[163]ibid, p.27.

Nagas should be free to decide their future. This memorandum was attached with an ultimatum that if no reply was received within 30 days, Naga territory would cease to be a part of the Indian union from 06 December, 1947. Immediately, after this all the Naga Magistrates were served with anonymous letter advising them to resign else they would be shot. Similar threats were issued to Government servants as well but that was not liked by the Aos for they wanted to take the recourse through constitutional means. Paradoxically **Phizo**, an archrival of Aliba Imti, failed to dislodge him from the post of the President of NNC, was against the ultimatum. When he finally didn't succeed to be the President of the NNC, he resigned and declared that he would have nothing to do with it so long as Aliba was in it.[164]

Finally, Phizo got a breakthrough and had an opportunity to meet the Governor of Assam on 05 May, 1948 but certainly not as a deputed leader of the NNC. Though, the meeting was of no consequence so far as the setttlement of ongoing problem was concerned but this meeting changed his position from an unwanted leader to more of an accepted leader of the Nagas.

Meanwhile, the administrative machinery was geared up to implement the Agreement but in certain sections the rumour was milling around that the government was not sincere enough to implement the provisions of the said agreement. Finally, the Government of Assam issued a written assurance that it was sincere to honour the Agreement vide Memo No: 88-c/47-570-72 dated 22 June 1948, almost a year after the signing of the Agreement. The statement was signed by Hydari, the Governor himself and Gopi Nath Borodoloi, Premier of Assam.[165] While these developments were taking place, Phizo was placed under arrest because he was trying to sabotage the efforts of the NNC and Government of Assam to bring about a just solution to the problem.

---

[164]Ramunny, op.cit, p.27

[165]Mar Atsongchanger, '*Unforgettable Memories from Nagaland*', Mokukchung, Nagaland, 1994, p.16.

Naga Hills District: Provisions under Constitution of India

Based on the recommendations, all the tribal areas including the Naga Hills district provisions were made in the Fifth and Sixth Schedules of the Article 244 in the Constitution of India. The fifth schedule deals with the states other than Assam and the Sixth Schedule is dedicated for the administration of tribal areas of Assam, out of which 'Part A' deals with the 'Excluded Areas' of the hills districts of Assam e.g. Khasi, Jaintia and Naga Hills whereas 'Part B' deals with North Eastern Frontier including Baliapara Frontier Tract, Tirap Frontier Tract, Abor Hill Districts and the Naga Tribal Area. The details of administrative set up as envisaged in the Nine Point Hydari-NNC Agreement has been enshrined in the Constitution of India. The Nagas were given autonomy in matters of local administration, however, within the Indian Union.[166] It is also to be worth mentioning here that the Nagas enjoy much more autonomy, which other states of India do not, through constitutional Article 371(A), which is yet to come, shall be discussed later.

Though all the provisions of Nine Points have been covered in the Sixth Schedule, but it does not talk of the revision of the agreement after ten-year guarantee period. Some of the Naga leaders, branded as pro-Government, such as Hokishe Sema (ex Chief Minister of Nagaland) felt that the Sixth Schedule provided all the safeguards for the Naga people as per Nine Point Agreement. He opines:

> "While all Naga demands contained in the Nine Point Agreement were included in this Schedule (Sixth Schedule), yet the confusion created by the conflicting interpretation of the ninth point of the Hydari Agreement continued to exercise and agitate the minds of Nagas."[167]

It is believed that actions due on ground lacked sincerity and seriousness especially after death of Sir Akbar Hydari.

---

[166]Mar Atsongchanger, op.cit, p.47. (Later Article 371(A)has been given to the Naga state, defacto autonomy, will be discussed subsequently).

[167]Hokishe Sema, *'Emergence of Nagaland'*, Vikas Publishing House, New Delhi, 1986, pp.89-90.

Possibly, the Government of India got unduly occupied in unwarranted war on Kashmir due to Pakistan's aggression in 1947-48 and resettlement of refugees' alongwith consolidation of Indian princely states. The provisions of the Sixth Schedule could not be used to form an interim government for the Nagas within Indian Union, thus, moderates in the NNC failed to explain it to the people that the provisions of the Nine Point Agreement had been achieved through the constitutional means.

India became a democratic Republic on 26 January, 1950 and the Constitution became effective, the Nagas found that they were given just short of what they expected i.e. a constitutionally Independent status specially as envisaged by some of the moderate Naga leaders, however, demand of extreme group could not be met for obvious reasons. They also knew fully well that they were demanding more than what they could have bargained for while Hydari Agreement was being put to vote. Even Phizo had admitted in his writing that:

> "This (Clause Number 9) was not a clear promise of self determination. But it was an acceptable start to a majority of the Naga National Council, and both sides formally agreed to this document".[168]

Demand of a Sovereign State

For the very first time the NNC openly declared that they wanted nothing but separate sovereign state for the Nagas on 05 April, 1950 and denounced to accept the sixth schedule. Finally on 15 May, 1950 the NNC followed up with another statement that they did not like the word 'District Council' in the Constitution of the Republic of India. To top it up, 'the Government of India decided that nothing would be done in future which might in any way be regarded as an official recognition of the nine point Agreement'.[169] Thus, the seeds of discontent sowed manifested as a bloody insurgency in which future generations were to suffer.

---

[168]Nirmal Nibedon, *'The Night of the Guerillas'*, Lancer Publishers, New Delhi, 1983, p.31.

[169]Nirmal Nibedon, op.cit.

4

The Naga National Council: Insurgency and Violence

The Backdrop

The genesis of the Naga problem, role of the Naga National Council in the Naga politics (till 1947) has already been discussed in the previous chapter. In this chapter, we will discuss the post independence period, specially after the new Constitution was accepted and India began its journey as a Republic among the comity of nations.

Although, the entire nation was jubilant, but it was not at ease for there were many problems to be addressed at an emergency basis. Thus, the government in Delhi was beseeched with many other things from nation building to political consolidation alongwith resettlement of millions of refugees from East and West Pakistan. Many issues which were also of importance, got very little attention at the apex level and so was the case with entire North East i.e. Issues in Assam state. On the other hand, the NNC leadership was not patient enough and began non violence movement and conducted a plebiscite in haste. Till then the government agencies had been silent and all peaceful political activities were permitted. But there was an unfortunate and bizarre incident that took place during the visit of Indian and Burmese Prime Ministers to Kohima, compelled the law enforcing agencies to clamp down on the NNC. Fear of repraisal forced the NNC cadres to go underground. Then the movement began in more assertive manner and the NNC formed a government called it as Hongkhin government.

The situation so formed, started deteriorating fast due to actions by the law enforcement agencies inviting vigorous reactions from the NNC and vice versa, that made the situation precarious beyond the control of state police hence the army was deployed. With this began a long drawn and protracted insurgency, in which the Trinity (i) the government, (ii) the people and (iii) its army badly got embroiled. Heat of that emergency can be felt even today i.e. after almost six decades. In this chapter, an effort will be made to study these aspects leading to deployment of army to quell the violence and effects thereof.

Section–I

The Plebiscite: Prelude to Violence

It may be recalled that the NNC consisted of a group of people, mainly government servants, had grown from a club into a political party. Till early 1950s, it was in the hands of moderates but was gradually taken over by hardliners led by Phizo. The ugly turn of events threw the Naga Hills into an array of socio-political disharmony. **Mao** has attributed this problem to ignorance and suspicion of the people in the Hills about the people of plains based on rumours and much of it were false propaganda about the Hindus, Muslims and Buddhists with whom they would not be comfortable. The British and the American Christian Missionaries also contributed to turn the Nagas against the plains people of India by circulating concocted stories. These were exploited by the separatists who were also the victims of similar kind of misinformation campaign.[170] Role of Missionaries were questionable, however, inaction on the part of central government has no logical and

[170] A.D. Mao, *'Nagas: Problems and Politics'*, Ashish Publishing House, Delhi, 1992, pp.35-37.

sound answer. May be action against Missionaries would have invited criticism from civil population which they could ill-afford at this stage.

The events that followed the British withdrawal from India in general and the Naga Hills in particular, were certainly unfortunate. By December, 1950, the NNC fell firmly in the grip of the hardliners, when Phizo took over the mantle as the President. The peaceful Nagas were led towards a path of violence without realising the impracticability of establishing an independent sovereign state in a small land-locked area, covering 6000 sq miles with a population of barely 2,13,000 souls. Phizo was a man of high ambition but politically not matured enough. His political ambition had caught, the fancy of the people and crushed any new school of thought cropping up against him ruthlessly. **Gundevia** articulated on **Phizo:**

> "To me it has never been a coincidence that **Angami Phizo**, who was always having second thoughts after each of the agreements, came from Khonoma. The powerful Angami village of Khonoma had… a history of militancy and defiance which must have bred a non-conformist psychology…"[171]

Plebiscite and the Controversy

Certainly Phizo was obsessed with independence and held plebiscite. The tactics adopted by Phizo and his aides during plebiscite vote meeting can be understood by Ramunny's account in which he quoted from the diary of Phizo. According to Phizo, over 6000 (Six thousand) people from all corners of Naga Hills came to Kohima to give their verdict on 16 May 1951. 'Phizo delivered a speech first in English and then in Nagamese for over an hour to the people who came for Plebiscite. There were two booths, one for those in favour of Naga-Independence and one for those Nagas who wanted Nagaland to remain in the Indian Union. The booth for the supporters of the Indian Union was empty.'[172]

---

[171] A.D. Mao, op.cit, p.63.

[172] M. Ramunny, op.cit, p.35.

However, the eye witnesses who attended the plebiscite meeting lay a claim contrary to the above and say that 'not more than a thousand were present including a large number of representatives from the bigger villages around Kohima.'[173] Thus, it was only the Angamis, who supported Phizo wholeheartedly. It is believed that Phizo did say during his speech:

"The white government has gone ; a black government has come. This black government will take away your land; they will tax your houses, your cows, your pigs will be counted and you will be asked to pay according to the number of pigs you keep. You will not be allowed to eat beef or pork. You will not be allowed to drink. Do you want such a government, or 'Independenti' (meaning independence)? If you are independent, you will enjoy life as we had before the British came."[174]

The people, of course, would have given the answer in unison for their '**independenti**' for obvious reasons. Surprisingly, the plebiscite was allowed to be held by the local administration and apparently there was no direction from the centre either. There were some basic flaws in conducting this plebiscite. Firstly, women participation was absent, thus violating basic norms of seeking a plebiscite. Secondly, it could not include all the male folk either, because of undeveloped terrain and non-communicability of one tribe to another. Also some elderly people who took part in the plebiscite used to say that a large number of finger prints were forged. The conspicuous absence of media for such a historic event (if at all it was!) as they claim till date, leaves much space for speculation. However, the Naga scholars claim it to be the expression of collective will of the Naga people. Aosenba writes:

"The people of Nagaland held a national plebiscite in May 1951, whereby 99% of the population renewed their commitment to sovereignty."[175]

---

[173]Ramunny, op.cit, p.35.

[174]ibid.

[175]Aosenba, '*The Naga Resistance Movement: Prospects of Peace and Armed Conflict*', Regency Publications, New Delhi, 2001, p.45.

Mis-Interpretation of "Sovereignity"

Here Aosenba's interpretation of sovereignty and the common folk's sovereignty has wide disparity in understanding. Being political science scholar, he has chosen to ignore the political dimension of sovereignty in its real sense, however, for a common man who gathered for plebiscite, 'sovereignty' meant or only hovered around to live life as before without any infringement. It is also true that the plebiscite was conducted in Kohima town and in Mokukchung, but the District of Tuensang in which approximately 150,000 people resided, was excluded from this referendum exercise, whereas only 1,89,671 was total population of Naga Hills in 1947. Thus approximately 75% people did not even know of the same. To conclude a plebiscite conducted throughout the Naga Hills in 1951 is merely an exaggeration and till date Naga people are fed with a liberal dose of plebiscite as a living cause. Lt Gen **JR Mukherjee**, a veteran soldier of Indian Army and also an authority on North Eastern states holds similar opinion. He comments:

> "In 1951 Phizo organized a controversial plebiscite in Naga Hills District to determine whether the Nagas wanted independence or merger with India. He then claimed that 99% were in favour of independence. In fact, the so-called plebiscite was held only in Kohima and Mokokchung with limited attendance, and women and other areas of Nagaland had been excluded. These realities are little known to all including the Naga public at large."[176]

However, immediately after the so called Plebiscite, **Phizo** sent a communication to the government claiming the success of the same. Basic premise of independence on which plebiscite was held is different as per Naga understanding which is not more than 'to live life as before without any interference'. **Kanwar Randip Singh**, who had long association with the Nagas as an administrator asserts the same:

---

[176]Lt Gen JR Mukherjee, *'Insurgency in India's North East'*, Anthem South Asian Studies, London, 2005, p.32.

"They need a strong government, as they had in British days, so that no inter-tribal head-hunting of the past is repeated (most of them believe that the Nagas themselves could never control this practice). There was to be no interference whatsoever with their ways of living, customs and general social organization. No other taxes than the customary house tax was to be imposed. Their lands would remain with them."[177]

Phizo's articulation about independence was different when he spoke to the Naga people who were misinformed for the fact that no Naga at that time could have understood the actual meaning of plebiscite, but voted for their governance as per customary laws and traditions in vogue. A common Naga understood very little about so called '**independenti**' or independence in those days as he would always say in the same breath that he was most loyal to the government and at the same time, wanted independence for the Nagas, which is contradictory.

Boycott of General Elections

Close on the heels, India was getting ready to embrace the democratic process of first general elections for its governance. The NNC declared boycott and people were intimidated against participation in the elections. **Elwin** writes regarding the election:

"No Naga sought election to Parliament or the Legislature of Assam and no Nagas exercised their right of voting. Government, however, went through – It had to go through – the full procedure of a General Election. Electoral rolls were prepared, election-booths were established everywhere, ballot boxes and papers were provided and Election Officers were placed in position. Yet there were no applications from anyone, no nominations from any side and no candidates to vote for."[178]

---

[177]Kanwar Randip Singh, '*The Nagaland*', Deep and Deep Publication, New Delhi,1987, p.63.

[178]K. Maitra, '*The Rebel and Insurgency in the North East*', Vikas Publishing House, New Delhi, 1998, p.19.

The boycott was total and effective, whether it was due to the spontaneous popular support or otherwise, could not be ascertained. The NNC and subsequent NSCN documents claim that the people rejected the general election *en masse*. **Maitra** writes about the election in the following manner:

> "The boycott was a complete success. **Bimla Prasad Chaliha** (the then president of Assam Pradesh Congress) toured the interiors of the Naga areas in September, 1953. He observed that, apart from the plebiscite, the boycott of the general election was sufficient proof of unanimity of the Naga people for independence and their singleness of purpose."[179]

While it can be said that plebiscite was a sham for the reasons that it was not based on universal adult franchise but the boycott was certainly total. It was due to both, fear of the NNC cadres who had issued whip against participation in elections in any manner and also to support the NNC call for Naga national cause. The atmosphere in the Naga Hills continued to be tense and it was apparently under the grip of the NNC cadres. They were successful in sabotaging the efforts of the administration.

Visit of the Premiers of India and Burma: Ended in Fiasco

Under the prevailing circumstances, Prime Minister Nehru visited Naga Hills accompanied by **U Nu**, the Premier of Burma (now Myanmar) on 30 March, 1952. The aim was probably to settle the issue and calm the people. Both the premiers were extended very warm welcome all the way before reaching Kohima from Imphal and it was really befitting to their stature.

One press report as quoted by **M. Ramunny**:

> "Both the Prime Ministers received an exceptionally warm welcome from wayside Naga villages. Though there are not many of these on the 90-mile route, yet wherever road passed a village it was a thrilling sight to see crowds of Nagas, the men

[179]Rh. Raising and Angelus Shimrah, *'Nagas in the Historical Perspective'* (*50 Years of Resistance*), NSCN (IM), 1999, p.31.

in their picturesque battledress complete with spear, shield, and ornate head dress cheering the party."[180]

The NNC also had planned to extend a formal ceremonial welcome as per Naga traditions and customs to the visiting dignitaries in most befitting manner, but unfortunately, the events took an ugly turn, which had a long term impact in the lives of the people of the Nagaland. The Naga people who gathered to welcome both the premiers, suddenly there was a communication passed through voice (ear to ear) from the NNC leaders, were told to quit the ground by the NNC volunteers, as they were not allowed to submit a memorandum to the Prime Minister in the public meeting by the Deputy Commissioner, **Barkataki**. Apparently, a show down took place about which the Deputy Commissioner said:

"The memorandum, a draft of which was submitted to me last night, may be handed over to me by the representative of the NNC in my house for submission to the Prime Minister, through the Chief Minister of Assam."[181]

In addition he had sent another note to the NNC that the Prime Minister had agreed to meet with the NNC representatives during the tea party and the memorandum could be given to him there as handing over of memorandum in public would have been a bit cynosure in front of the foreign dignitary, hence, advised accordingly. This might have created suspicion in the minds of the NNC leaders and thus NNC volunteers drove the people out of the ground. It was also felt that if the D.C. or his staff, concerned people understood Naga psyche better and handled the situation with maturity, the inevitable could have been avoided.

This sudden but unfortunate incident had a pronouncing effect on the policy of the government as the highest level of decision making authority of India and Burma (now Myanmar) were offended. This couldn't have gone down well and can be inferred from the actions undertaken by the government authorities soon after the departure of visiting dignitaries.

---

[180]**M.Ramunny**, p.38. (*The Statesman*, 31 March 1952).

[181]ibid.

Section-II

The Beginning of Violence

The visit of both the premiers ended in a fiasco, left a deep scar in the psyche of all concerned. The common people were apprehensive about the reaction of the government, and NNC leaders correctly anticipated it that the government would take serious action against them and decided to go underground. Certainly, the reaction was stern from the government agencies. It was felt by the latter that missionaries were behind the agitation and hence, the foreign missionaries were ordered to leave the Naga Hills and monthly newspaper of the 'NNC' i.e, the 'Naga Nation' was banned. Due to these two actions and absence of media, rumour spread like jungle fire. Shortly on the night of 04 April, 1953, Assam Police raided the house of T. Sakhrie, the then secretary of NNC. Thereafter, villages (Viswema, Jakhama, Kigwema, Phesama and Khonoma) were raided, guns were seized and a number of innocent people were arrested. These suppressive actions of the government created the required conducive atmosphere for launching an underground movement by the NNC. Aosenba writes:

> "Unable to live peacefully, the apprehensive policy adopted by the Government led the Naga leaders to evade arrest and compelled them to go underground, which sowed the seeds of the insurgency movement."[182]

The decision to drive the foreign missionaries out of the Naga Hills was based on the understanding of Nehru, who had presented a memorandum in October, 1952 at Mao village in Manipur about which **Nehru** was of the opinion that:

> "...the Naga National Council memorandum given to him at Mao last October, could not have been drafted by Nagas. No one who knew what India was and stood for, could have drafted this."[183]

---

[182]Aosenba, op. cit, p.49.

[183]M. Ramunny, op.cit, p.38.

Though one can question the apprehensions of Nehru but his assertions cannot be ignored as a biased opinion or rejected because of the dubious distinction the missionaries had earned in India specially when working and engaging themselves in social work in the name of Christ for betterment of tribal people in India.

High Profile Visits

While the administrative machinery was busy to quell the voice of dissent, simultaneously efforts were made to understand the socio-political dimension of the problem with more pragmatic approach through visits by high profile political leaders and by establishing contact with the underground leaders. One of such visit by **B.P. Chaliha**, the then Congress President of Assam province, achieved its aim and facilitated establishing contact with some of the undergrounds whose names were withheld by Chaliha himself as per understanding they had arrived. Later, it was revealed that they were Sakhrie, Jasokie, Silie Haralu and Thinuniu. However, present day NSCN (IM) documents refer to this as a matter of treason and total sell out to India. They agreed on some of the important issues such as recognition of no bloodshed and resolving the problem through peaceful negotiation, but there was no deviation from the demand of independence.

There were some other leaders who visited the Naga Hills during this period as well. **Rajkumari Amrit Kaur** toured the entire Northeast region and held talks with a number of Naga leaders in November 1953. She did explain to the Naga delegations who met her at Imphal, Manipur that their demand of complete secession was untenable, however, she urged the members of the delegation to join hands with the government in the reconstruction of Naga Hills.[184] **G.B. Mavalankar**, the Speaker of the Lok Sabha (Lower House of Indian Parliament) also visited the Naga Hills in January, 1954 for the same

[184]A.D. Mao, op. cit, p.52.

mission. In fact, the central leadership was working for one nation by consolidating on the much fragmented provinces and princely states. Since the Naga demands appeared to be contrary, they were advised to reach some common meeting point so that issue could be resolved through political negotiations. It appears that it was the failure of both the sides to understand and articulate their view points as they already held the common ground of '**independenti**' but differed on semantics.

Meanwhile, hostility continued and the government employees were under serious threat. **Elwin** writes about the life in general in the Naga Hills:

> "Government employees specially Naga employees, were threatened by posters and letters, denounced at meetings, sometimes attacked and killed. Some were kidnapped and held to ransom. Roads were damaged, bridges cut and official buildings were burnt."[185]

Return Visit by Naga Goodwill Mission

The outcome of the visits by the political leaders of Assam province and centre was that a return visit of Naga Goodwill Mission was organised which visited other parts of Assam and interacted with a cross section of people and politicians. This visit was to bring the NNC leaders back into mainstream of national politics and shed the demand of independence whereas the latter wanted to press home their agenda of secession. The Goodwill Mission wrote in their Mission Report:

> "Our Mission has failed so far to the extent that it failed to bring home to those shooters of epithets that it could not be a case of separation when the connection, in the first place, had been non existent just as much as there could be no 'separation' among the parties of an unmarried couple. Separation could arise only when there had been a union. In our case there was no 'Union' which would give ground for calling our national struggle to regain the former sovereignty, a 'separatist movement' much

[185]Elwin, op. cit, p.54.

less an 'anti Indian' movement since the claim of our national independence is not a force for the opposition of India."[186]

Beginning of Insurgency

Phizo was busy in organizing people in Tuengsang area with a popular slogan of 'No House Tax' which led to violence in Akubami, a village near the border under the administrative area of Aghunato. Dobashi (Interpreter) of Assam Rifles patrol was severely injured in an ambush while passing through the village, though the patrol commander did not return the fire and the issue was amicably settled by the political officers. The NNC also started motivating the *Gaonburhas* (village headmen) for non cooperation with the government.

Rise in tension generally results in violence, which happened in this case too, but **Elwin** asserted that 'the NNC never officially approved a policy of violence', but it was organizing for armed struggle against the Government in the remote areas of Tuengsang. Not a single opportunity was wasted by the NNC to encash any situation to earn political mileage whenever a common man was questioned, interrogated or harassed by the government agencies, and locked its horns with the Government. On 08 September 1953 the NNC decided and declared that Nagas would not be the first party to seek negotiation with India. Thus, both the parties were on a wild goose chase of each other. Meanwhile, Pangsha village was raided wherein few NNC cadres were killed. The NNC tried to defame the government and exploit the situation and accused the later of having intent to finish the NNC hierarchy, wherein none from the government were involved, and appears that government agencies were clueless about the incident. In fact, it was a punitive expedition to punish the villagers against the age old tradition of head-hunting, about which **Elwin** writes:

"Yengpang, a village on the Burma border, who could not afford to even out with another village called Kojok, took the

---

[186]Luingam Luithui and Nandita Haksar, '*Nagaland File: A Question of Human Rights*', Lancer International, New Delhi, 1984, p.83.

assistance of Pangsha, a powerful village. Pangsha villagers did the raid on Kojok, hence a punitive expedition was undertaken against Pangsha in 1936, but Yengpang was spared. The old habits and Naga enimity die hard. In 1954, son of one important leader of Pangsha was ambushed. Since Pangsha could not be sure that who could have done it, all the indicators of success and suspicion pointed to Yengpang. Hence the punishment was meted out on 15 November 1954 and Yengpang lost fifty seven heads, before the information could reach the administration and necessary precaution could be undertaken. At that time there was no official and no security personnel anywhere in the area; and the incident was perfectly normal act of revenge on the part of Nagas themselves."[187]

Incidentally, in this expedition of **Yengpang**, NNC leader **T Temjen Ao** was also killed. **Phizo**, of course blamed it on the authorities, as if, it was launched by the government expecting him to be present in that village. Bendangangshi, a Naga scholar and NNC activist, who is more vocal against the government, sees a high level of conspiracy by the government of India to finish the race altogether. He wrote:

"The campaign of Indian terrorism and genocide came in two stages. The first stage involved beating, thaping (slapping) and torture of the Naga leaders. The second stage was indiscriminate massacre aimed at annihilating the Naga freedom fighters from the face of the earth. As stated, the first one to suffer the full onslaught of Indian Army was the free Nagaland. And on November 15, 1954 Indian armed forces raided the village of Yengpang in free Nagaland and killed 60 men, women and children at a time."[188]

Though, expeditions were common practice against the erring villages during the British rule wherein brutality used to be at its prime; neither punishing the savages of Yengpang or Pangsha can be morally or logically supported nor can it be propounded as a policy of the state. The opinion of Bendangangshi is naturally biased and should be seen

[187]Elwin, op. cit, p.55.

[188]Bendangangshi, *'Glimpses of Naga History'*, Private Publication of Sopungwati Ao (Revised Edn), Mokokchung, 2000, p.73.

in its correct perspective as the same story has been stated by Haimendorf in the chapter 'Yempang's Black Day' and subsequent chapters.[189] He himself participated in that expedition against Yempang village and presence of NNC cadres was purely incidental of which the authorities were totally unaware. But no one can deny that harsh measures were taken in order to clip the wings of the NNC by the authorities in the entire Naga Hills.

Certain special legal provisions were made for the police to operate with impunity. The proclamation of the 'Assam Maintenance of Public Order '(Autonomous Districts Act), 1953, was to empower the law enforcement agencies with wide range of powers. The provisions of this law allowed imposition of collective fines on inhabitants of any area who harboured, or failed to discover and apprehend people who engaged themselves in activities prejudicial to public safety, maintenance of public order. Actually, this act was a very powerful tool in the hands of government agencies to check anti – government activities and one could be arrested without a valid warrant. All offences under this act were punishable with imprisonment of upto two years with additional fine. The act was certainly meant to drive the NNC cadres out of the public life and quell the violence, but the aim could not be achieved as most of the NNC workers went underground with greater resolve.[190]

Phizo and the NNC leadership were committed and certainly facing lot of hardships in their personal lives, desperate to see some results but they could not compel the government to pay heed, so they started organizing the NNC cadres in Tuengsang Frontiers. The aim was to launch armed rebellion against the government initiative to extend the administration

---

[189] Heimendorf, *Return to the Naked Nagas*, John Murray, London, 1976, pp.152-270.

[190] Kaka D. Iralu, *'Nagaland and India'*, Pvt Pub, 2000, p.78. *Also see* Nirmal Nibedon, *'Nagaland: The Night of the Guerallas'*, Lancers, New Delhi, Reprint, p.48, Laxman Murthy and R.N. Kumar, *'After Four Years of Ceasefire'*, Civil Society Initiatives on the Naga Peace Process, New Delhi, 2002, p.47.

and thus could exploit the mass sentiment in its favour. Since the government agencies were quick and successful to extend the administrative help to the people in those remote areas, much against the NNC's wishes, stage was set for a conflict. Sporadic violence of initial days kept on increasing with frequency and intensity. Violence was perpetrated to one and all and even the schools were not spared. 'On eleven occasions the hostiles attempted sabotage on the lines of communication or burning down government buildings including schools, dispensaries and offices.'[191]

No government can ignore violence perpetrated on common people and it's officials, hence, additional troops of Assam Rifles (a para military force organized on the lines of Indian Army) were deployed. However, Aosenba feels that they (NNC) were left with no option for peaceful negotiation as any prospect of negotiation with the government was completely belied with the decision of government to refuse any further discussion on Naga Independence issue.[192]

During this period of uncertainty, violence was the order of the day because neither of the parties accepted the reverses on their side. The NNC workers attacked Assam Rifles personnel and hence called for brutal and repressive retaliation in the form of raids and burning of villages etc. Situation was desperately tense and authorities had realised that it was beyond the capabilities of poorly equipped state police and the Assam Rifles. There is another side of the story, which claims that it was the government which dealt with the whole situation as a **'Law and Order'** problem rather than a political one. People were arrested, 'properties of leaders were confiscated and auctioned, crops in the fields were destroyed and wives and children of several leaders were arrested and detained in jails... As a result, even the *Gaonburhas* returned their prestigious red blankets and went into hiding.'[193] Though it was true that the *Gaonburhas* had returned the prestigious

[191]**M. Ramunny**, op. cit, p.46.
[192]**Aosenba**, op. cit, p.49.
[193]**Kaka D. Iralu**, op.cit, p.65.

symbol of honour, the 'Red Blanket', but whether all of them did this on their own or were threatened to do so by the NNC, remains to be established.

Federal Govt. of Nagaland: Mysterious!

Meanwhile, the NNC announced the installation of an Independent Republican Government of Free Nagaland at Kautaga, an imaginary place in Tuengsang Frontier Division on September 18, 1954 with Hongkhin as the president. **Phizo** kept the identity of 'Hongkhin Government' separate from NNC and even told the NNC workers in Kohima regarding non-violent activities of 'Hongkhin Government' (Hongkin means 'get out' in Chang tribal language).Though, Federal Government of Nagaland (FGN) was formed but its date and place of origin stands clouded in mystery, since there were no media or any other agency to record the event. A.L. Ao confirms the date of formation of said government. He writes:

> "The Naga freedom fighters did not remain silent to defend their motherland from foreign aggression, on September 18, 1954. They declared 'Free Nagaland' as sovereign Republic. In addition, they reorganized their government and formed the 'Federal Government of Nagaland' (FGN) on October 16, 1956."[194]

But most of the authors date the birth of 'Hongkhin' government on 22 March, 1956.

The Launch of Indian Army

The Indian Army was called in aid to the civilian authorities in order to restore the situation on 22 August, 1955. The army was deployed once the Naga Hills was declared as 'Disturbed Area' on 20 July, 1955. By then underground activities had taken a serious turn and violence was increasing day by day, some of the moderate NNC leaders declined to tow the line of violence enunciated by Phizo, and requested the government

---

[194] **A.L. Ao**, *'From Phizo to Muivah'*, Mittal Publications, New Delhi, 2002, p.67.

to maintain law and order for peace. A Naga delegation met Bishnuram Medhi, the Chief Minister of Assam at Shillong on 15 August and signed a declaration which condemned violence and terrorism and promised to use peaceful methods for the redressal of their grievances.[195]

The NNC was also undergoing internal problems as evident from above and it was realized by a few moderates that the path of violence adopted by Phizo would rather be counterproductive. When questioned by some young NNC leaders, **Phizo** emphatically stated that the NNC stood for a policy of non-violence and attributed the violent activities in Tuengang to the so-called free 'Hongkhin' Government of Tuengsang, which had nothing to do with the NNC and Naga Hills (administered areas). This was the dichotomy, probably a tactics to protect the NNC activists from the wrath of the Indian Army.

Some of the friends of **Phizo**, who did not like the violent ways to achieve the aim, were **Sakhrie**, **Jasokie**, **T. N. Angami** and they also had following in the ranks and files. Since his own people did not approve of violence, surely people on the streets must also not have been with **Phizo** on this account. However, all Naga undergrounds see this change of mind of moderates as an act of sell out to India for personal benefits. Two years later, on 22 March, 1958, Hongkin Government assumed new form in Phenshuniu, a Rengma village, located northeast of Kohima. The 'Naga Federal Government (FGN)' was restructured with a detailed organization. It had planned a Tatar Hoho (Parliament) with 100 tatars (members) and the president was to be elected by the people and his cabinet would be of 15 kilonsers (ministers) led by Ato Kilonser (prime minister) *(refer to Appendix 'E' for the organization of FGN).*

It is believed that the so called 'Yezhabo' (the constitution) of the 'FGN' was authored by none other than **T. Shakhrie**. The Naga Home Guards was organised in 1954 in Tuengsang under the '**Chang**' leader, Thungti Chang, a retired soldier of the Indian Army. The Naga Home Guards were armed with

---

[195]Kaka D. Iralu, op.cit, p.71, and Ramunny, op.cit, p.47.

the left over arms and ammunition of 2nd World War and of course, some looted arms of the police and the Assam Rifles.

'Azha': The Death Sentence

The 'Naga delegation' which visited Shillong in August 1955, generated goodwill and some kind of understanding was developed between the Assam Government and the delegates specially with Sakhrie. A statement signed by Chaliha jointly with Sakhrie said 'that the deadlock in Nagaland should be resolved amicably through negotiations and without bloodshed'.[196] This agreement became the turning point in the history of the NNC wherein one group of NNC parted ways and denounced violence.

The inevitable happened. The duo separated on ideological differences, **Phizo** could not withstand this as the NNC hierarchy believed that Sakhrie was bought by Indian agents and thus, Sakhrie was ordered to be eliminated and reportedly, the '**Ahza**' i.e, the 'instruction for killing or death sentence' was issued by none other than **Phizo**. The souvenir of NSCN (IM) confirmed the same. It says:

> "...The Government of India was then secretly planning to create division among the Nagas by wooing some Naga leaders. Very soon some leaders of NNC were caught in the trap laid by India. T Sakhrie, the then General Secretary of the NNC, and his colleagues, in connivance, with the Government of India, clandestinely decided to split from the NNC and get themselves ministerial berths in various ministries of Assam Government and other lucrative posts of the Indian Government. But the secret move got leaked out and NNC president Mr. A. Z. Phizo, in order to nip the unholy plan in the bud, had to eliminate Mr. Sakhrie."[197]

'Ahza' was passed down and Oking's (Headquarters) execution squad picked up Sakhrie from the house of his

---

[196]R.N. Kumar and Murthy, op.cit, p.47.

[197]**NSCN (IM)** Souvenir, *'50 years of Resistance'*, Private pub of NSCN (IM), 1999, p.22.

lady love in village Chiechama and brutally killed him on 18 January, 1956. Phizo and NNC continued with the agenda of violence beyond a point of no return for which many were to be sacrificed in the years to come.[198]

Indian Army's Philosophy in Combating Insurgency

The Indian Army, much reduced in strength due to partition of India, further depleted due to low priority to defence sector because of utopian concept of universal brotherhood and peace adhered to by the central leadership, was called for to help restore the situation for civil authorities in the Naga Hills. The philosophy of counter insurgency operations is a much recent phenomenon.

Though Indian Army had fought the bloody battles in the same terrain against the much powerful Japanese forces in which the Nagas supported the Allied Forces in an exemplary manner, the army in conventional operations is psychologically tuned to turn the opponents to ruins where the quantum of force is of no consequence. Moreover, the Indian Army, in the early 1950s was led by the officers with very less experience, worse; none were trained in combating the insurgency being a new form of conflict which was hitherto unknown. The same Army under the British rule had conducted the expeditions in the Naga Hills to punish the Naga villages, hence; developed and practised the principle of application of extra ordinary force to quell the violence. With this back drop in mind, we will study the deployment of the army and fallout of counter insurgency operations.

The Naga Home Guards and Naga Safe Guards who constituted themselves to form an army with the similar rank structure, uniforms and insignia to that of the Indian Army, clashed head on. The strength of the Naga hostiles in the beginning was about 300 men but by the end of 1956, Phizo had organized approximately 3000 men and thus, intensified his

---

[198]Nirmal Nibedon, op.cit, p.71. Also R.N Kumar and Murthy, op.cit, p.47.

campaign with extreme ferocity. The villagers were compelled to cooperate with them and this provided them with money, rice and other essential supplies, without which they could not have thrived the way they did.[199]

Psychological Challenges to Fight Insurgency

Here it would be prudent to mention some of issues related to armed forces when deployed for counter insurgency role. More often than not, they face bullets from an unknown quarter along-with various allegations like murder, rape, torture, use of third degree and gross human rights violation, notwithstanding majority of the cases are found to be exaggerated. In this case too, allegations of inhuman behaviour, torture and rape were common but no one can say that those were without provocation. In addition, once deployed in combating insurgency albeit with constitutional mandate and support, they lose battle-worthiness and subjected to fight with one hand tied behind, psychologically much more challenging than fighting in actual war. On the other hand, the human rights of a soldier can be violated anytime by an unsuspected but omnipresent insurgent. He can be written off for his decision dilemma, whether to shoot or not at a person suspected! If he does, may kill an innocent inadvertently but if he doesn't, then what? A soldier is accountable for his action to the nation but not an insurgent, sad but it's true!

Army in 'Catch 22' Situation

The Army was severely crippled due to lack of hard or actionable intelligence and often led them to a trap and hence, suffered casualties. Such betrayals by agents met with harsh actions. In fact, it was a catch 22 situation! Neither all the Nagas were with Phizo nor with the army, but they were caught in the crossfire. They (soldiers) were housed in the government

---

[199]Hokishe Sema, *'Emergence of Nagaland'*, Vikas Publishing House, New Delhi, 1986, pp.92-93.

buildings specially schools which remained closed for years and this led to dissatisfaction and frustration of the villagers, as narrated by **Bendangangshi:**

> "...Throughout 1953-1954, villages were raided, ransacked the houses and the inhabitants were beaten up mercilessly by Indian troops... schools were closed down and hostel buildings occupied by Indian Army... mass flogging was being freely administered in all the villages ... every where raping took place... of course, human decency prevents narrating such acts of lustfulness which reflected the history of Indo-Naga freedom struggle hitherto unknown to the Nagas."[200]

Promulgation of Armed Forces Special Powers

These claims are not totally baseless, may be they are exaggerated. Many villages were clubbed together (called as concentration camps), copied concept from the counter insurgency operations in Malaya to provide security to the villages against hostiles and cut off the insurgent from their logistics support bases but these were more often then not resented. Certain acts were also passed to strengthen the hands of the Army and other government agencies. Besides the Assam Maintenance of Public Order Act, 1953 and Assam Disturbed Area Act, 1955, following acts were also passed and applied:

1. The Armed Forces (Special power) Regulations, 1956.
2. The Armed Forces Special Power Ordinance, 1958.
3. The Nagaland Security Regulation, 1962 etc.

Out of all the Acts, the Armed Forces Special Powers Act (Commonly known as AFSPA) gives sweeping powers to the armed forces and till date, it is in vogue in all disturbed areas against which all the human rights groups are vocal and fighting to get it repealed.* But in absence of these powers life

---

[200]Bendangangshi, op.cit, p.69.

* This Act and related issues will be discussed in seventh chapter. Here it is discussed to present a comprehensive picture of the situation.

of a soldier is always at stake. An insurgent always has the advantage to appear on the scene from nowhere, hit the target, be it a civilian or an army Jawan and just merge with the crowd or melt away in jungles.

Absence of Media

One aspect that has been not discussed i.e, role of the media or conspicuous absence of it, which came much later. There could be two reasons i.e. firstly the entry to Nagaland was regulated by Inner Line Regulation Act of 1873. Owing to this, any outsider specially people from plains had to take permit to travel in the Naga Hills. Secondly, the fear of being hunted down by the NNC cadres. Whatever had been reported by the media was generally presented one sided story. **Niketu Iralu** wrote that 'the Indian media has depicted the Naga struggle as a secessionist'[201] movement and rightly so Indian media held the view from the Indian perspective, whereas **Tapan Bose** opined that 'Indians for a long time have been ignorant about the Naga cause. Many ruses were used to keep the people in dark.'[202] At least in the initial years, the NNC's demand was seen as a secessionist movement of few disgruntled men because of its small support base among the masses, but as time passed by, NNC and its cause had caught the fancy of the people and was truly a mass agitation.

Role of Army: Politicised

The role of army has been lauded by many, including Nehru, which may be taken as natural, being the head of the state (Prime Minister), but Lohia, a Member of Parliament after visiting the Naga Hills had reported that rape by Indian troops and police was widespread.[203] The comment of famous socialist leader

---

[201]NPMHR, *'Embracing Hope and Dreams'*, Kohima, 2003, p.114.

[202]ibid, p.115.

[203]For views of Lohia, see N. Maxwell, *'India: The Nagas and the Northeast'*, Report No 17 (Revised edn), 'Minority Rights Group', 1980, p.6. *Also see* Aosenba, op.cit, p.54.

leaves much scope for introspection.* Notwithstanding the kind of environment, the army was operating in, their relation with the vast majority of the people were friendly. The human approach and friendly gestures, displayed by some of them under the circumstances were laudable. The way they often lived was anything but harder than those of the tribal people themselves. Their courage and enterprise had made them very popular through out the hills.[204] The truth must be between the two extremes of reported human behaviour, and therefore, discretion must be used for making an objective assessment of the situation under which soldiers would have acted/reacted.

The opposition group, the NNC, exploited any excesses that were suggested to have taken place. In its documentation for propaganda, they have brought out vivid details but not all are credible. One such charge of the NNC was:

> "... That out of maximum population of about one million the Indian Army in eight years has killed over 100,000, ... Phizo lodged documented charges with the International Commission of Jurists alleging 70,000 Naga deaths, but delegations insist that the figure is over 100,000. They say that some 400,000 Naga men, women, children are being held in 180 concentration camps and prisons in appalling conditions, so that exact figures can not be given ..."[205]

The above figures seems to be unbelievable, because during 1947, as per the estimates total Naga population in the entire Naga Hills district was 189,671 of which 183,766 or 97.4 percent were said to be tribal population.[206] As per Elwin, who estimated the population of Nagas (all tribes included)

---

* It is also known to the officers of the Indian Army that one of the Rajputana Rifles Battalion was removed from Naga Hills and ordered to march on foot as a punishment by their 'Colonel of the Regiment', General Thapar, who was the then Chief of the Army Staff. (Told to the author by one of the Regimental Officers of the same Battalion in 2005-06.)

204 Elwin, op.cit, p.61.

205 '*The Naga National Rights and Movement*', Kohima, NNC Publication,1993, p.105.

206 Kumar and Murthy, op.cit, p.14.

to be 357,000 in 1961. Thus, the population within one decade was doubled, if the other factors are not taken into account, the population of Nagas should have been reduced to half by 1961 due to alleged killings, well below 100,000, but it was otherwise.

The instructions from the senior officers at command were to maintain highest standards and operate with restraint. But as it's been an experience all over the world that excesses do take place and most of them could be avoided but those who do it are driven by the circumstances. It is unfortunate and there could be no justification either. **Kumar** and **Murthy** summed up the situation under which a soldier operates and the inevitable outcome, they remarked:

> ".. all impartial observers of the Indo-Naga conflict will testify, monstrous atrocities did occur, and victims were left without reparation. This seems to be the insistable outcome whenever armed forces, foreign or national, are deployed to put down separatist insurgencies, political uprisings or liberation struggles ... in all such situations, monstrous atrocities and human rights abuses invariably occur ... Perhaps more complex factors are also at work, group psychology, organizational loyalty, political cynicism and the loss of moral sensitivities resulting from being a cog in what is essentially an inhuman machinery."[207]

Humane Face of Army: A Report

It is worth mentioning here that the government agencies were trying to rehabilitate the people and restore faith and normalcy by doing developmental works. One of the field directors of the Angami Baptist Mission (1956) **Kenneth Kerhuo** said about the friendly gestures or humane face of the mighty and faceless Army:

> "Owing to the violent activities of the Naga Home Guards, most of the churches stopped functioning in Naga Hills sometime ago. The villagers were so terror-stricken that they

---

[207]Kumar and Murthy, op. cit, p.7.

could not even enter their own houses. How could they come to the churches? Thanks to the Army, confidence has returned to the villages and the peaceful Nagas are able to look after their affairs, unafraid. The Churches are having regular services attended by bigger congregations then ever. Quite a number of Army officers and men are christians. They make it a point to attend church services. I have heard nothing but the highest praise of Army Officers and men in general from several Nagas of different tribes. They all say that the way Army personnel rehabilitate villages and bring medical succour to the sick and the infirm shows that they literally implement the following words of the Lord: 'Love your enemies, do good to them that despitefully use you."[208]

Unfortunate Shooting of Dr. Haralu

These excerpts were not from the churchman from any other part of the globe but a missionary from Naga tribes. During those violent days, **Haralu**, the first doctor from the Naga Hills was killed by the soldiers by mistake but hostiles took advantage of it and made a serious effort to earn political mileage. In fact, **Silie Haralu**, son of slain **Dr. Haralu**, had joined the ranks of hostiles and deserted it once he realized the mistake for whatever reasons. 'The guerillas were after his blood. Silie's children were residing near the Kohima Cinema Hall. But **Silie** never spent nights there as he was mortally afraid of the guerillas. **Dr. Haralu**, his father, used to come from his residence to see his grandchildren. One fateful day he was going by road to Kohima and was ambushed by the guerillas in the morning. Some soldiers on guard saw **Haralu** coming and mistook him for a rebel and shot him dead. The soldiers were, of course, court martialled later on.'[209]

Conclusion

The violence perpetrated by either side was to get the situation under their control and in the bargain common Nagas were

---

[208]K.S. Maitra, op.cit, p.34.
[209]ibid, pp.29-30.

caught in the crossfire. The army wanted the information about NNC movement, locating hide-outs etc and NNC needed them for ideological and material support for sustenance. Open display of leaning on either side would have invited wrath of the other group. It was a desperate situation, terrifying and filled with disastrous consequences. The liberal leaders on either side sought to bring an end to the violence through peaceful negotiations, as people were fed up of violence. They were looking for peace and an atmosphere in which they could live happily without any fear.

5

An Era of Peace Initiatives

All sorts of popular movements are actually manifestation of unfulfilled desires, unequal distribution of resources or socio-political or ideological differences between two groups in any society or in a nation-state. In the case of the Nagas, it was between the government of India which presumably represented the majority of Indians, so-called people dewelling in plains and the tribes in the Naga Hills. Though, initial response to the call of NNC was benign or subdued but became spontaneous from the people at large specially around 1955-56 C.E. There were two issues which were not in favour of the movement, i.e. firstly, common people who were mobilized in the name of sovereignty, understood it to be the freedom to live life as ever before, which is guaranteed by the Indian Constitution to all its citizens and the NNC articulated this sentiment in terms of absolute sovereignty and freedom. Secondly, viability of its existence as a nation state for which reasons have already been discussed.

It would be appropriate to say that the government of India approached and addressed the issue as a 'Law and Order' problem, in the beginning and inept handling turned it into a full blown insurgency. After couple of years of serious violence, the people reached a state of saturation. On the other hand, the insurgents were also weary of fighting in the jungles. Battle fatigue had set in and mood of the cadres could be gauged by rational thinking people within the NNC as well. A beginning was made to get all the tribal leaders to a common platform and discuss it out. The government also pressed its officials to deal with the issue and resolve it.

In this chapter, an effort has been made to study the peace initiatives which led to the statehood and much needed peaceful environment. The ceasefire, however, broken after few years by the hostiles and finally the army operations created conducive situation for talks, culminated in the name of Shillong Accord, which is most hated and controversial till date.

Section-I

Initial Efforts for Peace

In the middle of insurgency and violence, **T.N. Kaul**, from External Affairs Ministry visited Kohima to get a first hand report of the ground situation. It may be noted that affairs of the North-East Frontiers were being Prime Minister Nehru's subject under the 'External Affairs Ministry' and many undergrounds still cite this example in support of their claim when they demand sovereignty. The reasons for keeping the area under the Ministry of Foreign Affairs and not under the Home Ministry was politically motivated. Although it was damaging to an extent. **Gundevia** writes:

> "Naga affairs were the preserve of the Ministry of External Affairs, indeed virtually the personal preserve of Prime Minister Nehru himself; no one else had much say in the matter."[210]

Whether it was politically motivated decision or not, it's a matter of debate, however it has been proved very costly time and again as China also has been reminding India about the previous status of NEFA (present state of Arunachal Pradesh) as if, it was alien to India. Notwithstanding, **Kaul** on return in his report indicated that:

---

[210]Y.D. Gundevia, *'War and Peace in Nagaland'*, Palit and Palit, Dehradun and Delhi, 1975, p.71.

> "Phizo's demand for independence could not be entertained, nor could any government worth its name be threatened by a violent movement to accept a dictated solution..At the same time, he felt that the government should consider the desirability of finding a political solution to this delicate problem."[211]

Subsequently, some of the liberal Naga leaders visited Delhi in September, 1956. They were **Jasokie, Salsu, T.N. Angami, Khekiye, Silie Haralu** (whose father was shot dead by soldiers by mistake). There was fervent appeal to the common Nagas to reject **Phizo** as a leader. They said:

> "in the interest of our people, we had to ask you to throw off his leadership, because for years by his stubbornness and desire for personal power he has led us into negative paths of disaster. He has changed the whole meaning of independence which the Naga National Council and he himself defined in the beginning when we accepted the 1947 memorandum. By independence, we mean freedom to enjoy our Naga way of life. In this crisis, the time has come to find an honourable settlement before more blood flows and the land ruined."[212]

Peace Initiatives by NBCC

Not only these liberal Naga leaders came forward for peace but Naga Baptist Church Council (NBCC) also condemned the violence and appealed to the common Nagas to work for peace. As a result of these efforts, first Naga Peoples Convention (NPC) was held in August 1957. Imkongliba was the President and J.B. Jasokie was Secretary of the Convention. The first Convention of Kohima was attended by 1760 delegates from the 15 tribes. About two thousand other delegates were also present.[213]

In this session, a resolution was passed on August 26 to solve Naga problems politically within the framework of the

---

[211]**M. Ramunny**, op.cit, p.67.

[212]ibid, pp.67-68.

[213]**K.S. Maitra**, *'The Rebel and Insurgency in the North East'*, Vikas Publishing House, New Delhi, 1998, p.48.

Indian Union,[214] the ultimate aim of the Government. But the Convention was held amidst lot of confusion and the hardliners of the NNC tried to disrupt it by opening fire from a distant hill, when the Convention began in Kohima (Assam Rifles ground). Though, the convention was organised under the aegis of government, duly backed by peace loving Naga leaders but it was better represented than **Phizo's** plebiscite meeting. **Ramunny** writes:

> "The representatives of all the tribes had been elected according to the Naga custom. Every village sent their representatives to the tribal meetings where the tribal representatives were elected unanimously by consensus and they attended all tribes meetings at Kohima with the full mandate from the tribe as a whole. This meeting was far more representative and much more democratically elected than any meeting held by Phizo. Even so called plebiscite held in 1951 ..."[215]

Political Settlement: Controversy Still Lies

The Convention ended with a resolution for political settlement of the problem within Indian Union, but not without a controversy. **Vizol**, who later became the Member of the Parliament, alleged that the word 'within Indian Union' was introduced at the behest of representatives tutored by the government agencies. He wrote:

> "The first sitting of Naga Peoples Convention was addressed, among others, by Kevichusa, the first Naga IAS (retired). Kevichusa introduced a draft resolution (which) was received by the delgates with a wide acclaim and it was about to be adopted without much discussion. But the meeting was cut short by an announcement from the chair for lunch break. When the house reassembled in the afternoon some delegates tutored by the government agencies brought an amendment. The amendment was for the inclusion of the word 'within Indian Union' after 'political settlement' in the first resolution ... Kevichusa seeing

---

[214]K.S. Maitra, op.cit, p.49.

[215]**M. Ramunny**, op.cit, p.73.

the hands of the government in the convention withdrew from the convention."[216]

This process of bringing the political settlement to the problem had mixed reactions, while the moderates welcomed it as a positive step; undergrounds on the other hand condemned it and they intensified their operations. Apparently the Convention was being tutored or remotely controlled by someone from the government to find a solution within Indian Union. The hardliners of the NNC did not accept the view of the moderates and blasted it as simply rubber stamping of Indian proposals.[217] These Naga moderates were invited to Delhi for discussions with Nehru. In this meeting, the proposals put forward by them were accepted and based on this, on 01 December, 1957, **Naga Hills Tuensang Area** (NHTA) was formed, combining the Naga Hill Districts of Assam and Tuensang Frontier of NEFA (North East Frontier Agency). This area later was to become the state of Nagaland.

Second Convention: Options kept Open

The second Naga People's Convention (NPC) was held at Ungma (village of Ex Chief Minister S.C. Jamir) in May, 1958 attended by much larger number of people. In this convention, a proposal was made that all efforts be done to bring the undergrounds to over ground and join the mainstream for which the NPC was to initiate a process and the government had to drop all the operations for the time being. But in case, if things were not moving as desired then the option of tough (say military) actions were kept open. The NPC leadership made an earnest effort to persuade the undergrounds, but they didn't succeed. Thus, the NPC leadership called for the third convention.

---

[216]Vizol. '*On Sovereignty and Human Rights: An Unconditional Dialogue*', Private Circulation, Kohima, pp.22-23.

[217]NNC, *Naga National Rights and its Movement*, Kohima, 1993, p.62.

The Third Convention: 16 Points Resolution Accepted

The third and final Convention was held at Mokukchung in October, 1959. This was also attended by approximately 3000 Naga delegates. After the deliberations 16 points resolutions were passed. These resolutions were finally accepted by the government with minor modifications (**Refer Appendix 'F'**). This agreement paved the way for formation of the state of Nagaland and as usual, it could not have gone uncriticised. The Naga scholars allege that the Government of India for hob-nobbing with moderates and to drive a wedge between the rebels and the former. **Subir Ghosh** called it as a half hearted treaty. He writes:

> "Far from resolving the Naga contretemps, the 16 point Agreement of 1960, only served to appease the moderates. More important, it ensured that the chasm between the rebels and the moderates had become unbridgeable. A piecemeal solution was offered by the agreement. This half hearted treaty was essentially aimed at marginalizing the insurgents."[218]

S.C. Jamir*, ex Chief Minister of Nagaland state and veteran Congress leader; who happened to be the Secretary of the Reception Committee of the NPC at Ungma, his own village, has expressed the views contrary to that in election manifesto (July 2000) 'Bedrock of the Naga Society'. He expressed candidly that – "it was possibly the best solution to the imbroglio under the situation at that time, which later he affirmed". He said:

> "The 16 Point Agreement of 1960 came about (when) the Nagas were going through the worst times. But it was also one of the best things to have happened to the Naga people because it led to the birth of statehood on whose firm foundation, our society is built. In a larger form of things, due to the agreement, for the first time, the world recognized the territory of the Nagas as Nagaland."[219]

---

[218]**Subir Ghosh**, *'Frontier Travails'*, McMillan, New Delhi, 2001, p.210.

* **S.C. Jamir** was interviewed by the author on 17 August 2003 at Kohima.

[219]**S.C. Jamir**, *'Bedrock of the Naga Society'*, Publication of Indian National Congress, Kohima, 2000, p.5.

Of late, there has been an increasing tendency to criticise the 16 Point Agreement that led to the creation of Nagland State in December, 1963. When carefully analysed, much of this criticism was bereft of historical facts and emanated from a section of politicians solely for the sake of narrow political and personal gains. However, few impartial people seem to believe that the Agreement compromised the demand for a sovereign Naga nation.

Formation of State of Nagaland: An Apt Solution

Despite the dis-satisfaction of some people, in next general election, 75 percent of the electorate exercised their franchise. Failure to achieve peace could be attributed to the failure of moderates to motivate the NNC leadership to join the NPC and thus, resolutions passed by the NPC. In fact, the President of the NPC was assassinated for having signed the Agreement. **Chandrika** feels that:

> "the creation of Nagaland as a constituent state fulfilled the long cherished demand of the right thinking and nationalist Nagas, but this in itself was not the panacea for ills that the land and its people were ridden with."[220]

J.H. Hutton felt that the Nagas were conferred aptly and met the demands of the majority. He wrote:

> "It seems to me that by the formation of the state of Nagaland, protected as it is by the clauses in the Constitution of India, the Nagas have, in fact, got more than what had been expected or even desired; complete internal home rule financed by the Government. Indeed they have won the war, but to take advantage of their victory, the underground Nagas must be persuaded to surrender their arms and peace and order must be restored."[221]

---

[220]**Chandrika Singh**, *'Political Evaluation of Nagaland'*, op.cit, p.97.

[221]**J.H. Hutton,** *'The Assam Tribune'*, Guwahati, August 18, 1966 (Quoted by Chandrika, op.cit, p.97).

The formation of Nagaland state, the mission of moderates and the government was certainly a successful move although failed to win over the other group of NNC. So, they stepped up their violent activities which derailed the development process and affected the state adversely. Again peace loving people or one may call them right thinking citizens made another bid to broker peace. Curiously, this time initiative was taken by **Baptist Church** in its **Wokha Convention** held from 31 January to 02 February, 1964. A resolution was also adopted in which it was requested that both the parties i.e. government and the undergrounds to come forward and resolve the impasse.

Phizo Moved to U.K.

Meanwhile, **Phizo** crossed over to Dacca, East Pakistan (Now Bangladesh) and to London via Karachi with the help of Pakistan* and Rev. Scott. Phizo was not given visa by the British initially as they could ill afford to antagonize India being the most important nation in the Commonwealth. Rev Scott intervened with British authorities and fought his case. He argued that **Phizo** was a British subject before 1947 and thus, he had a right to enter. Thus, **Phizo** was permitted visa for entry in Britain and from there, he was controlling the NNC and the movement. He was running all the major issues that included procurement, shipment of arms, training through inimical neighbours of India, lobbying with foreign governments including U.N. *(this aspect will be covered in greater detail in the seventh chapter).* The Government of India was also aggressively trying to bring Phizo back for negotiation through diplomatic means and track two channels but proposals were limited to within the framework of Indian Constitution. As per **Gundevia,** Phizo was contacted through the High Commission in London and was promised safe passage to India. He was welcome for talks but there was no progress after that. He writes:

---

* **Hekiye Sema** of Naghutomi village, also visited Karachi for training, who met the author and confirmed this.

"Guarantee of a safe conduct was communicated to Phizo. But we never heard anything further from Angami Phizo and he never came. What stopped him, I do not know."[222]

Church's Initiative for Peace

Not only the Government of India was conscious of this fact that most important issue was to bring peace but also all the people who were associated with the Nagas including the Church, which took initiative to get the issue resolved. Regarding the Church's initiative, **Gundevia** writes:

"The Baptist Church, to which virtually the entire Naga Christian community belongs, had by and large, stayed out of politics. However, it was being obviously whispered around that the Chief Minister (Shilu Ao) was in touch with Phizo and some of the Church leaders felt that the time had perhaps come for them also to take some hand in trying to bring about peace. Needless to say, we welcomed the Church move."[223]

The Church had proposed constitution of a Peace Mission wherein four names of very famous personalities, who excelled in their public life and respected by people, were recommended. They were Shri **Jayprakash Narayan**, a true Gandhian and Sarvodayee* leader, who later led a political movement against un-democratic practices of one of the Prime Ministers of the country, Shri **B.P. Chaliha**, the Chief Minister of Assam, a man of transparent sincerity, **Shankarrao Dev**, a prominent social servant who was not available due to his ill health and Rev. **Micheal Scott**, a famous missionary who worked for the Indian under-privileged in South Africa and a friend of **Phizo**. **Gundevia** liked the composition of the Peace Mission. He writes:

"One must give full credit to the Church leaders for picking the names for the composition of a Peace Mission: one an Assamese, but after all Chief Minister belonging to the ruling

---

[222] **Y.D. Gundevia**, op.cit, p.106.

[223] ibid.

* **Sarvodaya**: Sanskrit term meaning *'universal uplift'* or *'progress of all'*. The term used by Mahatma Gandhi and is known as one of his philosophy.

party, and the other, a critic of the ruling party, but a respected critic 'and a god-damned pacifist,' as a Naga described him."[224]

Scott was selected as a spokesman of the 'other cause'. It was a long and arduous journey to peace most of which was being traversed by Scott, being the only available able bodied member (57 years of age) of the Peace Mission and most trusted friend of the undergrounds. Soon it was realized by all those who were involved that without cessation of hostilities, progress of the peace negotiation would be very slow because of very primitive communication (road and tele-communication in the Naga Hills), official protocol based hierarchy which was further impeded by counter insurgency operational hazards. It took approximately five months to hammer out the differences and reach an agreement for cessation of hostilities. Finally, on 06 September, 1964, Ceasefire Agreement came into force. This ceasefire facilitated suspension of all types of operations e.g. jungle operations, raids, patrolling beyond 1000 yards from the security posts, searching of villages, aerial actions, arrests and forced labour by the security forces and sniping, ambushing, imposition of fines, kidnapping, forcible recruitment, sabotage, raiding, firing on security posts or towards administrative centers and moving with arms or uniform etc activities banned.[225]

Scope of the Ceasefire Agreement

Under this agreement, ceasefire was to cover all the areas inhabited by the Naga people including Mao, Tamenglong and Ukhrul sub divisions of Manipur. Further, the ceasefire also covered the protection to the convoys and columns of security forces. Also there was a provision that Indian forces would not patrol the Burmese (Myanmar) border as long as the rebels gave an assurance that no arms would be

---

[224]Gundevia, op.cit, p.111.

[225]M. Aram, *'Peace in Nagaland'*, Arnold Heinmann Publishers Pvt Ltd, New Delhi, 1974, p.26.

imported from abroad during the peace talks.[226] The draft agreement was signed by the members of the Peace Mission and five underground representatives. This was referred to the respective higher authorities viz. 'Tatar Hoho' (the Naga parliament) and to Delhi.

The **Tatar Hoho** ratified the agreement but there were three technical problems which came up as an impediment, such as the Government was not ready to recognize the Federal Government of the undergrounds (FGN). Secondly government would reserve the right to patrol the border if it was required and the state government of Nagaland must be associated in any settlements. In fact, the term 'ceasefire' was also objected to. Truly in classical sense 'ceasefire' can be signed between two sovereign nations (a norm of that period), whereas undergrounds were not recognized as an independent nation as they thought to be. There were recommendations to change certain words in the agreement. **Chandrika** opines:

> "There were two serious flaws in the agreement. First it gave the impression that the underground Nagas had a sovereign government claiming an equal status of sovereignty as was implied ... Secondly, the underground Nagas wanted to side track the lawful government of Nagaland ... It was thought that the proposals were no doubt, objectionable but they were just means to an end, the end being the cessation of hostility."[227]

On the other hand, it was alleged that the agreement signed was a total surrender by the government. Though, government conceded some of the untenable demands of the underground Nagas but it cannot be termed as total surrender as the government never compromised on certain basic and fundamental issues. It always maintained that the solution of the problem has to be found within the frame work of the Indian Union. Notwithstanding, on 06 September 1964, the cessation of hostilities came into force and this day is known as **'Peace Day'** till date.

---

[226]Gundevia, op.cit, p.117.

[227]**Chandrika Singh**, op.cit, p.105.

Phase of Final Solution after Ceasefire

Soon after the 'Ceasefire', the talks for final solution began. First meeting was held at Chedema (which was a hostile village) on 23 September 1964. Probably the Naga leaders wanted some safe place like Chedema and not Kohima. **Y.D. Gundevia** was the leader accompanied by **Shilu Ao**, Chief Minister of Nagaland. Brig **D.N. Sen**, Legal Advisor, Sri **U.N. Sharma**, Chief Secretary and Shri **N. Suntook**, Deputy Secretary, Ministry of External Affairs, Government of India, were participating. The other side was led by **Zashei Huire**, accompanied by **Issac Swu**, self-styled Foreign Secretary of FGN and **Thinuselie** (self styled Brigadier of Naga Army). As soon as they met, there was a deadlock; Under-grounds objected the inclusion of Chief Minister of Nagaland, as they did not recognize the statehood. Finally, deadlock could be removed by the intervention of Peace Mission and they agreed on inclusion of **Shilu Ao** as a representative of Government of India, rather than Chief Minster. **M. Aram** writes:

> "The Peace Mission stepped in and suggested that it was agreed previously that each side was free to choose its own delegates and so the right to include any particular person should not be questioned. Why could not the underground look upon Shilu Ao as a delegate of the Government of India?"[228]

Zashie Huire insisted upon the presence of foreign correspondents and foreign representatives which **Gundevia** rejected straight away. Once they were made to understand and accepted the position of Shilu Ao, they did not insist much on foreign correspondents and observers' issue. Inclusion of Suntook, Deputy Secretary of External Affairs Ministry, in this meeting was official necessity as the case was still being handled by the Foreign Ministry despite formation of the state and the local state Government.

There was not much progress in the talks. Moreover, there had been other problems too such as language, its interpretation

---

[228]**M. Aram**, op.cit, p.33.

and absence of principal leaders of the Nagas from the talks. As they stayed away from the conference, reasons were best known to them only. Mostly the delegation circulated letters signed by them. On 23 September's meeting, they released a statement of **Kedhage** (self styled President of FGN) in which he stated: **'we can give everything to India which is required of us, but our sovereignty we shall not.'**[229] Finally, they broke off to reassemble again on 10 October, 1964. The Naga undergrounds put up their demands. As per the press reports, Naga undergrounds asserted that Nagaland should be made independent and the armed forces of India should be immediately withdrawn from their land.[230] However, Gundevia is silent on the demand of independence but speaks about this in the following manner. He writes:

> "In the second round of talks, Zashei Huire said that to establish peace and to 'open up avenues for political negotiations', the Government of India must take three steps: they must close down all 'concentration camps'* release all 'political prisoners' and withdraw the Indian armed forces from Nagaland. After considerable discussions it turned out that the 'concentration camps' was a reference to some villages which the Nagaland Government had taken over as a special measure to protect them against hostile raids. ... There were no 'Concentration Camps' in Nagaland, Chief Minister said emphatically."[231]

During this meeting **Jayprakash Narayan** proposed that both the parties should agree to renounce the violence. **Zashie Huire** told that they were prepared to renounce armed struggle and lay down arms. The leader of the other side, **Gundevia** said:

> "if the Nagas were prepared to lay down their arms, the government would be glad to withdraw the troops from Nagaland, retaining only such units as might be necessary

---

[229]**M. Aram**, op.cit, p.33.

[230]*The Statesman*, Calcutta, October 13, 1964.

* Grouping or clustering of villages is being referred to as – *Concentration Camps.*

[231]**Gundevia**, op.cit, pp.133-134.

for the protection of the international border. The internal law and order situation could be left to the Nagaland state government."[232]

Proposal to Surrender Arms: Rejected by Tatar Hoho

The news regarding the acceptance of the proposal to lay down arms went around and celebration started for the forthcoming 'lasting peace.' The Peace Mission had drawn out a detailed plan for surrender of arms by the undergrounds. As per the plan, the Government was to intimate the number of the forces stationed for the security and submit a plan of withdrawal and NNC was to declare full list of arms and ammunition in its possession and plan for depositing these arms and ammunition to the Peace Mission.[233]

This proposal was welcomed by the public but **Kaito Sema**, brother of **Kughato Sema** (self styled Prime Minister), stuck to demand of independence being very powerful as head of military wing of the NNC and possibly duo were aiming to unseat **Phizo**, being in exile. **Kughato**, categorically rejected **Phizo** as a leader could not represent the underground government. He was of the view that the Naga people will have to come to terms with the Government of India and not Phizo.[234]

The proposal of the Peace Mission was then referred to the **Tatar Hoho** which rejected the proposal. Contrarily, the Hoho passed a resolution saying that the Naga Army would not surrender arms till a political settlement based on a sovereign Nagaland was accepted.[235] This U-turn from the previous stand taken by **Zashei Huire**, could not be due to poor translation or even lack of proper vocabulary in Naga dialects but something more which was yet to unfold. **Gundevia** writes:

---

[232]**Gundevia**, op.cit, p.134.

[233]**M. Aram**, op.cit, p.35.

[234]**Ramunny**, op.cit, p.118.

[235]**Chandrika Singh**, op.cit, p.115.

"It was also strongly rumoured that Zashei Huire had been taken severely to task for talking, apparently without authority, about renouncing war and laying down all arms. Or was this, once again, a typical instance of impossibility of translating high sounding English words into relatively less developed languages spoken in the hills?..."[236]

Chandrika Singh, however, reasoned it in the following manner which appears to be more logical:

"...the purpose behind this outright rejection was obvious. The rebel Nagas had collected a good number of arms and ammunition from some foreign countries. Had they surrendered these arms to the Peace Mission, that would have totally exposed these foreign countries which were assisting the underground Nagas. The hostiles did not want to let down their supporters. It was also apparent that the rebel Nagas wanted to internationalise the Naga issue..."[237]

The Peace process was also derailed due to suspicious conduct of Rev. Micheal Scott. His neutrality came in the way and he is believed to have lost his main aim of being mediator of peace. He apparently sympathised with the undergrounds and at times failed to reason out the FGN allegations which he was supposed to have verified. Many a times, his vision was found to be coloured and contrary to the role he accepted to play.

Another development took place on 17 November, 1964 wherein the undergrounds issued a letter to the Peace Mission and reiterated the demand of a sovereign state. In addition, they wanted to seek justice from International Court of Justice to uphold the right of people to self determination as **Scott** had collected lot of documents from villages about the sufferings and violence in the hands of Indian Army.[238] The letter was circulated to the press by Scott carried some serious allegations. In one of the reports it was alleged that in Sema

---

[236]**Chandrika Singh**, op.cit, p.138.

[237]ibid, p.116.

[238]**Ramunny**, op.cit, p.120.

area 34,244 Nagas have been killed between October, 1952 and September, 1960.

Ramunny says that Scott should have verified the population of Semas in Nagaland, which were not more than 12,000 men, women and children. He would have realised how absurd it was to suggest that 34,244 were killed and about 800 were alive.[239] At the end of November 1964, another meeting was held at Chedema. This was the fourth round and without the Peace Mission. Nothing worthwhile came however, undergrounds were told by **Gundevia** that if they did not stop going to East Pakistan for arms and ammunition and the collection of forcible donation from the people, as was decided by the **Tatar Hoho** on 20 October, 1964, the Peace talks might be broken.

As mentioned earlier, Scott was indirectly advocating the cause of the undergrounds. He had approached the British High Commission in India for obtaining British travel documents for delivery of some underground leaders to London to meet **Phizo** without informing the Government of India. The government authorities did caution him about his partisan conduct. It is apparent that **Micheal Scott** must have had first-hand account of gross violation of human rights by the security forces during his close interaction with the villagers, moved him so much that he was prepared to work for the cause of hostiles even if it was against the charter of his duties. In fact, his stature was that of a Messiah for the common villagers whom he lent patient hearing which explains his changed behaviour. **Kaka D Iralu** writes:

> "The Naga people, suffering in silence, because the Indian Government had so effectively sealed them off from the rest of the world, looked to the presence of Rev. Michael Scott (a member of the Peace Mission, 1964-69) as an avenue of salvation. They poured out their grief to the Englishman and after the report (they were) quite convinced that he would be able to bring a permanent solution to all their woes."[240]

---

[239]**Ramunny**, op.cit, p.120.

[240]**Kaka D Iralu**, *'Nagaland and India: The Blood and the Tears'*, Private Publication, Kohima, 2003, p.128.

Fresh Round of Conferences

Another round of talks began on 29 December 1964 in Chedema. In this meeting, delegates from undergrounds asked for some more time for deliberations, hence, the meeting was postponed for January 21, 1965. They met next on the due date at Chedema, Government delegation accepted the Peace Mission proposal and reiterated that a peaceful solution in Nagaland could only be found within the Indian Union with more autonomy to fully satisfy the aspirations of all sections. The undergrounds had nothing new to offer but made a request to shift the venue of the talks from Chedema to Khensa. Since the Chief Minister was an Ao, the choice probably fell on Ao village of Khensa. On 24 February, 1965, the delegates met at Khensa, for the seventh round of talks. In the opening session **Jayprakash Narayan** said:

> "... We tried to give the background of the conflict and to state the both cases as impartially as we could; we then stated what seemed to us 'the fairest and most practical' solution ..."[241]

During these discussions, the undergrounds held on to letter addressed to the Peace Mission on 09 February 1965 which emphasised on Naga right to self determination and asked permission to hold plebiscite under the supervision of an international body. But on the question of joining Indian Union on their own volition and negoriating the terms for further greater autonomy or further relationship, **Issac Swu** said:

> "We have referred the matter to parliament. We can not go beyond the reply that they have given without referring back to them." [242]

Another suggestion by the undergrounds was to bring **Phizo** to Burma for consultation which was straight away rejected by the government as he was no more an Indian Citizen.

---

[241]**V.K. Nuh** and **Wetshokhorlo Lasuh**, op.cit, p.281.

[242]ibid, p.288.

Though, there could be no progress in the talks at Khensa but they agreed to have neutral observers for monitoring ceasefire violations.

The Peace Observers

This idea was further consolidated in the next meeting in April, 1965 and proposed the names of **M. Aram**, a Sarvodaya worker from Coimbatore, Miss **Marjorie Sykes**, another well known Sarvodaya worker in South India and Nabo Krishna Chaudhary of Orissa. This observer group did not have the powers to investigate the incidents that could have undermined the responsibility of the local officials.[243] The undergrounds called for special session of the 'Tatar Hoho' to discuss the progress on 24 March, 1965 at Wokha, was attended by the Peace Mission for explaining the Peace Mission's proposals on which delegates were unable to put forward any comment/ suggestions and thus, ended without any progress. During this meet, **Scott** was said to have explained to the **Tatar Hoho** in the following manner:

> "We want the Federal Government to accept the proposal as a basis for future negotiations. By accepting the proposal, the Federal Government is in no way committed to India. It is a package deal ...The Peace Mission is asking you to discuss the possibility of participation in the Indian Union. Various forms of relationship may come up for consideration... If at the end, it becomes impossible to reach an agreement, you would be no worse off than you are now."[244]

At the end, the **Tatar** had asked some questions with respect to their understanding of the problem. The questions were specifically whether they considered the problem to be a political one or as a law and order problem. In response, **Jayprakash Narayan** had answered:

> "There can be no doubt whatever that the struggle led by the NFG (Naga Federal Government) can be regarded merely as

[243]Chandrika Singh,op.cit, pp.121-122, also Gundevia, op.cit, pp.153-154.
[244]M. Aram, op.cit, p.43.

problem of 'law and order'. It is most certainly a struggle for national freedom. It does not aim at over throwing a government, but it certainly aims at throwing out a government namely, the Government of India which it regards as established here by force."[245]

During the discussion **Jayprakash Narayan** also advised and cautioned them that even if they wish to take help of some foreign governments, they (foreign governments) will not do it without considering their own benefits. He said:

"no doubt, you may get help but there is a danger in that those people who help you will exploit you and make you the tools of their purposes, for there is no altruistic government in the world."[246]

Section–II

Talks with the Prime Minister

Once the Peace Mission members left Wokha, ***Tatars*** continued its session for three days but nothing concrete was communicated to the Peace Mission. Later in the first week of April, 1965, when the negotiation for settlement resumed, a letter from the **Tatar Hoho** was delivered to the government delegation. This letter had completely ignored the Peace Mission's proposals and expressed that they would like to settle the problem through peaceful negotiations once their right to self determination was accepted. The representatives could not comment more than what was written in the letter and thus, negotiations came to an end at Khensa. However, it was agreed to continue to cessation of hostilities for another three months and thus, ceasefire was further extended till 12 October, 1965.

Meanwhile, **Gundevia,** the leader of the government delegation was replaced by **Dharam Vir,** but underground

[245]M. Aram, op.cit, p.45.

[246]ibid, pp.46-47.

leaders declined to accept him. They wanted to talk to the cabinet ministers preferably the Prime Minister[247] and not to the officers deputed by the Government of India, possibly they had developed confidence in **Gundevia** and didn't want any change. However, the talks could never materialize as authorities in Delhi were pre-occupied with Indo-Pakistan problems and war in 1965. It is a noteworthy fact that despite the army having left Nagaland for the war; the cessation of hostilities remained effective. Soon after the war was over, preparation for the talks began, but unfortunate death of Lal Bahadur Shastri in Tashkent, postponed the scheduled meeting with the Naga leaders on 12 January, 1966 till the appointment of next Prime Minister. Indira Gandhi, on assumption of the reign of the country agreed to talk to the undergrounds for which she came under serious opposition in the Parliament. Notwithstanding, on 16 February, 1966 Indira Gandhi received a five men Naga delegation at Delhi.

On the day of talks, one of the factions of the underground blew off the Assam Mail to coincide with the peace talks. May be the explosion was in a way a warning to the government that if they did not concede the demands of the rebel Nagas, sabotage activities (will be) stepped up.[248] In fact, the attack on Assam Mail was probably to draw attention of the Government of India towards the strength of the hostiles or may be the faction that was not in favour of talks was trying to warn the delegates that if they gave in to the pressure of the Government during the talks, they would face dire consequences.

The talks were held till 18 February 1966 despite the blast about which, **Kughato Sukhai**, leader of the delegation, denied the involvement of rebels. This meeting provided an opportunity to the undergrounds to pay a courtesy call to the Prime Minister without any cognizable result but set a precedence for all insurgent groups to demand for talks with the highest possible political authority in India. This level up-gradation was a morale booster for the rebels. While they were

---

[247]**Y.D. Gundevia**, op.cit, p.164.

[248]**Chandrika Singh**, op.cit, p.125.

returning empty handed and nothing substantial to address their constituency, **Issac Swu**, self styled Foreign Minister of the FGN, raised the issue of sovereignty and independence at Calcutta Airport. He said:

> "if the government did not grant ... independence ... we may also be forced to seek the assistance of foreign countries to achieve our objective."[249]

However, **Kughato Sukhai** on 21 February, 1966 on reaching Dimapur airfield, expressed his hope that some lasting solution to the political problem would be found out, notwithstanding the fact that some sections of the underground were signaling a bloody repercussions in case government did not respond favourably towards their demand.

Mis-Interpretation of JP's Speech

Jayprakash Narayan, the leader of the Peace Mission for almost two years resigned because of misunderstanding. On 17 February, 1966 when the peace talks were ON, reported to have said that the Government of India could 'liquidate' the Nagas. He later explained the underground leaders that it was a wrong translation of what he said in Hindi and that actually he meant was the Government of India could put down the rebellion in Nagaland. This did not satisfy the rebel leaders and thus, displayed discourteous behaviour. On the other hand, Indian press was critical of Jayprakash Narayan for his suggestion that the Naga state could have its own flag and constitution while the centre would have kept for itself such subjects as defence, finance and communication.[250] This suggestion was also not liked by the Government either. Thus, he felt it appropriate and wise to resign once he had lost the confidence of both the parties. Though, Jayprakash Narayan resigned from the Peace Mission in February, 1966, but it continued to function with **Chaliha** and **Rev. Scott** for some

---

[249]**Chandrika Singh**, op.cit, p.127.

[250]ibid, op.cit, p.128.

more time. They participated in second round of talks with Prime Minister held from 09 to 12 April 1966.

Rev. Scott: Declared *personna non-grata*

On the other side, **Rev Scott**, on 15 February, 1966 wrote a letter to the Prime Minister, Indira Gandhi, for setting up an expert commission to examine the history of the Nagas to establish whether India had ever exercised control over them. He also wrote to the UN Secretary General U Thant for exerting pressure on the Government of India for inclusion of more foreign observers in the Peace Mission. He also wrote to Ne Win, Chairman of Burma Revolutionary Council protesting Burmese Government action against Naga rebels trying to cross over from Nagaland to East Pakistan (now Bangladesh) through Burma.[251] When these things became public, the Government of India declared him as *persona non grata* and issued an order (on 01 May, 1966) revoking his Inner Line Permit. These actions were beyond his charter of duties and sure enough, no government would have liked this. In fact, while leaving India, on May 04, 1966, Scott accepted that he was indeed sympathized with the Naga people for their struggle and said:

> "I was partisan in the sense that I had sympathized with many of the things for which the Nagas had been struggling (for) and things which they had been trying to resist."[252]

Achievements of Peace Mission

Following expulsion of Scott, the third member **B. P. Chaliha** resigned. Thus, existence of the Peace Mission came to an end. Although, permanent solution could not be achieved by the efforts of Peace Mission but brought much needed succour through cessation of hostilities, which was broken by one of the factions of the undergrounds later. There were *six rounds*

---

[251]**Chandrika Singh**, op.cit, p.129.
[252]**Ramunny**, op.cit. p.149.

of talks between the Prime Minister and the underground leaders. During this period, underground leaders (NNC) were allowed to visit London for consultation with **Phizo** despite strong opposition from the state Government of Nagaland. Gradually, it became apparent that they were at the deadlock and there was no possibility of further progress thus after the sixth round (05-07 October, 1967)' talks' were terminated. Despite the failure in achieveing any concession from the government, the undergrounds kept on maintaining the cessation of hostilities officially for another five years till it was broken on 01 September, 1972.[253]

Cracks within the NNC

While the Peace Mission was active in brokering peace in Nagaland, there were visible cracks which surfaced in the underground setup, specially between the military - civil wing hierarchy for control of power. The undergrounds Army mostly consisted of the **Sema** tribes but political leadership was with the **Angamis**. **Kaito Sema**, self styled Commander-in-Chief of the underground army and brother of **Kughato**, was looking for dominance. He was ambitious and daring, considered to be the best among the undergrounds. As such, the Semas are said to be the bravest of the braves of all the Naga tribes where Angamis are bestowed with mastering of weapons alongwith skill of politicians.

Angami's Tactics: The **Angami** political leadership must have noticed his ambition and thus would have decided to sideline him. They did it with élan and sent a group to China for training commanded by **Thungti Chang**, created a competitor to him. This was last nail on the coffin, outraged **Kaito** raided the rebel 'Naga Army Headquarters' in June, 1967 at Gaziphema, for which his brother **Kughato** was held responsible. Meanwhile, it could also be said that **Kughato** had mellowed down while

[253]**Chandrika Singh**, loc.cit, pp.130-133.

he was engaged in talks with Prime Minister Mrs. Gandhi. It is believed that there was a discussion between the Prime Minister and **Kughato Sukhai** without any aides on 11 and 12 April, 1966. **Kughato's** associates **Issac** and **Ranogo** did not like the exclusive meeting. What transpired in the meeting is not known but it did create a breach among the close associates, a statecraft learned from the British.

A rumour spread that after having accepted bribe from India, Kughato had abandoned the demand for Nagaland's independence.[254] Hence, **Thangkul Muivah** was brought in to neutralise the **Kughato's** hold over the underground. **Muivah**, since then got prominence over **Kaito**. As mentioned, it appears that underground leaders (Angamis) were trying to sideline the Sema brothers (**Kughato** and **Kaito**) which **Kaito** would never have liked as he was challenging the authority of **Phizo** and his fellowmen over the leadership of the NNC. The Sema-Angami feud became much more visible in the coming months wherein **Kaito** lost his life and **Kughato**, his position of **Kedhage** (President of the FGN) to Mhiassiou. Probably **Kughato** lost due to his idea of favouring a peaceful solution within Indian Union. By that time, there was one rebel group led by Thinouselie was undergoing training under PLA of China.[255] Once the talks failed, another batch of guerillas (350) was marched to China under command of **Issac Swu** and **Mowu Angami**.

On June 06, 1968, Indian Army raided Jotsoma Camp and captured good number of Chinese arms and ammunitions, documents, diaries, medicines and photographs of guerillas in Chinese uniform at Yunnan. After securing these documents from Jotsoma Camp, the Chinese charge-de-affairs in New Delhi was summoned and a strong protest was lodged for interfering in the internal affairs in India.[256]

---

[254]**Kiran Shankar Maitra**, op.cit, p.87.

[255]General **KV Krishna Rao**, *'Prepare or Perish: A Study on National Security'*, Lancer Publishers, New Delhi, 1991, pp.262-263. Also *The Eastern Mirror*, Dimapur,07 August 2003.

[256]**K.S. Maitra**, op.cit, p.99.

Formation of RGN: Sema-Angami Feud

After the murder of **Kaito Sema** by the Angami guerillas, Khonoma village was raided on 03 August, 1968. Semas (Kaito's brothers: Zuheto, Kughato and Scato Swu) founded Council of Naga People on 01 November, 1968 and posed a serious challenge to the NNC as many anti-Phizo rebels joined them to form Revolutionary Government of Nagaland (RGN)[257] to match with FGN. The triumvirate Semas raided Chedema Camp of FGN and captivated **Mhiassiou** (President) and **Z. Ramyo** (Prime Minister) of FGN. Actually on 06 March, 1969, **Mowu** had managed to escape the onslaught of Burmese Army and entered Nagaland through Somra tract near Kiphire, and he wanted to meet **Zuheto**. But on 16 March, 1969, **Mowu** was captured 'while attempting to reach a secret jungle-camp north-east of Kohima, along with 200 guerillas who had come from Burma border earlier. He was immediately flown in an Indian Air Force plane to New Delhi for interrogation by Army Intelligence.'[258] Regarding the capture of **Mowu** there is a bit of mystery. **Ramunny** writes about his capture in the following manner:

> "On March 14, the gang entered the Phesama Camp of the 11th Battalion of the Naga Army (Revolutionary Government). They found it impossible to go through any village as most of the Federal Camps had already been destroyed by the army. Scato hearing about the entry of the China gang under Mowu sent for Zuheto and asked him to proceed immediately to their camp in Aghunato. Zuheto left in the middle of the night and arrived at 'Lt Col' Zhukiye's camp. He found Mowu and his group had arrived there. ...Mowu and his second -in-Command were received well with all courtesy by Zukhiye in his camp. By this time the security forces had closed in, Mowu initially thought of fighting it but later decided to surrender. Hokishe Sema had a lot to do with the peaceful surrender and there was no bloodshed."[259]

[257] **K.S. Maitra**, op.cit, p.102.

[258] **Gundevia**, op.cit, p.181.

[259] **Ramunny**, op.cit, p.177, also K.S Maitra, op.cit, p.106.

Kiran Sharkar Maitra has narrated the story in a similar manner. It is clear that Sema group enjoyed the patronage of the Government of India (through Nagaland Government led by **Hokishe Sema** and the Army). Due to this none from the Revolutionary Government of Nagaland (RGN) was captured from that camp which belonged to that group. Even after 34 years of that event, some Nagas blame the collaborators for his capture. When **Mowu** died on 05 Aug, 2003, a report that was published:

> "… while Th. Muivah remained in China, General Mowu and Brigadier Thinouselie left China and returned in the later part of 1968 after receiving full military training and equipments. History took a crude turn when his group was betrayed by a section of Naga collaborators of Nathami village under Zunheboto district on March 16, 1969, the entire group of Naga patriots underwent long incarceration in several jails in India including Nowgong (now in Nagaland) and Mawlai Jails, Shillong until February 1976 when they were released unconditionally…"[260]

Though, **Mowu Angami** was captured, but another group under **Issac Swu** managed to sneak in and kept on fighting the security forces, albeit with heavy losses on their side. **Mhiassiou** and **Ramyo** were freed after eight months in captivity on July 15, 1969, but they were kept in house-arrest and remained as suspects. Meanwhile, **Phizoites** attacked the Chief Minister **Hokishe Sema's** house, who was elected in the 2nd general election in the state early in February, 1969. Notably, this election also was boycotted by the NNC, but people did not pay heed to the call. The Naga society was divided: moderates were for peace and a solution within Indian Union whereas there were many who supported the NNC's view for Independence.

No War–No Peace

Though, there was no ceasefire and neither was it abandoned

[260]**Savi Liegise**, 'General Mowu Passes Away', *The Eastern Mirror*, Dimapur 07 August 2003.

officially but skirmishes continued. Undergrounds were ambushing army convoys and terrorising common people who supported liberals including the state government servants. On the other hand, the army was raiding the camps with major or minor successes. There were surrenders from the underground ranks as well. **Gundevia** writes:

> ".... The Chief Minister, Hokishe Sema, told the Assembly on August 10, 1969, that since the cessation of operation in September 1964 about 1,800 rebels had surrendered but the total number of arms accounted for did not exceed 237 weapons of all kinds nor in the casualties among the Security Forces. In one month, August, 1969, there were at least four serious encounters..."[261]

The situation was not much different in 1970. Parliament elections were held for Lok Sabha (the Lower House of Indian Parliament) in March, 1971 followed by crisis in East Pakistan. Though events in East Pakistan overshadowed the problems in Nagaland and almost entire army was again withdrawn from Nagaland, the state government had a tough time to keep the situation under control with Central Armed Police and newly raised Naga Police battalions. The Chief Minister tried to maintain contact with the underground leaders and ensured no serious breach in peace during Indo-Pak war.

Though, peace initiatives so arrived could not achieve yet these struggles provided much needed relief to the people who enjoyed peaceful environment for about a decade. With the ambush of **Hokishe Sema**, the eerie calm that was prevailing in the Naga hills, also came to an end in August, 1972. The Naga Hills again slipped in the grip of insurgency and violence.

---

[261]**Gundevia**, op.cit, p.203.

6

Shillong Accord to Framework Agreement

Review of Preceding Study

As it has already been discussed, creation of Nagaland, a constituent state of India with special provisions in the constitution it was felt that the Naga aspirations, long cherished dream of freedom of the Nagas to live freely with their age old traditions and customs without any infringement or external influences was fulfilled. It is the matter of fact that none of the laws passed by the Parliament in Delhi is applicable till Nagaland Assembly ratifies it; *defacto* autonomy has been granted and enshrined in the Constitution of India.* Creation of the state was the outcome of the hard work of Peace Mission but could not prove to be a final solution to the problem till all the groups participated in it. It would be incorrect to say that Peace Mission was a failure; rather, it was great success under the circumstances they worked and brought succourr to the people. It had achieved peace for eight years, a great achievement indeed!

It was an irony that both the sides viz. the Government of India and undergrounds could not encash the opportunity to settle the issue despite best efforts by the Naga Peace Mission.

* Refer 7th Point: 16 Point Agreement (Appendix 'F') and Article 371(A) of the Constitution of India.

In case the undergrounds participated and negotiated with matured outlook, the problem could have been resolved with the formation of state. Since the Peace Mission ceased to function, a Peace Commission* was set up which kept on functioning in a similar manner. The flag bearers of the Commission did their best to keep the parties away from conflict. But that was also rendered ineffective and guns again started booming after the failure of six rounds of talks with the Prime Minister. Following the failure of ceasefire, both sides got engaged in an unending spate of violence till the signing of the Shillong Accord in 1975.

In this chapter I shall make an endeavour to cover the politico-military situation in Nagaland after the failure of ceasefire and pressure mounted by the security forces which culminated in signing of the Shillong Accord. Non-acceptance of the Accord by the majority of undergrounds gave birth to another new underground outfit named **Nationalist Socialist Council of Nagaland** (NSCN), its subsequent vertical split into two parts viz. **NSCN** (Issac-Muivah) and **NSCN** (Khaplang) and their role in insurgency and violence till the signing of ceasefire instrument separately by each group with the Government of India in 1997. The ceasefire culminated in signing of the '**Framework Agreement**' in August, 2015 between **NSCN(IM)** and the Government of India.

Section-I

Pre Shillong Accord Period

The sixth and last round of Peace talks was held on 05 October, 1967. The Prime Minister of India, Indira Gandhi categorically informed the underground leaders that there could be no common meeting ground if the problem can not be settled within Indian Union, which was unacceptable. Both the sides had stuck to their stated positions and thus, negotiations were

---

* Peace Commission comprised of M. Aram, Marjorie Sykes and Naba Krishna Chawdhary.

called off. With that all the hopes for a peaceful solution to the Naga problem were dashed to the ground. Four years of parleys between the Government and the underground leaders resulted in complete failure.[262]

Failure brings gloom and pessimism, uncertainty and fear of unknown and it appears that nothing was done right. Was it really true if seen in correct perspective? **M. Aram** also held a similar opinion regarding the parleys from 1964-1972, the years of Peace Mission (later Peace Commission) with which he was closely associated with. He opines:

> "Does this mean the eight years of efforts for reconciliation has gone in vain? Does this mean that many rounds of talks in Nagaland between the Government of India representatives and the federal* representatives and the six rounds of talks at Delhi with Prime Minister Indira Gandhi were a waste of time? No, between 1964 and 1972, much progress has been made towards mutual understanding and mutual good-will. Political reconciliation has been difficult but personal reconciliation has been possible..."[263]

Efforts to Peace Continued but Ceasefire Broken

But this failure did not dampen the spirits of either side. The Central government continued its governance and development activities through the state government, followed by general elections and political process continued unabated. The undergrounds on the other hand, renewed their activities and when they ambushed the convoy of Nagaland Chief Minister, **Hokishe Sema**, on 08 August, 1972, in which his bodyguard died on the spot and daughter, **Kaholi**, suffered bullets but survived, ceasefire came to an end.

As violence became the order of the day, the Government started clamping the undergrounds down with series of acts

---

262 Chandrika Singh, *'Political Evaluation of Nagaland'*, Lancer Publication, New Delhi, 1981, p.133.

* Federal' means FGN (NNC).

263 M. Aram, *Peace in Nagaland*, Arnold-Heinemann Publishers, Delhi, 1974, pp.315-316.

to empower the Security Forces. On 01 September, 1972, the 'Unlawful Activities Prevention Act' in addition to most powerful and potent law i.e. the Armed Forces (Special Powers) Act, 1958 which is mainly applicable for states like Tripura, Mizoram, Manipur, and the Union Territory of Arunachal Pradesh, was enforced on 31 August, 1972. This gave sweeping powers to the security forces to operate with impunity in the 'Disturbed Areas'. Certainly, the government had taken a stand and was not in a mood to give any further concessions to the undergrounds.

Transfer of Naga Issue: External to Home Ministry

During this period, the Government of Nagaland became stronger and could manage to establish itself. The Chief Minister **Hokishe Sema** got the Angamis sidelined or weakened and encouraged Semas in the FGN, set up through his political and social influence. He successfully got created another government named Revolutionary Government of Nagaland (RGN) led by Sema brothers and that helped establish peace in two ways,firstly, Angamis lost the grip over NNC and secondly Phizo could not return back. Thus, elected government of Nagaland became stronger to deal with the situation.[264] The Government of India did a major policy change, by transferring Nagaland from External Affairs Ministry to the Home Ministry, however, protested by the State Government through a resolution against the decision. The Naga Army was considerably reduced by sustained operations and the situation was desperate for the undergrounds. There was total black out on the press but intensity and effect can be gauged by the occasional press reports. **George N Patterson** wrote:

> "while the India Government's official policy was announced as 'the Army has not to fight a foreign enemy but to restore order among their own kith and kin whatever might be attitude of the hostiles', there was an official black out of information,

[264]**M. Aram**, op.cit, pp.194-195.

press correspondents being forbidden to enter the area. But reports and not only from the Nagas, but from other reliable Indian sources stated that punitive pressure was being brought against the non-combatant population, indiscriminately and deliberately applied through the grouping of villages."[265]

Creation of NPC Amidst Heightened Insurgency

Meanwhile, there were changes in the over ground politics as well. The RGN surrendered and come over-ground. A new organization named Nagaland Peace Council (NPC) was formed by the Baptist Church in May 1974 and acted as mediator between the Government and the undergrounds to broker peace. On 14 August, 1974, **Rev. Longri Ao** met the Governor and proposed Kohima as 'Peace Zone'.

In one of the raids on 04 September, 1974 in Iganumi and Lasami village in lower Sema area found a 'congratulatory letter' from **Micheal Scott**, who had sent a message through **Miss Billieu**, sister of **Rano Shaiza**. This had been passed on to the undergrounds in time for their independence day celebration.[266] This was attended by **Zovepra**, Chairman of the Regional Council, Kohima who came to attend the function in a government vehicle despite being a public servant. Apparently one gets impression that almost all the politicians across the board have contacts with their underground brethren and they help each-other and survive, partly because the leaders need them for political battles and undergrounds need money and shelter. This is an open secret that many a times underground leaders found to have taken shelter in the houses of ministers or members of legislative assembly or parliament when the security forces are doing jungle bashing for them. In fact, it is difficult to comprehend who is not with the undergrounds!

By the end of December, 1974, as the activities of the undergrounds were in full swing, they dispatched another batch of recruits to China under the leadership of **Thangkul Muivah**. These groups trained by China used to return and

---

[265]**George N Patterson**, *'Far Eastern Economic Review'*, May 13, 1966, p.205.
[266]ibid.

enter India by sneaking in small splinter groups. On the other hand, the newly formed NPC met Home Minister in Delhi. The response from the Government was favourable to the proposal for talks once they were assured of NPC's neutrality and certain underlying principles confirmed, e.g. integrity of India would not be jeopardized. Once these two factions were agreed upon in principle and the peace process moved forward. It may be noted here that Indira Gandhi was the Prime Minister and certainly the pressure on the undergrounds would have been very severe to come to terms, which we will discuss later.

Signing of the Shillong Accord

From 01 May 1975, the talks began with the help of NPC and Liaison Committee. **Keviyalley**, brother of **Phizo**, became the point of contact, who took great risk of coming out of jungles even when ceasefire was not 'ON'.[267] The Government was against any concession to undergrounds as they were utilizing peace zones to their advantage. Though, people believe that **Keviyalley** did participate on his own, contrary to the truth, he was nominated by none other than the **Zashei Huire**, President, Federal Government of Nagaland under a written authority submitted to the Governor, which is duly documented by various authors. The deliberations continued for couple of months and finally, six members of FGN duly authorized by **Zashie Huire** participated in the final talks with the Governor and his advisers on 10 and 11 November, 1975. On 11 November the undergrounds made it clear about their 'decision to unconditionally accept the constitution'.[268] Finally, they reached an agreement and put their seal of acceptance by signing in the same document known as '**Shillong Accord**'. Salient features of the Accord were: firstly: the NNC representatives on their own volition accepted, the Constitution of India without any condition, secondly: they

---

[267]**George N Patterson**, op.cit, pp. 205-206.

[268]**Ramunny**, op.cit, p.25 (**Ramunny** participated in the Talks as Advisor to the Governor).

agreed to lay down arms and deposited with the government and thirdly: It was agreed that the underground organisation should be given reasonable time to formulate other issues for discussion for a final settlement.

Rejection and Failure of the Accord

There have been large number of accords or agreements signed between the Government and ethnic groups in India, but none have been so poorly accepted by the people like this one. The people of Nagaland, whether overground or underground, rejected it completely. This Accord has been named as blatant and bizarre 'betrayal' by the NNC leadership. The Shillong Accord had divided the Nagas in two parts, and hence, the outcome was a forgone conclusion. General **KV Krishna Rao** remarked:

> "Unfortunately, the Shillong Accord did not result in an end to the insurgency. The gangs which were in China, on their return to the Burma border, denounced the Accord, and declared their intention to continue with the struggle for independence."[269]

However, for the government authorities it was a great success. Consequent to the signing of the Accord, 368 undergrounds laid down arms and they were suitably rehabilitated. It may be mentioned here that approximately 1566 RGN and 316 FGN personnel had also come overground in August 1973 and were rehabilitated,[270] which were much higher than what this Accord could bring. The undergrounds (specially the China trained ones) did not accept the Accord and blamed it on the NNC officials who were the signatories of the Accord. **Issac Swu** while addressing the cadres in Jordan Camp in 1989, denounced it. He said:

> "...signing of Shillong Accord between the Indian Government and NNC-FGN on 11 November, 1975, shocked the whole Naga nation while the adversaries celebrated with unprecedented joy. It was the most ignominious sell out ever made from within

[269]Gen **K.V. Krishna Rao**, op.cit, p.265.

[270]ibid.

the national organization itself. Indeed, such a fatal blow of disgrace to the prestige of the nation marked the beginning of anti-climax."[271]

Phizo's Silence: Acceptance of Ground Reality

Despite serious opposition, there were at least one section of the NNC that accepted the Accord and that includes Phizo. In fact, Phizo was approached to condemn it, but he remained silent, due to which many Naga nationals treat him with disdain. Rh. Raising and Angelus Simrah expressed in the following manner:

> "People at home did urge him number of times to declare that the Accord was the work of the traitors and he had nothing to do with it. But A.Z. Phizo, in his perfidious high-handedness, placed himself all the more above the people and above the national cause and contemptuously refused to condemn it right upto the time he went to grave in 1990."[272]

There was a special meeting called by the breakaway faction of the NNC and they condemned all the office bearers. The Naga National Assembly (**Tatar Hoho**) was called to session and deliberated on this from 15-17 August, 1976. The Assembly condemned the Accord once and for all as the work of traitors (to the Naga cause). It also condemned the **Zashei Huire** ministry.[273] Here it would be pertinent to mention that the 'other group' who condemned the accord probably would never know the pressure on the Huire ministry to accept the offer of talks within the frame work of Indian Constitution. There is no doubt that the acceptance of Agreement was under duress. There were serious pressure from the government and Indian Army that the NNC-FGN leadership were compelled to accept such a solution. Probably they had no other alternative at that moment. **SC Jamir**, ex Chief Minister of Nagaland

---

[271]**Issac Chisi Swu**, *'A Brief Account of the Transitional Period: 50 years of Resistance'*, NSCN (IM), Pvt Publication, 2002, p.12.

[272]**Rh Raising** and **Angelus Simrah**, *'Nagas in the Historical Perspective, 50 Years of Resistance'*, NSCN(IM) Private Publication, 2002, p.36.

[273]ibid.

expressed similar views during interview that it was done under pressure and he said:

> "...it was Nagaland Government decided to put pressure on the villagers ...'if you do not bring out the villagers who are underground, we will not allow you to harvest'... That kind of pressure was mounted on the villagers and Army was brought in and almost all the districts were cleaned up barring Chekhesang and Kohima... So they told the remnants that instead of surrendering you are made to sign the Shillong Accord."[274]

Section-II

Birth of NSCN & Resurgence of Violence

The Accord was rejected by the majority of the undergrounds, but Indian people at large were made to believe that the Shillong Accord was a great success and served its purpose. Subsequently, the undergrounds (the faction which did not agree or the China returned group) left no stone unturned to blame NBCC and NPC for their initiatives. But the withdrawal of operations had positive impact on the lives of common Nagas. The Army stopped doing Cordon and Search operations, government returned the collective fines which were imposed on the villages and no more curfews were imposed on the villages. While some of the underground activists deposited arms to the NPC members and on the other hand, government released 800 Naga political prisoners.[275] It was a great relief to common people but for the hardliners, it was a bizarre surrender.

Adinno, daughter of **Phizo**, who leads the NNC (Adinno) faction, tried to explain her father's stand on the Shillong

[274]**Jamir** was interviewed by the Author, 17 August 2003 at Kohima (Refer Appendix 'D').

[275]**Kenheth Kerhuo**, The Role of Nagaland Peace Council in the Indo-Naga Peace Talks, Nuh and Lasuh (ed), *'The Naga Chronicle'*, Regency Publications, New Delhi, 2002, p.343.

Accord and its background but her explanation was hardly accepted. She said:

> "Naga civilians in villages who lived through the period from 1972 to 1975 poignantly recall their experience as horrendous at the hands of evil people. As in 1963, the Nagaland Baptist Church was forced to intervene but this time its sponsored Nagaland Peace Council took the role of peace brokers. It culminated in the unofficial talk between the 'underground organisation' and the Indian officials to take advantage and coerced the Naga representatives at the talk to sign alleged Shillong Accord. We are bored with unsubstantiated frenzy of allegations and recriminations over the years.... our leader AZ Phizo refused to be drawn in to the politically contrived allegation which he knew had no legality."[276]

It is also true that Adinno knew it better than anyone else about the legality of the signatories from both the sides and her claim is nothing but a political compulsion in changed circumstances. Moreover, Phizo's silence was considered to be an acceptance, howsoever, mute it was. The reality cannot be wished away as there was nothing which could stop him from denouncing the accord, as others did; if he so desired. Was it a ground reality that Phizo was compelled to accept it with stony silence?

Post signing of the accord and resultant turmoil, the NNC leadership in Nagaland was not only in a state of flux but they were rudderless as well. As discussed previously, Naga underground Assembly was called to session, which had condemned the Accordists and termed them as traitors. Another meeting (on 15-16 Aug, 1976) was held in which they elected **Issac Chisi Swu** as the Vice President of the NNC. It is notable here that they had not selected/elected a new President for the group; hence, **Phizo** remained as the head of the organisation. It appears that despite **Phizo's** silence on the Accord, he had tremendous clout and hold over Naga underground ranks and files.

---

[276]**Adinno Phizo**, The Naga National Council: Meeting the Challenge Time and Again, *The Nagaland Post*, Dimapur, 09 December, 2003.

Clearly, there were two groups: Those who signed or supported Accord and the other group who denounced it. The Accordists, however, kept on pressurising other group people to come overground and surrender. The logic given was since the President **Phizo** has not condemned the Accord, means he also wants others to follow. Soon there was rift in the NNC and a *coup de etat* took place and a so-called martial law was declared within the ungrounded faction. Personal account of **Swu** tells us:

> "Very soon, they (Accordists) hatched a plot and staged a coup led by Maj **Subung Ao** and declared martial law. Six of the top leaders including Lt Col **Pruning** were arrested. They at once forced the leaders to hand over the powers of the NNC and the Federal Government to the martial law administrators... **Messers Issac** and **Muivah** were held in custody for one and half years."[277]

Subsequently, there was rift among those so-called martial law administrators of NNC and **Khaplang**, a **Hemi Naga** from Burma, was requested to be the President of the NNC. But he joined hands with **Issac Swu** and Thuingaleng Muivah and they formed National Socialist Council of Nagalim* (NSCN) on 31 January, 1980. It is noteworthy here that it took five years for non-Accordists to regroup and form another outfit to continue.

From the government side, efforts were 'ON' to bring the breakaway faction to the negotiating table and also to bring NNC and NSCN together. But it is said that NSCN had let the terror be spread all across and punished those who supported the Shillong Accord. The signatories of the Accord were systematically routed out. According to Thomas:

> "Issac-Muivah group had killed all those who opposed them and formed so called National Socialist Council of Nagaland

---

[277] Address by **Issac** and **Muivah** to the cadres on 07 July 1989, Handout published by Government of Peoples Republic of Nagaland, p.13. Republished in *Nagaland Post*, Dimapur, 'The Abortive Coup Attempt of 1988' 26 July 2003.

* Nagalim: Means Greater Nagaland comprising of all the Naga areas in India and Myanmar.

(NSCN) on 31st January, 1980. Since then they had killed more than two thousand of NNC people. They did everything to malign the Accord and were heavily engaged in false propaganda; killings, extortion and loot etc in order to keep their organisation alive, and sowed the seed of hatred and enmity among the Nagas."[278]

By now, many of the NNC cadres have settled down to active overground politics over the years. Since there was no other player in the underground to challenge them, NSCN established its supremacy and grew from strength to strength. In 1986, the Army operated vigorously in conjunction with Myanmar Army, the NSCN was put on the back foot but they managed to survive. The NSCN was reduced in size and strength but yet remained a formidable outfit to ignore and had been calling shots over the Naga population and thus, leadership was not yet reconciled to negotiate within the framework of Indian Constitution. As Thomas said:

> "Several peace missions were sent to the NSCN leadership but there was no concrete response from the NSCN. The NSCN had made it known that they would hold peace talks with Indian government without any preconditions while the government wanted it within the frame work of the Indian constitution. As both sides had different opinions, no headway could be made in this regad."[279]

Offer of Conditional Talks: Rejected

At this juncture, NSCN could afford to ignore the offer for conditional peace talks due to its clout among the population and strength of its armed cadre. The next offer for peace came in the year 1987 and government was able to convince one of the sections of NSCN leadership to accept the invitation for peace talks through Chingang Konyak. Since other group was either ignorant or otherwise, wedge was created. It was in the

---

[278]Thomas, 'Know the Cause of Our Problem and Work for Peace and Unity', in Nuh and Wetshokhorolo (ed), *The Naga Chronicle*, op.cit, pp.385-386.

[279]**P.Tarapot**, op.cit, p.124.

month of December, 1987 an emergency meeting was called by the Chairman of NSCN to discuss the issue. In the words of **Issac Swu**:

> "We (Issac and Muivah) moved our Council HQs to a place above Hangshen village. We discussed there, among other things, to hold an emergency session and to give a reply to Chingang Konyak, a member of go between. There was information from Chingang that the Indian Government wanted to hold talks with the National Socialist Council, 'within' the frame work of Indian Constitution, which was a deliberate back out from the previous unconditional approach of Indira Gandhi."[280]

It is important to note here that this meeting was not attended by **S.S. Khaplang**, Vice Chairman. Meanwhile reply to Chingang was dispatched by stating that:

> "NSCN would have no talks whatsoever with the Indian Government on any conditions and he should not take the risk of reaching us for information of conditional talks."[281]

During the meeting of NSCN council, this point had been discussed and **Issac** believes that there was no room for misunderstanding[282] despite the conspicuous absence of **Khaplang**, his deputy. It is apparent that differences among **Khaplang** and other duo (**Issac** and **Muvah**) did exist prior to this proposal.

NSCN: Deadly Differences and Break Up

It was felt by the close associates of Vice Chairman, **SS Khaplang** that the Chairman **Issac** and Secretary **Muivah** were prepared to talk to the Indian Government to settle the Indo-Naga issue within the Indian Union,[283] and thus, was his absence. On the other hand, **Issac-Muivah** accused **Khaplang** was trying to usurp the NSCN leadership by spreading wrong information. Both the factions blamed each-other but **Tarapot**'s assertion

---

[280]Address by **Issac Swu** and **Muivah**, mentioned in footnote 277.

[281]ibid, p.2.

[282]ibid, p.3.

[283]**P. Tarapot**, op.cit, p.117.

could not be proved comprehensively. While addressing his followers, **Khaplang** said:

> "NSCN was also not free of danger within. During the later part of 1987, formerly the two most senior leaders, Issac and Muivah, then chairman and general secretary respectively, had secretly conspired to sell out the rights of the Nagas through a negotiation with New Delhi which was to accept a settlement little higher than the Shillong Accord. One step on from what is popularly known as 'uncle Suisa's (Chingang Konyak) proposal'."[284]

Relation between these two groups went sour so much so that, Khaplang supporters attacked NSCN Central Head Quarters (CHQ). The bloody internal clash was the final straw in the fragile relations. **Tarapot** writes about the clash:

> "Over 100 NSCN members mostly belonging to Muivah and Issac's group were killed in the worst ever bloody internal clash..... The incident took place at Taka, Kake and Lhasa areas-all around CHQ. About 230 NSCN activists mostly women and children survived the onslaught."[285]

Issac-Muivah faction battered by **Khapalng** faction and the Burmese Army. Finally, they were reduced to only few men. In late October, 1988, only 40 men survived to reach Manipur-Nagaland border. Though, the clash and split of NSCN was their inter tribal feud, NSCN (IM) group in its souvenir claims that it was the creation of Indian intelligence agencies which could neither be ruled out nor ascertained. If it was the handiwork of Indian Intelligence agency, it can be said that it was well executed. **Rh. Raising** wrote:

> "The whole conspiracy was a well organized one, directed by the Indian Intelligence Bureau (IB). They concocted the story that Messers Issac Chisi Swu and Th Muivah are progressing to work out a solution with India (within the Indian Union) and, secondly, to do away with all the Konyak and Pangmi national workers to seize all arms to surrender them to India. S.S.

---

[284]**S.S. Khaplang**, 'The Weekly Journal of NSCN (K)',03 July 1991, internal circulation.

[285]**Tarapot**, p.123. Also **Issac** and **Muivah's** Joint statement, pp.11-13.

Khaplang and his mercenaries became the tool of the adversary in spreading this sheer fabrication among the workers and villagers, whipping up bitter antagonism..."[286]

Khaplang: Proximity with the State Government

In fact, **Khaplang** is more pro-Indian then **Issac-Muivah** group when it comes to negotiation/settlement. Another plausible reason that was also very vital for **Khaplang** or northern group, mostly comprised of **Konyak** tribe, provided the bulk of the cadres but were ignored when it came to sharing the hierarchy or assigning appointments, where they were always ignored. This could have provoked the north group to take over the control by eliminating south group. Thus, it appears that tribal antagonism or cleavages were mobilised against the other group, if at all it was a conspiracy. On the contrary, it is also an open secret that '**Khaplang** group has been armed, financed and sheltered by the Indian agents and the Nagaland State Government under the Chief Minister **S.C. Jamir**'.[287]

NSCN(K) concentrated its operations in the northern districts of Mokokchung, Mon and parts of Tuensang and Zunheboto districts, while NSCN(IM) remained dominant in the rest of the state with substantial influence in Manipur specially in Ukhrul, Senapati and Tamenglong districts. Both the groups initially consolidated in respective areas and later, they started campaign to increase the area of influence. Thus, stage was set for conflict i.e. Inter Factional Clashes (IFC) basically to control the territory and milking of support from the local population including recruitment. These events have also been confirmed by Lt Gen **Mukherjee**. He writes:

"The 80s witnessed a split in the NSCN, partially on ethnic lines and a blood feud leading to a power struggle between the two factions of NSCN. The Issac and Muivah (I & M) and Khaplang (K) groups (named after the leaders) to gain control

---

[286]Rh. **Raising**, op.cit, pp.39-40.

[287]**Luingam Lithui** and **Frans Welman**, 'Naga History: Chronology of Recent Events', *The Nagaland Post*, Dimapur, 28 December, 2002.

over Nagaland and Naga-inhabited areas in Manipur, Assam and Arunachal Pradesh."[288]

Rise of NSCN (IM): A Formidable Group

NSCN (IM) regrouped within two years and reorganized well in the hill districts of Manipur and its bordering areas in Nagaland. Once they reorganized themselves, started widening its network and also established a 'base' in Bangladesh where other extremists organisations such as PLA of Manipur were present. In late 1991, intelligence inputs pointed out that about 200 NSCN activists were sent to Bangladesh and procuring arms from various sources from the soil of Bangladesh.[289] In fact, 'Alee Command' or foreign command headquarters of NSCN (IM) functioned from Bangladesh since 1990. In addition, they made all out efforts to internationalise the issue at world fora.

Since 1991, the insurgent operations escalated to such an extent that it resembled with the 1960s. The spurt in the violence due to growing belief of the NSCN(IM) that stiff resistance is the only way to achieve independence as Muivah himself told NSCN cadres on Republic Day celebration of NSCN (21 March) in 1989 that 'while outside aid is helpful, it is self-reliance that is decisive'.[290] Initially, the money required came from government treasury and that was being done by laying ambush for security forces convoys carrying money. *The Clarion* reported this incidence in the following manner:

> "... the members of the National Socialist Council of Nagaland (NSCN–Muivah group) ambushed a convoy of vehicles off Likchao, about 80 km from Imphal, their main target was money being carried in the steel trunks to the border town of Moreh. They managed to kill 11 Central Reserve Police Force (CRPF) personnel and also took away a big cache of automatic weapons from the accompanying security personnel, (which) was just a bonus."[291]

---

[288]Lt Gen **J.R. Mukherjee**, op.cit. p.33.

[289]**P Tarapot**, op.cit, pp.128-129.

[290]ibid, p.130.

[291]*The Clarion*, Imphal, 16 December 1991.

This kind of success could not be achieved without hard intelligence that too from someone within the government agencies, which they subverted and without any doubt exists till date.

Daring Move and Giant Strides: NSCN (IM)

Killing of Army Personnel: In the beginning after split, Khaplang faction was strong and Issac-Muivah faction had difficult time but with the Likchao ambush, however, Muivah (IM group) re-emerged as a major security threat in the states of Nagaland and Manipur.[292] By the end of 1992, they had gained formidable strength to strike back. In the month of August, they gunned down 13 army personnel of 1/5 Gorkha Regiment including one Lieutenant Colonel, one Major and one Second Lieutenant who were traveling in a bus.[293] The killing of army personnel after picking them up from a bus was to prove their mettle. Military success and in search an image of big brother, it started training and helping all other groups who are fighting for secession in the North Eastern states of India. Lt Gen Mukherjee opines that this was due to Pakistani motivation to NSCN (IM) which was certainly a great morale booster for the smaller groups and simultaneously provided the former with bigger area of influence. He felt that the aim was to engineer secession of entire north east, wrote:

> "There were also changes in the pattern of insurgency. NSCN (I&M)'s Pakistani mentors managed to convince its members that success was feasible only if they operated conjointly with other insurgent groups and that their philosophy needed to change to secession of the entire North East. This led to NSCN (I&M) becoming the mother organisation ... in the region."[294]

Formation of United Front: A new underground front called 'Self Defence United Front' of the south East Himalayas was floated by Th. Muivah wherein seven underground groups

---

[292]*The Clarion*, Imphal, 16 December 1991.

[293]**Tarapot**, op.cit, p.132.

[294]Lt Gen **J.R. Mukherjee**, op.cit, pp.33-34.

joined hands. 23 members of all the seven outfits signed the formal declaration on November 30, 1994. The members of this front were Kanglei Yawol Kannalup (KYKL) from Manipur comprising UNLF (Oken faction) KCP (Ibobi Singh), PREPAK (Khomba), National Socialist Council of Nagaland (Issak-Muivah), Hyuniewtrap Achik Liberation Council of Meghalaya (HALC), Karbi National Volunteers of Assam (KNV), Hmar People's Convention (HPC) and National Democratic Front of Bodoland (NDFB). Thus, NSCN (IM) became a dangerous outfit in the region, alongwith members of the new front with deadly striking power in entire North East India.[295]

In a similar move, NSCN (K) also entered into an agreement with UNLF (Meghen) and ULFA to form IBRF (Indo-Burma Regional Front). Khaplang started consolidating in the Eastern Naga Hills and Upper Myanmar area, where he was supreme commander. IBRF group became a dead horse before it could take off, as Khaplang was allegedly hobnobbing with the Government of India. They even went to the extent of charging him that his representatives were camping in New Delhi, though unascertained. To make matter worse, another top functionary of the IBRF, Kalpajyoti Neog of ULFA surrendered with his followers. Even ULFA supremo Rajkhowa was held responsible for starting the dialogue with the Government of India but persuaded by the hawks to leave it halfway.[296]

However, the NSCN (IM) kept on growing and its geographical coverage of the area also increased, an added advantage for trans-shipment of arms, ammunition and movement of cadres from Bangladesh through Meghalaya or Tripura to Manipur and Nagaland, because of the front affiliation. They started running parallel administration in their respective areas of influence and were successful in extraction of money from all employees, businessmen and common people. Moreover, it was quick enough to understand the spin offs in drug trade and exploited it to the maximum due to

---

[295]**Jacob Shaiza**, Threat from the Front, 'North East Sun', 28 Jan – 03 Feb, 1995, p.10.

[296]ibid.

change in the international route of smuggling. In 1990s, drug barons of the golden triangle (Myanmar, Thailand and Laos) were forced to change the route due to stringent drug offence laws in Thailand and Singapore. The new route ran through Manipur/Mizoram, Silchar, Karimganj and on to Bangladesh.

The Kachin area of Myanmar was also developed into a major poppy growing area and the trade was controlled by the Shan and Kachin rebels. Since the NSCN (IM) has had considerable influence in the Naga dominated (Hill areas of Manipur) and at entry points like Moreh and Chandel, exploited the opportunity to its advantage. Naga-Kuki ethnic cleansing wars were essentially a struggle for control of the lucrative narcotics trade only.[297] Even the money sent from Delhi to the state for development, it is alleged that they managed to get a fare share from it for running their organisation to fight India only. State Government machinery specially in Nagaland was subverted and 'in rare cases, the funds were properly used. Interestingly, the diversion of funds had not only affected rural people and developmental process, but various government departments for which the state government claimed to have spent lions share of its annual budget regularly, were also affected.'[298] But nobody for sure can explain as to what happened to that money, obviously, the money went for the purpose it was not meant for! The Indian leadership must be in know of these realities but ignore these drain on exchequer for larger national interest.

Killing of D.C. Kohima: Early in April 1995, **LV Reddy**, DC of Kohima was shot dead in a daring move by the undergrounds, thus it was declared 'Disturbed Area'. But there was wide spread protest against the decision. Naga Peoples Council staged statewide 'bandh' (complete shutdown) on 06 April, 1995, and *Gaonburhas* (village headman) union organised a peace march in Dimapur. Though, the peace was being

---

[297]Colonel **Bhaskar Sarkar**, VSM (Retd), *'Tackling Insurgency and Terrorism: Blue Print of Action'*, Vision Books, New Delhi, 1998, p.59.

[298]**Suvendu Roychoudhary**, 'What Ails Nagaland', *North East Sun*, March 25-31, 1995, p.12.

shattered by the NSCN factions yet the common Nagas were against the decision to invoke the **Disturbed Area Act**, despite the situation was beyond control of authorities. *The Nagaland Herald* wrote:

> "This momentous and disastrous decision to invoke the provisions of the Disturbed Areas Act was necessitated by the vitiated atmosphere caused by rampant killings, extortions and failure on the part of the law enforcement agencies to contain law and order, the latest incident being the gunning down of DC, Kohima, L.V. Reddy in broad daylight by unknown assassins."[299]

The Naga cause and the morale of the NSCN (IM) were further bolstered when they were heard in the conference of UNPO (a misleading name: Unrepresented Nations and People's Organisation, located at Hague) and it has nothing to do with United Nations. I shall dwell here on efforts and successes of the NSCN(IM) in raising the issue in international fora.

Efforts to Internationalise the issue: The NSCN (IM), as discussed that they went all out and pressed its machinery to get wider recognition from other organizations across the globe. Close on the heels, NSCN (IM) got an opportunity to participate in the UN Working Group Consultation Meetings on Indigenous People at Geneva, Switzerland. In 1994, Angelous Shimrah and Rh. Raising were sent to USA for generating awareness as part of a campaign and to muster American support as well. It was successful in KWIA, Belgium, who passed a resolution in favour of the Naga Movement on 30 July, 1993, in Geneva, KWIA declared:

> "The Naga People as a whole has the right to determine its own future, its own political institutions... We respect and support the Naga resistance by all legal means, including armed resistance as authorized by international law."[300]

---

[299] *The Nagaland Herald*, Kohima, 10 April, 1995.

[300] Shimrah and Raising, op.cit, p.42.

There were few more organisations that supported or sympathised with the Naga cause. These were the Society of Threatened Peoples (Germany) and International Human Rights Association of American Minorities (IHRAAM) who assisted them in international lobbying. NSCN (IM) had a major breakthrough in internationalising the cause when the Secretary General, UNO, officially received the written statement about the Human Rights situation in 'Nagalim' and circulated in accordance with ECOSOC Resolution 1296 (XLIV).[301] This was the first time the UN officially accepted any statement in respect of Nagas as these efforts were also made by Phizo many times but to no avail. Moreover, NSCN (IM) also got an opportunity to present its case when they were called to address the 54th session of UN Commission on Human Rights (16 March–22 April 1998). However, by then NSCN (IM) had already signed the ceasefire agreement with the Government of India.

Military Operations and Talks: Side-by-Side

Back home, the government after having declared 'Disturbed Area' launched military operations to contain the insurgency. It is worth mentioning here that successive governments have been keeping channel for Talks open. By the fall of mid 1990, Narshimha Rao government sent feelers for the talks to the undergrounds, specially NSCN (IM) and since it had one condition that talks be held outside India and without any binding pre-conditions. The Prime Minister of India, Narshimha Rao, met the NSCN (IM) leadership in Paris for the first time on 12 June, 1995. Series of meetings were held in New York, Bangkok and Paris with the Prime Minister's emissary, **Amar Nath Verma**, who happened to be the Principal Advisor to the Prime Minister. Again Prime Minister Narshimha Rao met them in September, 1995 in New York and had preliminary talks on a prospective peace process.[302] However, the talks

---

[301]Shimrah and Raising, op.cit, p.42.

[302]Luingam Luithai and Frans Welman, 'Naga History: Chronology of Recent Events', *The Nagalad Post*, Dimapur, 28 December, 2002.

were stalled for some time, once the Congress government in the centre got changed.

So far as Rao government's actions were concerned, it was holding talks outside India and kept it secret from the general public and in addition, it was successful in bringing the most powerful faction to the negotiating table. However, talks were going as per NSCN (IM)'s terms but Army operations, specially since 1995 kept the militants on the run. Operation 'Golden Bird' of 1995 in Mizoram, for instance, was conducted after reaching a tacit understanding with the Myanmar Army,[303] which broke the rigid stance of undergrounds.

Talks were again resumed by the Prime Minister **Deve Gowda** in 1997 and sent Minister of State for Home, **Rajesh Pilot** to Bangkok for a feeler meeting, following which, he met **Muivah** and **Swu** in Zurich on February, 03.[304] Deve Gowda also pursued a couple of rounds of talks with NSCN (IM) at various locations outside India. Later, on 4 March 1997, during the Budget Session, Mr. Deve Gowda announced in the Parliament that the government has been engaging the underground groups without any pre-conditions as committed. He informed the nation that the government was holding talks with NSCN(IM) in order to find a political solution which would ensure durable peace in the region. He said:

> "... It was also my assessment that the common people in all these areas genuinely desired restoration of peace and normalcy so that they could pursue their vocations without hindrance and unemployed youth could find employment. My call was responded to by the National Socialist Council of Nagaland and I had a meeting recently with Shri Isak Swu, Chairman and Shri Muivah, General Secretary of this organization. It has been agreed that further talks would be held."[305]

It may be recalled that initially Narshimha Rao had offered for unconditional talks in 1995 in a public rally at Dimapur, but **Muivah** had rejected the proposal by saying:

---

[303] **R. Prasannan**, 'Watching the Nagas', *The Weekly*, New Delhi, July 27, 1997.

[304] iLid, also see Vashum, op.cit, p.79.

[305] **Luingam Luithai & Frans Welman**, op.cit, also http://nscn.livejournal.com/79350.html

"such proposals for peace talks are simply gimmicks by the authorities to buy time and confuse the real issue, our negotiations have to be political. There can not be just peace talks. We will agree to make peace only if we are certain that it will help negotiations."[306]

Santanu Ghosh opines that the turn around by NSCN (IM) was due to military operations and arrest of its top leaders in India including **Angelous Simrah, Queheve Chisi Swu** and **V Horam** which had put the NSCN (IM) on the back foot. Moreover, they were under pressure from Bangladesh to flee to Myanmar and their bank accounts were also frozen. He also opined that NSCN (IM) was not ready to lay down arms until and unless the demand for a separate homeland is met. Although, no substantial progress could be made in these talks, but it was a welcome change for the common population of India in general and Nagaland in particular.

Later on, I.K. Gujral became the Prime Minister of India. He gave further push to the peace talks. His Principal Secretary, **Satish Chandra**, met the NSCN leaders in Geneva on 26 May 1997. Finally Gujral also announced in the Parliament (Lok Sabha) on 25 July, 1997 and informed the nation that the government and NSCN(IM) have mutually agreed to ceasefire for three months with effect from 01 August, 1997 and initiate discussion at political level.[307]

Khaplang's Secret Parleys with the Government

While these talks were progressing, **SS Khaplang** also started secret parleys with the Government as he was also keen to settle the differences with the NSCN leaders, **Issac Chisi Swu** and **Th. Muivah**, in the interest of peace and Naga unity.[308] There could be two reasons for change of heart so far as offer of truce was concerned to his rival faction whom it wanted to decimate in 1989. Firstly, IM group had become a powerful

[306]**Santanu Ghosh**, 'Peace Mover', *Sunday*, New Delhi, 24-30 November, 1996, p.61.

[307]**Vashum**, op.cit, p.80.

opposition with growing clout and secondly he did not want to remain in the sidelines and keep on suffering from paranoia that he may be left out of the political settlement. Though, he did not give any indication that he wanted to be part of dialogue straightway.

The Ceasefire Agreement: Signed by both the Groups

The Naga movement has been the most faction ridden insurgency if compared to any other insurgency movement anywhere in South Asia. These divisions pose a serious problem in bringing a permanent solution. In this case, if government talks to IM group , Khaplang feels left out and Naga National Council (NNC) also wants the share of pie because it is the mother organisation. If others are engaged, IM group feels uncomfortable being militarily strongest. It was the real politick sense of the government which kept the secret channels open for all groups. Finally, after hard bargain between **K. Padmanabhaiah** (Home Secretary) and **VS Atem** of NSCN (IM), terms and conditions for ceasefire were reached on 12 December 1997. There were three important conditions in the Agreement, those were as follows:

> " ...(a) The talks shall be without conditions from both sides..... (b) at the highest level; that is at the prime ministerial level, (c) the venue of the talks shall be anywhere outside India. The objective will be towards finding a peaceful honourable political solution to the problem and the agreement comprises all the Naga areas."[309]

To govern the ceasefire, there were 10 clauses and certain rules were formulated. The were known as Cease Fire Ground Rules (CFGR). Though the ceasefire was initially agreed for three months only, but it was being periodically extended every three months till 31 July, 1998. Since 01 August, 1998,

---

[308]**Pradeep Parik**,'Nagaland: Give Peace No Chance', *Sunday*, 31 Aug-06 Sep, 1997, p.61.

[309]Dr **Gairiangmei Maringmei**, *Indo-Naga Second Ceasefire, 1997: An Analysis*, http://e-pao.net/epSubPageExtractor.asp?src=news_section.Naga_Peace_Process_Indo-Naga_Talks_2012.IndoNaga_second_ceasefire_1997

it has become an annual agreement and renewed every year on 31 July since 1998. To oversee the implementation of Ground Rules, it was also agreed upon by both the parties for monitoring the ceasefire process by drawing members from both the sides viz. from the Government of India and from the NSCN) including some Non-Governmental Organisations.[310] This group is known Ceasefire Monitoring Group (CFMG), generally headed by a retired General of Indian Army.

While the government was officially engaging NSCN (IM) for ceasefire, other group specially **Khaplang** was not in favour of such arrangement till two groups were united. **Kitovi Zhimomi** of **Khaplang** faction told in an interview that 'Unity among Nagas is our first priority. Till then, the ceasefire, with the Indian Government holds no meaning.'[311] Notwithstanding, the stand of NSCN (K) group on ceasefire, the Government of India in a goodwill gesture unilaterally declared ceasefire with NSCN (K) for a month beginning August 01, 1997. Later, it was unilaterally extended by another two months to make at par with NSCN (IM). The government maintained its initiative to bring NSCN (K) also on to the negotiation and finally they reached similar agreement in 2001. On the similar lines of NSCN (IM), arrangement was made to monitor and observe the implementation of Ground Rules, Ceasefire Supervisory Board (CFSB) was created which is again headed by the same general officer heading CFMG.

Talks Continued

Atal Bihari Vajpayee, Prime Minister who succeeded IK Gujral continued the policy of his predecessors. His emissary, **Swaraj Kaushal**, former Governor of Mizoram continued with the talks with NSCN (IM) leaders at different places e.g. Bangkok, Zurich, Amsterdam (May-September 1998) and for the first time, there was official talk held in Netherlands from 24-27 March, 1999.

---

[310]Dr **Gairiangmei Maringmei**, *Indo-Naga Second Ceasefire, 1997: An Analysis.*

[311]**Nitin A Gokhale**, 'The NSCN's Lair', *The OutLook*, 01 December 1997, p.37.

Meanwhile, coinciding with beginning of ceasefire in Nagaland, from 28 July to 03 August, 1997, representative of all Naga parties got together at Atlanta, Georgia (USA) under the aegis of Baptist Peace Fellowship of North America (BPFNA). The meet was basically organised by the Baptist Church leaders of Nagaland. At the end of the meet, they released an appeal to all factions for unity and peace among the Nagas. The signatories of Atlanta meet appealed to all Naga factions and reaffirmed their commitment to reconciliation and peace. It said:

> "We urge a common commitment to reconciliation, particularly in overcoming bitter political rivalries and inter-tribal disputes.. In the pursuit of a just peace we will continue to meet, developing strategies to promote dialogue among our people. We reiterate the call of the Naga Hoho, as per the summit of 1996, to a complete ceasefire between the Naga groups. We also call for the adoption of a visual symbol to express the desire of Naga People for Peace and Unity."[312]

Though, all the factions committed themselves for working towards peace and reconciliation, but peace could not be achieved in so many years, despite both the groups having signed the ceasefire agreements with the Government separately. They keep their guns trained against each other and it is difficult to even predict, whether the guns will ever be silent? Although it may sound very cynical!

Section-III

Post Ceasefire Period (1997-2017)

It was great political acumen and hard bargaining, coupled with a sense of people's yearning for peace, the government finally articulated the terms and conditions for Ceasefire Agreement with both the NSCN (IM) and (K) group. But it is an irony that although both the NSCN factions signed truce

---

[312]Nuh and Wetshokhorlo (ed), op.cit, p.456.

with the Government of India, (their common enemy) but both the groups continued to clash with each other bitterly. This appeared to be settling political score over each initially other but most important reason was that both were trying to grab the area and increase their influence by using the conditions of ceasefire. This was to ensure smooth flow of funds and increase the cadre strength. A rough estimate was that NSCN (IM) and (K) had swelled the cadre strength to 5000 and 2000 respectively by the year 2003. **Sashinungla** writes:

> "... In June, 2003, a top security official based in Nagaland had claimed that the outfit was taking advantage of the cease-fire with the Government of India to strengthen its organizational base. Media reports of June 2003 had indicated that in the preceding five years, the group had raised its cadre strength from 3,000 to 5,000 and also increased its weaponry two-fold. ... The NSCN-K has an estimated strength of about 2,000 cadres."[313]

The internecine feud erupted resulting into serious losses of life and threw the Naga Hills 'law and order' situation into a tizzy. Although, it can be said that inter-factional clashes (IFC), now manifested was existing even before the Naga movement commenced. Unfortunately, the leadership question of the political struggle between the two NSCN groups took precedence and had taken an ugly turn. In a socio-cultural milieu of the Nagas, wherein the tribal affiliation is more important than the individual, it becomes apparent that, when one kills an individual from a particular group, it will be reciprocated with equal or more ferocity. These IFCs were very-very frequent in the earlier days of ceasefire (initial first decade) and the number of death and injured used to be too high. The CFMG and other law enforcement agencies had a difficult time to keep them under check. There are no authenticated figures available in public domain, but one such report is good enough to imagine the loss of lives that would have taken place in two decades of Ceasefire:

---

[313]**Sashinungla,** *Nagaland: Insurgency and Factional Intransigence,* http://www.satp.org/satporgtp/publication/faultlines/volume16/Article4.htm#*

> "In May and June (2008) alone, more than 40 insurgent cadres from the three factions as well as non-combatants have been killed in insurgent cross-fire. The worst fall out of proximate insurgent camps was never more visibly demonstrated than the June 4 bloodbath by the NSCN (IM) when it killed 14 NSCN (K) cadres between Aoyim and Xelhozhe villages near Siethekima, about 16 km from Dimapur where the NSCN (K) has an underground camp. In a similar attack on NSCN (U) camp at Vihokhu on May 16, NSCN (IM) killed 12 of the former's cadres."[314]

It may be noted here that here is another group NSCN (U) has surfaced as a new outfit. Just to conclude on the IFCs, it is heartening to see that these clashes have gone down drastically over the years and in 2016, reportedly, there has been no loss of life due to IFCs.

Birth and Death of NSCN (U)

There have been only two major armed groups operating post split in NSCN with whom the ceasefire was '**ON**'. These two groups were engaged in influencing the Naga people but in 2007, the NSCN (IM) witnessed a split when Azetho Chophy, a Sema leader of the outfit broke away and formed the NSCN (Unification). It came into being on November 23, 2007 wherein an inter-factional 'truce agreement' signed between the few cadres and leaders of the NSCN(IM) and(K). Here NSCN (IM) was being represented by Azheto Chophy and the NSCN (K) by C. Singson, holding important positions in the respective factions. The NSCN(IM) leadership rejected it out rightly. The NSCN(U) later formed a strategic linkage with NSCN (K) and participated in joint IFCs against IM group. Post 2014, this group has not been active and possibly does not exist.

Birth of NSCN (KK): The Central Group

In May, 2012; another faction was born, this time it was

[314]**Namrata Goswami**, '*A Way Out of Naga Factional Violence*', IDSA Comments, New Delhi, 23 July, 2008.

breakup of NSCN (K). Two senior leaders of NSCN(K), **Kitovi Zhimomi** and **Khole Konyak**, broke away to form a new outfit called NSCN (Khole and Kitovi). This group has put the NSCN (IM) at an uneasy position since beginning as both the leaders are locals from Mon district of Nagaland, unlike **Khaplang**, who can pose serious challenge to their leadership being on its home turf, given their greater social acceptance and provide legitimacy to their claim that they represent local Naga aspirations. Therefore, their demand to be included in the Naga peace talks with the Government of India holds far more gravity than that of NSCN (K). There is also likelihood that the Government of India may keep Khole and Kitovi faction engaged in peace talks on the sidelines, should the NSCN (IM) takes a tough stand as the sole representative of the Naga people in final agreement which is under negotiation at this moment. As expected or fear of being pushed out of the centre of gravity of Naga nationalism or being given lesser importance by the Naga people or for that matter Government of India, NSCN(IM) had numerous bitter clashes with NSCN (KK) group to wipe out the competition. On the other hand, NSCN(KK) group had similar exchanges with NSCN(K) as well.

Another Faction Formed: NSCN (R)

Latest in the series of Naga factionalism, another faction came into being when **Y. Wangtin Naga** and **P. Tikhak** of NSCN (K) announced the formation of a new political group and named as National Socialist Council of Nagaland (Reformation) or NSCN (R) in April 2016. **Wangtin**, was member of the Ceasefire Supervisory Board (CFSB) which keeps monitoring the ceasefire agreement with NSCN (K) and Government of India, and **Tikhak**, a senior functionary of NSCN (K) expelled by NSCN (K) supremo as they were not in agreement with the Chairman over recent abrogation of ceasefire with the Government of India. The duo, wanted to continue with the ceasefire maintaining that violence has never served a good purpose and the Naga political problem can only be resolved through peaceful negotiation while **Khaplang** had it abrogated because the 14 years of ceasefire between NSCN (K) and India has become a mockery and futile exercise.[315] It is also true that while Government of India had 80 rounds of talks with NSCN (IM) group but they have not invited **Khaplang** even for once. Thus, Abrogation of the ceasefire can be said is an outcome of this neglect by the authorities in India for whatever reasons. Abrogation was followed by more than six attacks on the Indian Army in Nagaland, Manipur and Arunachal Pradesh (states of India) by the NSCN (K) Group. It is also to inform the readers at this juncture that passing away of Khaplang (on 9 June 2017 – Reported by all national/regional papers) may have bearing on ongoing Naga Peace Talks as majority of next level of leadership of NSCN(K) have left the group and formed their own group NSCN (KK) but nothing can be said with certainty.

Review of the Situation

It's not even worth saying that whatever has happened till date, is unfortunate and it will be further damaging if the Naga groups cannot maintain unity on slightest pretext or difference of opinions or perceived inequality on tribal lines within the factions. It has been seen umpteen times that until and unless, Naga reconciliation is in place, real peace cannot be achieved. It may be possible that all those who have taken up guns are driven by hallowed and idealistic but impractical thoughts live sovereignty and independence. Thus, there was a need felt by some serious rational thinking people within the Naga civil society and came up to bring these splinter groups to a commen platform and make them reconcile. It has happened in the past and this time too, *Gaonburahs* (Village Headmen) alongwith *Dobashish* (Interpreters) came forward and formed a Joint Forum of *Goanburahs* and *Dobashis* or the JFGBDB. It was this organisation that requested a ceasefire between the NSCN (IM) and NSCN (K) in July 2007, which was largely successful in bringing down violence in Naga inhabited

[315] *Morung Express*, Wangtin, Tikhak forms NSCN(Reformation), 06 April, 2016.

areas. Subsequently, another movement began under the stewardship of the churches, Christ being the common bond for all the Nagas.

The **Forum for Naga Reconciliation** (FNR) began its journey in February 2008, through the Shisha Hoho Prayer Ministry, comprising of all frontal Naga organizations, the Council of Naga Baptist Churches (CNBC), the Nagaland Baptist Church Council (NBCC) and the Nagaland Christian Forum (NCF).[316] After weathering intense and stormy initial stages of reconciliation efforts, FNR could make breakthrough after organizing couple of symbolic events such as the reconciliation soccer matches and the Naga National Choir etc. The **'Journey of Common Hope'** picked up momentum and a **'Covenant of Reconciliation'** was signed in June, 2009, by all the groups 'in the spirit of love, respect and understanding. These people began to see new hopes. This culminated in the signing of the 'Naga Concordant' in August, 2011 as 'having reconciled on the basis of the historical and political rights' and for which, the signatories resolved in principle to work towards the formation of one Naga National Government for a shared future. It has further asserted that a 'paradigm shift' has taken place in the reconciliation process with the Naga political groups 'transcending the past'.[317]

Looking back to the historical events within the last about a decade of the **'Journey of Common Hope'**, commendable achievements leading to the present situation have been witnessed. With cautious optimism, the Naga political groups had begun to tear down the wall of separation built over time by hatred, bitterness, malice and slander. Today, they have taken a courageous leap and have transcended the fences that divide and are sitting and eating at the table together and talking rationally on issues of a common future rather than be haunted and victimized by the past. For all these efforts, a sincere appreciation and loud applause to the Naga political groups is hailed by one and all. At the centre of the makings, was

---

[316]Rev DR. Wati Aier, *Naga Reconciliation: Journey of Common Hope*, http://nagalim.livejournal.com/20515.html, 06 March, 2010.

[317]http://www.nagalimvoice.com/news/forum-for-naga-reconciliation-an-appraisal/, 29 September 2012.

the historic signing of the **'Covenant of Reconciliation'** (COR), by the representatives of NSCN(IM), NSCN(K) and FGN, on behalf of the NNC (Adinno). Today, when the Government of India and NSCN(IM) has signed the **'Framework Agreement'** in August 2015, role of FNR has become more important as the other factions are not the party to this Agreement and thus there is a genuine fear that the '**Journey of Common Hope**' should not get derailed. Today the FNR is working towards the Naga unity and reconciliation as before.

FNR's Contribution

The FNR cautiously keeping all the groups engaged so that none of the groups resort to any kind of provocation or violence, if and when, any Agreement is signed and implemented. It has called upon the NSCN (IM) to maintain transparency with respect to the Agreement and future talks with the Government of India. For a decade FNR has been working relentlessly to bring all the Naga Political Groups (NPGs) together, as desired by the Nagas, for meaningful reconciliation, with the hope that an honorable political solution acceptable to both the sides.

The signing of the **'Framework Agreement'** was not an easy task 'but to make this treaty successful and binding will be an arduous task for both the Government of India and the Naga leadership. It may be a fallacy to assume that the NSCN (IM) is the custodian of the aspirations of the Naga tribes, and to believe that **Muivah** alone* will be able to unite all the Naga insurgent groups will be a delusion. Though the details of the Framework Agreement are yet not in the public domain, the government has clarified more than once that state boundaries are sacrosanct and a Greater Nagalim is unacceptable.[318] In this back drop, the NSCN (IM), the Naga community leaders including FNR, the states and the central Government of India, all will have solemn responsibility to work together to make it happen.

---

[318]**Narendra Kumar**, 'Naga Peace Accord: A Glass Half Full', *The CLAWS Journal*, Winter 2015.

* Issac Chisi Swu, Chairman of NSCN(IM) has passed away on 28 June 2016.

7

External Factors and Human Rights

Ethno-Political Conflicts: Similar in Nature

Ethno-political conflicts all over the world have many similarities specially in the genesis and that is socio-politico- or economic disparities. Also they have similarities in response mechanism by the majority group or the state and that is to control or crush it, initially through police and later armed forces but rarely attempted to address the root cause. During the transition from a small movement to armed struggle, the movement graduates from benign to bold, fragile to resilient when logistics and training, or material and moral support received especially from foreign countries. In India, involvement of external powers has been confirmed which is due to asymmetrical power balance in the sub continent and also for its geostrategic importance and geo-political alliances with the world powers. In this case of the Nagas, the undergrounds, out of sheer frustration and fear of being crushed, knocked the door of immediate neighbours for help in early stages of insurgency and later in late 1980s which were mostly limited to moral, material and training support.

This chapter has been dedicated to study the external factors, i.e. role of foreign countries and NGOs. In addition, it discusses as the human rights violations that took place in this conflict since the beginning of the movement.

Section-I

Role of Foreign Countries

Survival of any armed struggle greatly depends upon the material and moral support in terms of arms and ammunition supply. Since, these are difficult to manufacture and are very costly, procurement from international sources and shipment becomes key issue. Thus movement greatly depends upon external support. The Naga movement too, initially had World War II collections to begin their armed struggle but soon after the deployment of the army, it proved to be too meager a resource. So they had no choice but to seek international help specially for arms and ammunition, logistics support for food and shelter were met from the locals.

The NNC supremo, **Phizo** left Naga Hills when government stance became hardened and it was not easy to continue the struggle without external support. He visited few countries (Myanmar and Pakistan) to seek support for the Naga cause during which once, he was intercepted by the Burmese Police and released later.[319] Since then conscious efforts have been made by the NNC to garner support of foreign countries.

Pakistan's Intervention: Proxy War

On the other hand, Pakistan drew blood in its quest for annexing Kashmir immediately after independence. Since then (October, 1947) it hasn't been able to even out with India militarily, so extending moral and material support to all insurgency movements in India and followed a course fraught with disastrous consequences. As is known, Phizo contacted Jinnah, proponent of two nation theory, in pre-independence period before declaring independence on 14 August, 1947, which is celebrated as Independence Day by the undergrounds till date. Post independence, **Phizo** re-established contact with

[319]A.L. Ao, *'From Phizo to Muivah'*, Mittal Publishers, New Delhi, 2002, p.19.

Pakistani authorities through his emissaries. It was **Mowu**, self styled General of Naga Army, established first contact with Chief Minister of East Pakistan, **Ata-Ur-Rahman**, for sponsoring the Naga cause at the UN on 15 October, 1956, which was turned down.[320]

Later, Phizo himself entered East Pakistan (Now Bangladesh) and sought help from Pakistani authorities in December, 1956. Initially, Pakistan did not want to get involved in India directly. They suggested **Phizo** to go to London to raise the Naga issue in the UN but at the same time, they provided material and moral support, supplied arms and ammunition and extended training facilities.[321] **General KV Krishna Rao** (ex Army Chief of India) had the following to say:

> "They (Nagas) had established contacts with Pakistan and China and arranged for arms assistance. To start with, Pakistan provided arms assistance. A number of groups proceeded to Pakistan during the period 1962-64. These were under the leadership of self styled General Kaito Sema (100), self styled General Mowu Angami (73), self styled Brigadier Dusoi Chakhesang (202) and self styled General Zuheto Sema (1300). After training and indoctrination, these gangs returned with a large number of modern weapons."[322]

Subir Bhaumik, BBC correspondent, an expert on the subject with vast experience also opines that it was almost a spontaneous help that came from Pakistan, contrary to Aosenba's assertion. **Subir Bhaumik** in his article wrote that 'in 1958, **Phizo** fled to Pakistan to arrange for aid, which was soon forthcoming'.[323] It was quite clear that Pakistan was more than willing and allowed them to operate from insurgent camps in East Pakistan. Subsequently, from Dacca, **Phizo** went to Karachi (then capital of Pakistan) and finally reached London on 12 June, 1960 via Zurich with the help of **Rev Micheal Scott**. The aim of Pakistan was to keep Indian army tied down in

---

[320]Aosenba, op.cit, p.90.

[321]ibid.

[322]General K.V. Krishna Rao, op.cit, p.263.

[323]Subir Bhaumick, 'Farewell Phizo', *The Sunday*, 13-19 May 1990.

insurgency operation thereby reduce its fighting potential. India's sensitivity towards its North Eastern states was being exploited to suit Pakistan's geo-political ambition of annexing Kashmir and also to neutralise the threat to East Pakistan.

Chinese Support: Geo-Strategic Reasons

Initially, China was being perceived by Indian authorities as a friendly nation since independence and India ensured its entry into the UN Security Council and did remain mute spectator when later annexed Tibet and directly confronted with India on the borders in 1962. India, being weak nation then, further weakened militarily due to lack of budgetary support of the government due to the flawed concept of universal brotherhood, suffered ignominious and monumental defeat in 1962. China has unresolved border dispute with India which could not be solved till date and has kept vast tracts of Aksai Chin under its forceful occupation. In addition, Pakistan has ceded part of Pak occupied Kashmir (POK) for making Karrakoram highway. China today practices the policy of strategic encirclement of India along the boundaries and has made a deal with Pakistan for China, Pak Economic Corridor (CPEC) through Pak Occupied Kashmir (POK: officially Indian territory since 1947). It keeps India pin-pricking on diplomatic front on visa for Indian citizens hailing from Arunachal Pradesh (erstwhile NEFA) and also brazenly support international terrorists from Pakistan at United Nations. Today, Chinese stance against India is quite belligerent and overt on many other issues like opposing the membership of India in Nuclear Suppliers Group (NSG) despite being a close partner in BRICS (an umbrella organisation of five major countries viz. Brazil, Russia, India, China and South Africa) but in earlier times the support to the insurgents was covert. The Naga insurgents, when established contact with the Chinese authorities probably just prior to the War of 1962 through Pakistan, were extended full support. It is believed that **Kughato Sema**, wrote to the Chinese Prime Minister, Chou-En-Lai that the Nagas were willing to extend full support to the Chinese if later attacked India in NEFA

(Arunachal Pradesh). Surprisingly, Naga guerillas, fighting against India did not even lift a finger to help the Chinese army.[324] In fact, **Phizo** conveyed to the Government of India through press on 15 November, 1962, and offered support of 40,000 Naga army personnel to fight against the Chinese, if India agreed to grant independence to the Nagas.[325] Nevertheless, it shows desperation of the NNC for independence!

China had two pronged strategy: first to provide assistance for conducting guerrilla operations militarily and second, to indoctrinate the NNC cadres in socialist ideology which bears the testimony in the name of NSCN itself. First group, about 150 under **Thinouselie Angami** proceeded to China in November, 1966 for training and returned to Nagaland in January, 1968, with a large consignment of modern weapons. Another group of about 331 went to China in December, 1967 under **Mowu Angami** and re-entered Nagaland in March, 1969, again with large number of weapons.[326] These support were found to be true when the Indian Army raided Jotsoma Camp and recovered huge cache of arms and ammunition and captured 25 guerillas of these China returned insurgents.[327] **Issac Swu**, who led another batch of cadres, however, managed to escape in this operation.

Withdrawl of Support from China

It is said that **Thuingaleng Muivah**, then ambassador plenipotentiary of the FGN to China, visited North Vietnam (Hanoi) under the aegis of the Chinese, to have a first-hand experience on how Vietnamese fought USA. Even some of the guerillas were also sent to Hanoi from China itself for training in intensive guerilla operations. Somehow, due to ideological differences with respect to religion, Nagas could not go beyond a limit. Moreover, Indian Government took up

---

[324]**Aosenba**, op.cit, p.92.

[325]ibid.

[326]**Gundevia**, op.cit, p.190.

[327]**General K.V. Krishana Rao**, op.cit, p.263.

the case with the Chinese authorities and protested against its involvement in internal affairs. It is also believed that India had warned China that they would be entirely responsible for the consequences.[328] Probably, the Indian threat of consequence changed the Chinese stance since India has given shelter to the Government of Tibet in exile and could play a vital role in creating disturbance in Tibetan Autonomous Region (TAR). Though it was in their interest to keep the Nagas supporting but ideological/religious differences and Indian support to Tibetan people probably restricted the Chinese and subsequently, compelled them to withdraw the support.

Today, **Beijing's geo-political interests** in the region have increased and it is looking to control the Sea Lanes of Communications (SLOCs), vital to Chinese economy and majority of them passes through Indian Ocean. In addition, it has designs to keep India under check for its maritime interests in South China Sea. Thus China will continue its policy of strategic encirclement of India without confronting on borders, viable low cost option, which India can ill-afford to ignore. Towards this China has established good relation with Pakistan, Sri Lanka, Myanmar and Bangladesh. Moreover, eye on Arunachal Pradesh and claim over it keeps India under strategic pressure, Thus Chinese moves in respect of the North-East India cannot be just ignored.

Support from Bangladesh

Post creation of Bangladesh in 1971, Indo-Bangladesh relations had been having a roller coaster ride. Euphoric relations got subdued even while Mujib was alive. Soon after his assassination, Bangladesh started having problems with India and these were due to perceived threats despite geographic conditions, economic opportunities and ethno-cultural proximity. Moreover, the psychological debt on the part of Bangladesh was overbearing and Islamization of its polity brought it closer to Pakistan. Bangladesh got down to

---

[328] Aosenba, op.cit, p.93.

even out with India which it could not do overtly or sort out the differences be it on sharing of water issue or issue of the Chakmas. Hence, it can be said that from the beginning only, barring first four years of Mujib's regime, Bangladesh started harbouring insurgent groups in its territory.

Lt Gen (Retd) **Nayar**, who is a veteran of North East and was the Governor in Manipur, opines that Bangladesh was doing a tit for tat to India. He feels that 'while India is alleged to have trained Shanti Bahini of Chittagong Hill Tracts (CHT), Bangladesh has been playing host to a number of Indian insurgent groups'.[329]

In fact, during Mujib's time all the insurgent groups of North East India had to relocate their bases in North Myanmar and depended entirely on the Chinese. Once the Chinese began to reduce their involvement, the insurgent groups had to entirely depend on the Kachin Independent Army (KIA), who charged them heavily to their guests.

According to Gen Nayar, after Mujib's death in 1975, the pattern again changed and Bangladesh Intelligence–ISI links began to be gradually established. Today ISI operates a legal intelligence network out of its diplomatic establishment in Dacca and illegal ones under cover of business and fundamental groups.[330] The details of involvement of Bangladesh with the insurgents (all groups in North East India) and channels of acquisition of sophisticated arms and ammunition from Thailand with Bangladesh intelligence's connivance was outlined by the Border Security Force (BSF). Notes released in November, 1995 and the Annual Press Conference by DG, BSF on 27 November, 1997, which is an all open secret.

In fact, NSCN (IM)'s Alee command, located in Bangladesh did all the procurement of weapons and without tacit support of Bangladesh, it is just impossible. **Paresh Barua** (United Liberation Front of Assam-ULFA) had been staying in Dhaka since long and ran the outfit as well as his personal business

---

[329]Lt Gen **V.K. Nayar**, 'Insurgencies in the North East', *USI Journal*, Vol CXXX (No-540), Apr-June, 2000, p.300.

[330]ibid, p.301.

and maintained a good rapport with NSCN (IM) leadership in Bangladesh. E.N. Ram Mohan's account regarding the deal of Russian arms through an unknown dealer in Thailand, as told to him by one ULFA cadre who surrendered to BSF:

> "Thuingaleng Muivah and Paresh Barua had Bangladeshi names and passport given to them. Meeting with the ISI followed and held in Sayeman hotel in Cox Bazar where Thuingaleng Muivah, Paresh Barua alongwith ISI and DGFI officers."[331]

The emergence of military rule in Bangladesh ensured the revival of old link between Pakistan ISI and North East insurgents and this policy was continued till Begum Zia ruled the country. Actually, increasing Islamisation of society and politics, growing menace of fundamentalist groups like Al Quaeda, Jammat-e-Islami etc, are potential threat to India. However, there has been a welcome change in the policy of Bangladesh towards India after **Sheikh Hasina's** government returned to power. Thus, safe sanctuaries within Bangladesh and freedom to operate with impunity by the insurgent groups from North East India were the case of the past.

Role of USA

As regards USA, its role towards Indian independence was by pressurising UK during and post World War period. But in the beginning after 1947, Indian policy makers were highly impressed with the socialist philosophy and hence, adopted socialistic model of governance. Thus, influence of socialism brought India closer to erstwhile USSR and being the leader of Non-Aligned Movement (NAM) and Third world countries tilted the power balance against the USA and hence, Pakistan became a frontline state in US strategic interests. Since Pakistan kept its agencies deployed in the North East India, Central Intelligence Agency of USA extended their activities by supporting financially the Naga Movement.

---

[331]**EN Ram Mohan**, 'The Naga Insurgency', *USI Journal*, Vol XXXIII, No-554, Oct-Dec 2003, p.595.

It is alleged that in late 1960s CIA had 'handed the tribal leaders several million rupees, weapons and secret instruction prepared in Washington'.[332] There has been another allegation wherein USA had formulated an official research project named 'Project Brahmaputra' to study the conundrum of North East India including Sikkim and Bhutan.

According to the scope of the project, the research team was to conduct public opinion poll on the constitutional position in different North-Eastern states and find out the possibility of forming a new state.[333] However, there is no documentary proof to establish the veracity of the allegation or otherwise. It is said that the 'Project Brahmaputra' was the creation of KGB (USSR Intelligence Agency) propagated to keep India hooked on to USSR. There is no proof to claim or reject the suggestion that whether or not the 'Project Brahmaputra' was a brain-child of the KGB to malign the CIA and keep India hooked on to erstwhile USSR, but it can be said that in late 1970s and early 1980s, there was a fresh impetus in all insurgent activities and underground movements,[334] however, complicity of USA in any of these developments could never be established comprehensively.

Kirkpatrick Plan of USA

Contrarily, it is true that some of the politicians of USA had been directly or indirectly working against Indian interests at personal level. '**Kirkpatrick**' plan was one of those kinds, wherein Ms Kirkpatrick had 'advocated a policy to Reagan administration for dismemberment of India through active US support to the separatist movements'.[335] It can be inferred that since there is a segment of politicians who are hired by various countries for lobbying and furtherance of respective national interests and may be **Ms Kirkpatrick** was hired by any of the

[332]**V.I.K. Sarseen**, p.23, also see Aosenba, op.cit, p.95.

[333]ibid.

[334]**Gurudas Das** 'India's North East Underbelly; Strategic Vulnerability and Security', *Strategic Analysis*, Vol-26, No-4, Oct-Dec 2002, pp.542-543.

[335]ibid, pp.543-544.

inimical neighbours of India and should not be construed as official policy of the USA. Also another Democrat Senator from California **Barabara Boxer**, had helped NSCN (IM) to establish office at Washington DC, which surprised the people of USA and India both. 'In yet another significant revelations, highly placed sources said that former US President **Bill Clinton's** family was solely responsible for helping NSCN to set up their office'.[336] However, these reports could neither be verified nor were officially accepted by the Government of USA and possibly these kind of allegations are part of motivated mis-information campaign.

Role of UK

So far as official support to Naga cause was concerned, UK Government never openly sided either with NNC or NSCN groups except that, it allowed **Phizo** to continue to stay in Britain from the 1960s till his death which is fairly justified and in consonance with its policy of granting citizenship to the migrating population from any country specially those ones which were ruled by the British. However, some of the Britons, like David Ward championed Naga human rights cause as an individual, which will be discussed separately in human rights section.

Myanmar's Role

The **state policy of Myanmar** is entirely conditioned by two factors i.e. it's political requirement at the ground level and the limited capacity to fight insurgency in their own land. They were compelled to negotiate and settle the issue with most of the home grown insurgent groups by mutually convenient arrangements, as the state could ill afford to fight any insurgency. Since India always favoured pro-democratic dissidents, Myanmar allowed NSCN (K) to operate in the northern areas and NSCN (IM) in some other areas, may be they had little capability or the reach to tame these groups.

---

[336] *The Nagaland Page*, Dimapur, 17 August, 2003.

The response of the Myanmar government had been 'on' and 'off' throughout these years. Officially, Myanmar has never supported any insurgent groups but they could not possibly control them to stop using the Northern Myanmar area for their camps etc. However, insurgent groups of Myanmar e.g. Kachin National Army (KNA and Chins) had given all the help to the NNC, over whom the government has no control and these groups do it for money. Moreover, India's support to the Democratic leader Aung San Sue Ki, could have triggered the 'no' or 'negative response' of the military junta in the late 1980s and 1990s.

In the late 1990s, it was believed that the Chinese support had dried up; still arms transshipment from Bangkok had been taking place through land routes which passed through Myanmar. Despite the Headquarters of NSCN (K) being in northern areas of Myanmar, complicity of the government has never been established. In fact, there have been few military operations jointly conducted in past few decades. The Myanmar army operations in 1999, after the visit of the Indian Army Chief, were unilateral in nature. Though, it was a success, but it allowed many insurgents to escape into the Indian side of the international border. The Myanmar military Junta was not in favour of taking firm action against the drug traffickers (Naga undergrounds included), since their government is cash starved due to UN sanctions. Therefore, if the Myanmar government turned its eye away from these drugs trafficking mafia, it was more of economic compulsion rather than political or ideological one.

The relations with Myanmar have improved greatly due to India's 'Look East Policy' and present rule of democratically elected government with *de facto* leader Aung San Sue Ki. It may be noted here that India couldn't have been able to take on NSCN (Khaplang) in cross border raid inside Myanmar in August 2015 in retaliation to their attack on Indian Army wherein 18 soldiers were killed, had it not been her government in support. However, it is prudent to caution here that it is a friendly nation that needs India's support and thus inimical neighbours should be kept at bay specially China and Pakistan.

Section-II

Human Rights in India: A Perspective

Since Naga Movement has been the longest surviving insurgency and the very existence of this insurgency irrespective of its changes in the organisation, leadership, ideology or even modus operandi, proves one fact that they have been able to keep the cause alive and passed it to the next generation to continue the fight. This couldn't have been possible unless the cost paid by the Nagas was very heavy or in other words had there been no excesses or violation of human rights. Thus, it is important to study the same in its correct perspective and draw lessons for future.

In a country like India, which is multi-religious, multiracial and multiethnic, the human rights concerns stem from the claims made on the basis of perceived inequality and 'indigenous minority' status by communities within the nation state itself. The communitarian values take precedence over individualism, however, the political processes and state structures and principle adopted are 'west centric'. Thus, India shares its sovereignty also with a wide array of autonomous and largely self-governing community of communities, recognizing both individuals and communities as bearers of rights.[337]

Post colonial India, as a state, has taken care to protect the communitarian social structure, 'recognising' the sacredness characteristic of certain groups through enactments of a relatively 'differentiated citizenship' and creation of federal states on ethno-linguistic terms. Moreover, India had to reconcile and negotiate the claims of a 'community' and that of an 'individual', thereby the state attempted to provide for a dual structure of jurisprudence in its recognition of the **'Personal Law Code'** enforced by groups themselves and 'Civil

---

[337] **Rajesh Dev**, 'The Cultural Particularity of Liberal Democracy', in David Held (ed) *Prospects for Democracy*, Stanford University Press, USA, 1993, pp. 48-49.

Code' enforced by state. The cumulative result of these efforts is the natural recognition of groups, implicitly or explicitly as 'minorities/indigenous/disadvantaged' making them believe to certain legal claims and preferential policies that safeguards them from any social, cultural and economic compromises.[338] The recognition of these groups such as minorities/indigenous will continue to be determined by the vagaries of regional politics, which is a fallout of democratic form of governance.

Violation of Human Rights in Insurgency Prone Areas

Though, when we talk of violation of human rights in the context of insurgency ridden areas, all the parties seem to be the victims of misinterpretation of civil, democratic, fundamental rights. Since the origin of ethno-cultural conflicts based on relativism is a clear outcome of misinterpretation of fundamental rights or it can be termed as cascading effect of the definition of human rights, civil, political and even democratic rights, which are guaranteed in the Constitution of India. In the context of Nagaland, when we talk of violation of human rights, study is confined to the specific cases of violation of human rights at its grass root levels of execution and not at the conceptual level of discourse, since the origin of the movement, the conceptual distinction between civil, democratic, fundamental and human rights has remained somewhat blurred and even coloured within the intellectual and political discourses.[339]

It is also true that security forces operate against the rebels in a very restricted manner. They are compelled to fight with one hand tied behind due to which the faceless enemy can appear and strike at '**will**'. The imaginary quantification of 'minimum force' to avoid collateral damage severely affects the psyche of a soldier. In addition, more often than not security forces suffer from decision dilemma as to who is an insurgent and who is

[338] **Rajesh Dev**, op.cit, pp.47-49.

[339] **Aswini K Ray**, 'Human Rights Movement in India! A Historical Perspective', *Economic and Political Weekly*, Mumbai, Vol XXXVIII, No 32, August 9, 2003.

not! Whenever they carry out cordon and search operation, face serious allegations of rape, torture, fake encounters or custodial deaths etc. While some of the allegations may be true but many of them are manufactured to discredit and malign them, which in turn severely affects the morale. However, excesses against the common population amongst which insurgents hide, can neither be justified nor avoided. These are certain operational hazards and inconveniences caused to the people, generally termed as state terrorism. **Gen Samay Ram** opines:

> "Notwithstanding the dilemma of the security forces, the world at large has become sensitive to the issue of human rights violations. It is now believed that in response to private terrorism, the state cannot resort to state terrorism implying that the security forces behaviour cannot be similar to the militants, that violation of human rights by the terrorists does not justify state terrorism."[340]

Operational Necessity of AFSPA

India was a new born nation state, experienced cracks in subterranean fault-lines and the state persisted on short term measures to address the cracks and reactions were based on previous experience of the British era. There were certain laws passed to curb violence, which we have already discussed. Armed Forces Special Power Act of 1958 (AFSPA) (Refer Appendix 'G') was invoked alongwith Disturbed Area Act to quell the violence. In fact, the AFSPA's predecessor i.e. the Armed Forces Special Power Ordnance 1942 was enacted[341] to neutralise 'Quit India' movement. Today the AFSPA is the most powerful tool with the Armed Forces personnel and its use ought to be extremely judicious. This law was re-enacted to quell the violence and uprising in the Naga Hills in Assam in the year 1958, but yet to be repealed or revoked.

---

[340] **Aswini K Ray**, op.cit, p.90.

[341] **N Sanajaoba**, *'Human Rights in the New Millennium'*, Manas Publications, New Delhi, 2000, p.176.

On the other hand, security forces also now psychologically conditioned to the dependency of this law for operational necessity and safeguarding lives of the soldiers with checks and balances. Many a time, binding provisions are ignored because of non-availability/accessibility and even non cooperation of civil authorities; at times overlooked to keep the operational plans from being subverted. It has been the experience of Armed Forces that local administration officials do compromise the plan and get an ambush sprung. This is carried out by taking specific information about the impending operation, get detached discreetly en route at an appropriate time and place, and pass the information to the undergrounds and the undergrounds turn the table against Armed Forces. Thus, implementation of the provisions is necessary by ensuring that the human rights are not violated, be it that of a soldier or an insurgent, after all both are the citizen of India. However, **Imchen** advocates very strongly for repealing the law:

> "The standard of activities done so far by the armed forces in Naga areas does not tally with prudent rules of law which is granted by the democratic constitution of India; therefore immediate repeal of Armed Forces Special Powers Act 1958 is imperative in upholding the human values."[342]

There have been protests against invoking of AFSPA in all the North Eastern states of India wherever insurgency movements are alive. **Ms Sharmila Irome**, the Iron Lady, had been a crusader and fasting unto death against the AFSPA in Imphal (Manipur) since 02 November, 2000. Last year, she ended her fast on 09 August, 2016 and opted to join politics and continue the fight against the law.

In fact, Delhi is also weary of lifting the Armed Forces Special Powers Act and Disturbed Areas Act from all those areas which have been declared 'Disturbed', else how the government will ensure and protect the civil or human rights of a soldier whom they send to protect the nation and uphold the Constitution? As is known the common populace is scared

---

[342]**N Sanajaoba**, op.cit, p.176.

of AFSPA and such laws, but what about the troops who are empowered with this tremendous constitutional instrument? Majority of officers at all level feel pity for the local population, but they are adequately equipped because of their superior training and awareness level not to let it hinder with their professional functioning. 'The terrorist/insurgent is seen by many among the security forces, as a reaction to the social and political anarchy prevalent in the area. They even see him as fighting for a wrong cause but for just reasons'.[343]

However, a percentage of military men, who come from different socio-economic backgrounds and not adequately trained to reason out the ground realities, 'do appear to enjoy the feeling of 'high' and power that they experience as a result of their interaction with the local population from a position of dominance'.[344] The majority of troops are trained before induction for Counter Insurgency (CI) Operations and generally they do operate with humane attitude but those few who are psychologically inadequately conditioned to adapt to the ambiguity of the environment may fall prey to the emotions.

In fact, the behaviour of local population resulting from the emotional reactions in a soldier can be felt and experienced. The people's reaction (generally mute), has a telling effect on the behaviour of a soldier, for most interaction between the two actually occurs at individual level, which is subtle and self perpetuating and plays a strong determining influence on overall success or failure of operations.

Section–III

Human Rights Violation in Nagaland

All over the globe whenever Armed Forces have been deployed in counter insurgency role, there have been human

---

[343]**Capt Ashish Sonal**, VrC, '*Terrorism and Insurgency in India: A Study of the Human Element*', Lancer Publications, New Delhi, 1994, p.72.

[344]ibid.

rights violations. This is a historical phenomenon that has been observed and will continue in modern era as well. India is no exception, but most of the allegations against the security forces have been proved to be false and only five percent could be found true. Though, it can be said that the record of Indian Army has been outstanding in this regard; but was it so prior to 1975? The answer lies in soul searching! Prima facie, there are many cases which will fall into the category of 95 percent aimed to vilify the Armed Forces. But also there would be many of the cases about which people in the Armed Forces have no answer. In this section, some of those old cases will be discussed and for which no worthwhile proof could be gathered but they are true for the reason that these stories have survived in public memory for decades and are alive till date.

Do the Soldiers have Human Rights?

Unfortunately, when we talk about human rights, it is referred to the common man and to suspected/unsuspected insurgents, but none of the books/journals/periodicals talk about human rights of those soldiers who lost their lives or limbs. Many soldiers have lost their lives in ambush, raids or in such military operations. It may come as a surprise that the number of lives lost in insurgency is much higher than the casualty figures, of all the wars that India fought in 1947, 1962, 1965, 1971 and 1999, put together. Many have lost their lives when they went to answer nature's call behind nearby unsuspected bush, never to return to their loved ones. What was their fault? Just because he was donning the uniform and ordered to perform the duties to uphold the constitutional mandate of the country! The common proforma answer is 'it was his duty to fight'. Nobody remembers that he should be fighting against external aggression and not die for mistakes of the politicians, gross failure of administrators and police.

Why should a soldier fall to a bullet from an unsuspecting and innocuous looking hut while performing a routine patrol in aid to civil authorities? Nobody answers these questions; in fact nobody has an answer! An army soldier becomes victim for a task which does not form part of defined charter. Moreover, more often than not, the shooter would not know who the victim is! This is true for both the sides. But the fact is that, human rights of these people are flouted en masse. In addition, no published document is available to describe the details of human rights violation of any soldier, who were kidnapped, tortured and thrown in the jungles or on the road side in mutilated condition. However, some accounts are available as regards the total casualty figure who fell to the bullets of insurgents. Though, the archives of Army would be full of such cases, but till they are de-classified, world will have to wait.

Cases of Human Rights Violation

The human rights violation that took place in Nagaland during early stages of insurgency has been vividly described by the Naga people, **Rev. Michael Scott** was the first man from the outside world who heard or probably experienced those heart wrenching stories. It is plausible enough reason as to why he started behaving in a partisan manner when he was working as part of Nagaland Peace Mission under Jayprakash Narayan in early 1960s. The detailed excerpts which portrait the picture of human rights in those days needs no elaboration. A Sema Women's Organisation reported to the Peace Mission dated 16 June 1964 about the lustful behaviour of security forces towards the Naga women. An excerpt from the report:

> "... when we see Indians doing such unlawful deeds against women of Nagaland, they seem not to have been born by women. They have no nature of human beings. It must be perceived that humiliation of Naga women by Indian troops is a humiliation of all women in the world."[345]

Another report submitted by **Ms Tiala Ao**, Vice President, Naga Women Federation, Federal Government Nagaland (FGN) dated 02 May, 1964, which expresses similar feelings.

---

[345]**Kaka D. Iralu**, op.cit, p.128.

The fear of being humiliated, torture, rape or molestation loomed large on their faces and that is why they called the Army as an 'occupation force'. The terror that was allegedly perpetrated against the women and children by the soldiers of one of the most disciplined Army, if true, will put any civilized society to shame. Since the complaint was from the women wing of the NNC it can be said that it was motivated but the reality cannot be wished away. The anguish can be felt from the language itself:

> "... You will see too the subterranean feeling against the forcible occupation of our land by the Indian Army. Words fail to express the utterly incredible, inhuman, dastardly and wanton acts being perpetrated on our womenfolk. Acts of sucking babies being torn out of their mother's breast and thrown into burning fire; of unborn foetus being cut out of pregnant woman's womb and given to husbands; of women being rounded up and stripped naked in churches and being raped; of burning their private organs, or pouring powdered chilli in to them... and acts that will shock the civilized societies."[346]

After two months of touring through many villages and having acquired heart-wrenching first hand experience of horror stories, **Michael Scott** had submitted a report to the then Prime Minister of India, Lal Bahadur Shastri in which he had written:

> "...The whole story of Nagaland has not been told and will never be told now. But I am convinced that Jawaharlal Nehru was never given the true and whole picture of the tragedy that was being enacted here in all these years... If there is any reproach in the facts brought together in this report, it is a reproach against my country as well as yours, not only on account of our past connection with Nagaland. What is of such profound and immediate concern for all of us is the fact that Nagaland today constitutes a mockery of everything India has stood for and Britain and the West aim to defend..."[347]

---

[346]**Kaka D. Iralu**, pp.128-129.
[347]ibid, op.cit, p.129.

In another report entitled, **'Historic Hospitality'**, **Rev. Scott** narrates this moving experience he had with Rev. Kenneth* Kerhuo, the Field Director of the Angami Baptist Church Council, who served as an interpreter during Scott's term as a member of the Peace Mission between 1964-69:

> "One of the most moving moments I experienced in Nagaland was when an Angami villager came to tell his story of how he had been tied up by his ankles and beaten by the Indian Army. His wife had died and he had four children but was half crippled from all he had suffered. There was no thought of asking help. He had come from his villages solely in order to tell what had happened in case anything could be done to make Nagaland a better and happier place for his children when they grew up. Towards the end of what he was saying, Kenneth, who was interpreting for me, became silent, I wanted for him to go on. Thinking he was having difficulty in understanding or perhaps interpreting some piece of obscene cruelty, as interpreters often do here, I told him to leave that part. But still he did not continue. Then I found it was because he was struggling to control himself and suppress his tears. He was shaking all over and could only manage to say with pauses between words: It has been happening to our people so long... it...is...all...too much for us... to bear. And he walked away with tears running down his cheeks and left me with the old man and the problem of the grandchildren. Their father was serving with the underground and their mother had died and he found it hard with his crippled body to work enough to keep them fed and clothed. There was a rare dignity in the defiance of the old man who had come in from his village to make sure the truth was told."[348]

Matikhru's Black Day: Mourned Every Year

Matikhru is a village of only fifteen houses clustered together on a hilltop with a grand view of the Thetsu valley, which

---

* **Kenneth Kerhuo** praised the good deeds of Army as well. Refer chapter IV, footnote 208.

[348]**Kaka D. Iralu**, op.cit, p.131 quoted Rev Michael Scott's, *'Hostile Hospitality: A Report'*, p.4.

stretches into Myanmar after touching the fringes of Manipur state. Since the outbreak of hostilities in Nagaland in 1956, the villagers of Matikhru had also been actively supporting the struggle for freedom. Out of thirteen adult males in the village, three (viz. Wepulo, Nochutsu and Nuthokhu) were serving in the ranks of NNC and Ms Wenihilu was the Woman President of the region. The village was punished by the Army on September 6, 1960 but the cruelty that was unleashed over the hapless villagers was unimaginable. All the males were roughed up badly and all the women folk along-with their children were driven away to the jungle. Those unfortunates were probably beheaded before their bodies were thrown into the burning houses.One of the young lads named Zhiwhuotho (later a pastor of Pochury Baptist Church, Kohima) who fled into the jungles with the women and other children vividly recounted the horror story which he learnt from one of the survivors, who also succumbed to the injuries later.[349]

To this day, the Pochury Students Union observe 6th September as a *Black Day* every year to commemorate the sacrifices of their forefathers at Matikhru on September 6, 1960. The names of the nine victims, some of whom were beheaded and others who succumbed to injuries were Thah, Pogholo, Mezitso, Pongoi, Zasituo, Evethisu, Kezukhwelo, Thitu and Kekhwezu died a few days later but could narrate their story to the rest of the villagers before death.

Apart from these cases more such cases e.g. Assam Rifles punishment to Oinam village (Manipur) can be mentioned. There is no doubt that both the sides (insurgents and security forces) have violated human rights since the beginning and in the crossfire human rights of innocent civilians have also been trampled due to suspicion of being collaborator or sympathizer. Absence of media and government controlled reporting kept curtain for long over the issue. Moreover, the concept of human rights is still unknown to a large majority of the people inhabiting the region. In fact, human lives held

---

[349] **Kakd D Iralu**, 'Matikhru the Village that Refused to Die', *The Nagaland Post*, 07 September 2003.

a little value to them, the North East being nothing less than a 'war zone' where the Army ruled during day time and burgeoning militant outfits ruled at night.[350]

For long there was no voice raised from any quarters, till 1978, when Naga Peoples Movement for Human Rights (NPMHR) an NGO was formed. This is the only Human Rights group which is recognised by National Human Rights Commission. Other groups which are active in the field are Naga Vigil Human Rights group, founded in the UK in 1989. Some other organisations which are also active but classically they can not be defined as Human Rights group but actively involved in the Naga affairs e.g. Naga Students Federation (NSF), Naga Mothers Association (NMA) and Tuensang Mon Peoples Organisation (TMPO) etc.

NPMHR: Naga's Voice

The Naga Peoples Movement of Human Rights (NPMHR)[351] was formed on 09 September, 1978 in New Delhi, by a group of courageous and conscientious Nagas who had experienced enough of bloodshed and violation of human rights. It was during the post emergency period in India(1975-1977), when the whole Indian sub continent saw the containment and severe restrictions of civil rights at its most obnoxious form under the authoritarian regime of Indira Gandhi, ensuing the environment that had been created after overthrowing of Mrs. Gandhi's regime, Nagas, for the first time voiced, expressed and articulated the other side of silence.

Amongst other tasks which NPMHR took upon were to fight against all anti-democratic practices, socio-economic exploitation, against the practices of arbitrary arrest, detention, torture, execution and the use of unconventional weapons and safeguard people from political domination, military repression, imposition of undesirable alien legal systems and

[350]**Marie Laberge**, 'Indian Armed Forces Special Powers Act: A Denial of Human Security', *The Eastern Mirror*, 09 August 2003.

[351]NPMHR Souvenir, *'25 years of NPMHR: Embracing Hope and Dreams'*, September 2003 p.2.

socio-cultural concepts and ways of life in any part of the world, but factually, it is restricted to Nagaland only.

The NPMHR has been actively participating in generating public awareness within Nagaland and in international fora. It has participated at the various sessions of the UN Working Group of Indigenous population at Geneva (26-30 July 1999) and projected the case of Nagaland. They are champions in projecting the human rights violation cases in Nagaland and are successful as well. Despite being successful in projecting the human rights violation specially against the Naga people, NPMHR has categorically failed to raise any voice against the human rights violation of soldiers/security forces and non Naga civilians. Moreover, it has grossly failed to raise its voice against the human rights violation by various Naga factions against selective killings, factional clashes, extortion and even parallel and arbitrary judiciary of NSCN groups specially NSCN (IM). Thus, views/opinion expressed by the NPMHR can be considered as one sided story, if not biased!

NVHRG: The Radical NGO

The Naga Vigil Human Rights Group (NVHRG) is another NGO founded in the United Kingdom on 05 November 1989. This is a voluntary organisation concerned with highlighting the Naga cause and mobilising international opinion. The principal purpose was to document the human rights violation and make it available for research to the individuals and the NGOs. An interesting fact of this NGO is that it took birth in jail and one of the prisoners David Ward is the Coordinator of the group. This group works for the Naga cause in a voluntary capacity without any financial compensation. The membership is not open for the players in the given area of conflict although their offices are available for mediation as it is 'committed to peace and justice in pursuance of rights stipulated under international law. It's role being to be the voice of the Naga people themselves'.[352] The NVHRG has been radical in

[352]'NVHRG: Founding Precepts', *NVHRG Circular*, Kent, England, UK, March, 1996.

thoughts and actions since the beginning. It recognises the 'Nagas' as sovereign republic but it does not recognise the UN which it considers as an extention of P5 countries. In one of the releases, **David Ward** said:

> "We do not recognise the United Nations who we see as merely an extension of the United States and gang of five….. When this 'exclusive country club' realizes that there are significantly more than 170 old professed member states on the planet earth and Nagaland is free to take her legitimate seat within the international community of World Nations we will recognize UN legitimacy."[353]

The NVHRG also does not believe in following the international norms and refuses to seek valid visa, reflects eccentric views of its founder. In October 1991, David Ward alongwith another activist entered Nagaland to conduct fact finding investigative tour and claimed that they were the first foreigners to do so in last thirty three years without valid visas and travel permits from either Myanmar or India, but from the people of Nagaland. Thus, David Ward was arrested for various charges against him. Though, the NVHRG officials call themselves to be NGO and certainly they should be accepted as an NGO i.e. as it is 'a private association whose *raison d' etre* derives from the promotion and/or protection of one or more internationally recognised human rights'[354] but their conduct is not above board. Moreover, NVHRG identify them to be an aggrieved party and Ward's thought process is not apolitical. In one letter to Shimray of NSCN (IM), he writes:

> "The fact remains that there are factions in Nagaland, we must not be shy to admit our weakness, only in doing so will we be able to identify our strength and subsequently implement them to the betterment and good of the nation."[355]

---

[353]**David Ward**, 'The Naga Vigil's Stand', *The Nagaland Journal*, Kohima, 20 October 1994.

[354]**Laurie S Wiseberg**, 'The Role of NGOs in the Protection and Enforcement of Human Rights', in J Symonides (ed), *'Human Rights: International Protection, Monitoring, Enforcement'*, Ashgate Publishers Limited, UNESCO, Hans, England, 2003, p.349.

[355]**David Ward**, *The Nagaland Journal*, Kohima, 01 June 1992.

Reverberation Till Date

Though, there are large number of human rights violation cases that have had taken place in these seventy years, many may not be true but certainly those ones who still haunt the memories of the people would require no testimony or proof as they have survived in the memories of next generation all through these years and appear in the local/regional press regularly during their anniversaries, whether good or bad!

27th December, 1994 is said to be the most eventful day in Mokokchung, ever since the inception of this town. The nature and extent of this incident on that fateful day is regarded as the most terrifying experience of the people. The source of this information is a petition to Rangnath Mishra, the Chairperson of the National Human Rights Commission (Retired Chief Justice of Supreme Court of India), New Delhi, submitted after the Mokukchung tragedy.

As per the report, the Commanding Officer alongwith 21 Jawans of the 16 Maratha Light Infantry (16MLI) was shot down by the NSCN (K) near Chunghtia village in broad daylight at around 10:20 A.M. In retaliation, the 16 MLI (Maratha Light Infantry) battalion resorted to heavy firing in the market place and as the time of incident was just after the Christmas, thousands of people had gathered for New Year shopping. Many innocents lost their lives and the shopping complex was set on fire. The people who had taken shelter inside the shops were either dragged out or gunned down and those who were hiding inside their shops were roasted alive.[356] Neither the attack on the cavalcade of CO within the marketplace can be hailed nor the reaction in which many innocents lost their lives.

The Indian Army, sadly true, practised the age old tradition of burning of villages by their predecessors during expeditions. It is alleged that total of 40 villages were burnt 119 times during 1956-57 in the Ao Area only. These incidents certainly indicate that there were human rights violations by

---

[356] A.L. Ao, op.cit, pp.124-127.

the Army, which was more of an extension of British policy of punishing villages just a decade ago. Also by then no world army had developed any doctrine and training manual to teach the soldiers the nuances of operating in an Counter Insurgency role. Thus, the age old method of local legal jurisprudence might have been adopted, which appears dastardly and wanton act in the modern era, wherein operational philosophy has undergone a seachange.

Human Rights Violation of Soldiers

In this whole game, surprisingly these ideologues and human rights groups have grossly failed to bring out the Army casualties in ambush, raids on the posts, sniping of patrols etc. All the Naga human rights groups, which were formed only late in 1970s have published many stories of harrowing tales of the past in their handouts and pamphlets which are well recorded. Thus, it would be unfair not to have discussed the issue of human rights violation of the soldiers or even Non-Nagas by Naga insurgents. For this, an abstract of the report that appeared in a Souvenir of NSCN (IM), is given at Appendix 'H' which shows that insurgents have also equally had their fair share on human rights violation cases[357], unfortunately the gruesome fate the soldiers met, have remained untold and there is none to tell us that side of the story.

Delhi had its own limitations to tackle the problem being a democracy. The Army is deployed in 'aid to civil authorities' albeit with enormous power like Armed Forces Special Powers Act 1958 and without these powers how can a soldier operate? Do we have an answer to the questions put forward to **Subir Ghosh** by **Colonel Bhoparae** of Counter Insurgency and Jungle Warfare School? He tries to reason out:

> "There is a man. You have definite information that he is an insurgent. You know for certain, he has a gun under his shawl. You know as well that if you don't get him first, he is sure

[357]*NSCN(IM) Souvenir, '50 Years of Resistance'*, also see A.L. Ao, op.cit, pp.165-174.

> to get you. What do you do in such a situation? Wait for the arrest warrant to come five days later? Or do you run to safety? Colonel Bhoparae (of CIJW) was visibly agitated. What he did not comment on was the potential of its (the Acts) misuse. No Army officer does. But then he had a valid point. How else could a Jawan or an officer make the best of the situation?"[358]

Indeed it is a baffling question but without a reasonable answer! In fact, none has!

[358]**Subir Ghosh**, *'Frontier Travails'*, MacMillan, New Delhi, 2001, p.172.

8

Delhi's Dilemma: Compulsions and Complexities

It has been a long drawn battle of nerves for the Government of India and other agencies, who are engaged to ensure that the conflict is brought to an end. This is true for insurgents as well who are fighting for the cause of 'independence'. Each day that has passed brought sad stories, tense moments and rarest were events which came with flickers of happiness. Hopes and despair lived all through side by side since the day of independence, i.e. 15 August, 1947 in the Naga Hills, but there has been no respite till date. There is no confirmed indication that the curtain being drawn to a closure. Almost two decades of ceasefire with NSCN (IM and K groups, till abrogated by Khaplang group in 2015) and more than 80 rounds of peace talks (with NSCN-IM) and hard bargaining at times appeared to be fruitless.

Progress: Un-reported

The progress whatever has been made is not in the knowledge of public domain with respect to the '**Framework Agreement**' that has been signed by the NSCN(IM) in August 2015 with the Government of India, thus, many questions appear in one's mind. There are limitations for the Government of India as it can't go beyond the Constitution, fearing a trigger in similar demands from elsewhere in the country. These are certain issues which need to be discussed to resolve this complex and long standing conflict.

Section–I

Ignorance, Neglect and Apathy

It is unfortunate but true that composite Assam, which included present states of Assam, Meghalaya, Nagaland and Mizoram was called as Cinderella. It is said that the Centre could never pay the due attention to entire North Eastern states and treated them in a step motherly fashion like Cinderella.[359] It may not be entirely true, given the kind of problems this nation has been through since its independence, but it is perceived, more so, when compared with other states of India. The major problem which can be visualized is that the region is totally isolated from the rest of the country and the same is felt on ground. The affairs of North-East have been handled in an inept manner by the responsible political leaders and clueless officials who were ignorant and certainly lacked the understanding of socio-politically complex mosaic of the North-East.

The sense of alienation is so acute that the students of North-East in Delhi are seen as foreigners specially from South East Asian nations, worse, as Chinese. Reasons are basically very few. Firstly, there had been no systematic effort to bring the North-East people to the main stream of national life through socio-economic interactions. Secondly, the heart-land people were not encouraged to interact with the people of North-East and the area beyond Kamrup region of present day Assam (famous for Kamakshya temple) is hitherto unknown to them, despite North-East has been inalienable politico-social entity of India since Mahabharata period. Thirdly, the tribals of North-East were so weary of plains people that they seldom interacted and thus, sense of belonging couldn't be developed. **Nitish Chakravarthy** feels that the behaviour and

[359]Nitish Chakravarty, 'Reframing Look East Policy', *Yojana*, New Delhi, December 2005, p.19. (A step mother)

opinion of people at the policy making level was a great factor for increasing the sense of alienation. He writes:

> "This feeling coupled with statements inconsistent with facts, sometimes by people in high positions at the centre, has shaken the people's confidence, and retarded the process of bonding."[360]

The alienation has been felt more acutely because policy makers or their advisors were totally ignorant about their task and most of the decisions were knee-jerk reactions. They often relied on 'quick fix' solutions. It is felt by many that there has been a tendency in Delhi to consider the entire North-East in a common single basket which shows the decision makers unfamiliarity with the complexity of the issues.[361] This is partially true but lack of development also can be attributed for their splendid isolation in their own rugged sub-Himalayan region.

Gross Seclusion: Intolerable in N.E. States

Perhaps, North-Eastern India is the only place whose parallel is not seen anywhere in the world in terms of ethnic, linguistic and socio-cultural diversity within a comparatively restricted space. The seclusion is so pronounced in all these small states and the feeling is more or less anti-Indian, as if they do not belong to this nation. In fact, they didn't belong to any nation but to their tribe and village and their loyalty remained so till yesterday.

Lt Gen VK Nayar, however, puts the anti-India feeling as not an anti-population feeling but anti-government feeling. He said:

> "When we talk of anti-India feeling or sentiments, it is really anti-government, both local and central and is related to policy issues which are inflicted on them, more by default than

---

[360]ibid.

[361]**Nitish Chakravarty**, op.cit, p.20.

design. The root cause of this is an ignorant and unresponsive administration."[362]

India inherited a vast multitude of land divided into two politically torn nationalities, which triggered the religious frenzy and million lives were sacrificed. Delhi received not only the large number of states, princely states and sub nationalities but also received plethora of intertwined problems. The new leadership of India continued the age old British tradition of governance i.e. autonomy and segregation of the hill tribes from the main stream.[363] The complexities involved in integrating sub nationalities in the main stream were not understood well by the people who were at the helm of affairs and continued the policy of status-quo or so to say ethnic exclusionism.

Lt General J.R. Mukherjee criticized the policy of no administration in the name of traditional governance strengthened their belief of being separate which strengthened their resolve for autonomy and prevented their assimilation into the Indian mainstream.[364] The absence of education, poor communication system and absence of media, feeling of discrimination and alienation was not only the outcome but was the destiny!

Perception of 'Law and Order' Problem

As it has been repeatedly emphasized earlier, the Government of India treated the problem as **'law and order'** problem in the initial years. There could be a couple of reasons for looking at the problem in that manner. Firstly, there were only a handful of NNC members who were asking for separation and the leadership in Delhi assumed that the problem is only limited to few misguided people and they would be able to address the issue amicably. But the demand of so called unsatisfied

---

[362]**Lt Gen VK Nayar**, *'Threat from Within: India's Internal Security Environment'*, Lancer Publications, New Delhi, 1992, pp.196-197.

[363]**Lt Gen JR Mukherjee**, 'A Perspective on the North East', in Shekhar Basu Roy (ed) *New Approach*, Kolkata, 2002, p.47.

[364]ibid.

group of the NNC was also non-negotiable and could not be bartered for anything else. The pattern of agitation was same as that of Gandhian movement else-where in the country.

Clash of Perceptions

The leadership of the country and **Phizo** confronted on one basic issue i.e. inheritance of Naga areas within India. Inheritance of all the areas under British less Pakistan was given to Indian union and no less, thus Nehru and others were of the opinion that the whole of the country must form one nation; and since Nagaland had been part of British India, Nagaland had to be part of independent India too.

On the other side, Zapu Phizo was arguing that the Britishers may have conquered the Nagas but India had not. Thus, clash of perception and ideas became a flash point. The non-violent Gandhian civil movement ended with murder of Sakhrie. Subsequent crackdown by police and when it went beyond the capabilities of the police, the affairs were handed over to the Army. Application of Armed Forces could only contain the insurgency but can never finish.

Geo-Strategic Importance

Present day Nagaland state and the areas which are inhabited by Nagas are basically the peripheral areas of International boundary. The strategic location of Nagaland, the tri-junction of India, Myanmar and China catapulted its position in overall security matrix of India. China had been expanding its strategic reach by occupying Tibet. Since 'security dilemma is an integral component of the larger dictum of the world politics but one of its unique manifestation can be seen in Nagaland and other insurgency infested North–Eastern territories. The state identified with a quintessential function of paving the way for security.'[365]

---

[365]**Mohan Dwivedi**, 'Naga Imbroglio', in Dipankar Sengupta and Sudhir K Singh (ed), *'Insurgency in North–East India'*, Authors Press, New Delhi, 2004, p.104.

Moreover, the Manipur state of India is connected through Nagaland. The life in Manipur, specially, the Imphal valley is totally dependent on the National Highway (NH-39). In addition, entire trade to Myanmar is done by means of surface transport and the same passes through Nagaland. In this context, Nagaland assumes very high place in the entire security matrix of India. Since security concern of India is multifaceted, the early leadership of the country could ill afford to allow the NNC to secede. It is altogether a different issue, whether or not Naga inhabited areas could survive without India then or even today.

It would be futile academic discussion which had been done by many Naga scholars in favour of the independence. Nevertheless, their individual perception could be limited as they failed to recognize the potential threat i.e. China.

In early days after partition and independence, external threat loomed large in the minds of policy makers and leaders as they had seen two World Wars. **B.G. Varghese** has dealt the issue of holding onto the North-East areas in detail. He said:

> "External security consideration too had suddenly come into play with hostile (East) Pakistan and continuing influx of migrants from across the border (apart from Hindu refugees fleeing the 1950's holocaust), insurgency in Burma and the Chinese takeover of Tibet. Sardar Patel was particularly concerned about these matters and warned Nehru that the Himalayas could no longer be regarded as an impenetrable barrier and that the Tibeto-Mongoloid character of the population 'our northern and north eastern approaches (consisting of) Nepal, Bhutan, Sikkim, the Darjeeling area, the tribal areas of Assam and the penetration of communist ideologies into some of these areas, posed a new threat'. He urged a review of border policy and security, including internal security..."[366]

Security vs Socio-political Structure

Though, security concerns were paramount but they were

---

[366] **B.G.Varghese**, *'India's Northeast Resurgent'*, Konark Publishers, New Delhi, 2002. p.33.

conscious about the socio-political structures and the exclusive way of life of the North-East, they had catered for the needs of all the tribes of North-East, specially those who belonged to so called 'Excluded' and 'Partially Excluded' areas.

Thus, the Sixth schedule in the Indian Constitution came into being. Though, it may not have fulfilled all the aspirations of all the tribal groups of North-East. But these were the only available options to ensure self governance and it was not out of sympathy but to reassure the people of the area. In fact, 'the Sixth schedule represented an advantage over the 1935's Act as the Governor would now act on the advice of his Council of Ministers.'[367]

National Unity and Integration: Basic Need

Other security related concern for India immediately after independence was forging national unity among large number of splintered princely states and each one of them wanted to remain independent. Bringing them together was a difficult task by itself and couple of them was tamed by using military means. At that time, secession was a 'no-go' concept and called for stringent action against those erring states e.g. the states of Kathiawad and Hyderabad (India). Moreover, India have had its major problem in Kashmir valley. Thus, India can ill afford to talk about secession or self determination which could have triggered the process of fragmentation as a part of chain reaction. Thus, policy of the central government had been graduated in such situation, varied between appeasements to tough actions.

Ironically, those Naga elites or rational thinking Nagas were not with the secessionists and if they were very few, then NNC or other groups could have wiped them away. But that did not happen till date. Thus, it is a testimony that all Nagas were/are never in favour of secession. Otherwise, no occupation force can survive such a long time by force*, if the population is not in support of the Government. Moreover,

[367]**B.G.Varghese**, op.cit, p.35.

* Case of Russian invasion or otherwise in Afghanistan.

why elections do take place in Nagaland, however, fractured it may be! Certainly the truth lies somewhere in between.

Section-II

There have been intense and heated debates, passionate discussion all along these years as to what should be the possible solution to the vexed problem. There had been demand lists of the insurgent groups but the main issue is sovereignty or right to self-determination and integration of Naga areas. This issue has been discussed over the decades by the ideologues; scholars, politicians and general population in various forms e.g. total independence, autonomy and linkages with India, no interference in the traditional life style of the Nagas etc. But so far, there have been no consensus on these issues and among the various groups of Nagas. The concept of sovereignty also has undergone a change in last couple of decades. In fact, in the present day context it is obvious to draw an inference that while history is important but today the economy drives the present and future as well.

Issue of Sovereignty

While sovereignty is the major issue and every time reference is made to the Unilateral Declaration of Independence (UDI) held on 14 August, 1947 and plebiscite of 1951, both the issues have been discussed at length and it would suffice to say here that even if both milestones in the history of Nagas do not affect the present day decisions anymore but they will remain alive in various discussions. During the formation of state, Nagaland has been given special status under Article 371(A) in Indian Constitution, while it has not been accepted fully but any effort to abrogate the same will be resented. With this backdrop, let us study the issues that are involved before attempting to explore options for conflict resolution.

Sovereignty: A Bone of Contention

The question arises whether or not the sovereignty, a bone of contention today? The answer would be 'yes and 'no' both. It is 'yes' because this word is discussed in all fora in a very liberal and frequent manner. But when the nitty-gritty of sovereignty are being discussed, then the answer becomes 'No'.

In political science, sovereignty is conceptualised in various shades. It varies from internal to external sovereignty, titular (Monarch of UK) to actual (British Parliament), defacto to de-jure sovereignty and even limited and divided sovereignty. Whatever be the concept of sovereignty, many among Nagas including those who are arguing for it are yet not very clear. So far as political outbursts are concerned, the main underground faction NSCN (IM) had been going hyper and their stand on sovereignty in public although 'non-negotiable'. In 2006, Rh. Raising, then self styled Prime Minister of NSCN (IM) made a statement that 'if we chose to solve the Naga problem within the frame work of the Indian Constitution, it is not negotiation but a sell out and surrender'.[368] Since details of latest '**Framework Agreement**' signed in August 2015 are not known, if any other kind of arrangement is made then the leadership will be blamed and condemned like the Shillong Accordists, whom they have punished and executed brutally. On the other hand same **Mr Raising** in an interview, said:

> "Everybody is fond of talking of independence and sovereignty of Nagalim. But no one talks of the strategy or formula of how it is to be materialized. We look forward to solving the problem on the basis of the 'will' of the people. NSCN, is therefore, trying to explore any possible formula to bring a lasting solution. On the phase wise formula, it can be probable option depending on the objective condition we may go to that extent."[369]

From the above excerpts, it appears that NSCN (IM) may accept a mild sovereignty status which they termed it as **'Shared Sovereignty'**, a new terminology used by the NSCN(IM) in a press note dated 10 may 2017 (published by all the national and regional dailies), however, exact meaning has not been divulged. Does it mean an autonomous state within India,

---

[368]*The Nagaland Post*, Dimapur, 06 June 2004.

[369]ibid, 04 June 2004.

which is now an acceptable solution as some of the rationale thinking Naga people expressed in various fora! But today after a decade plus of the statement day (June 2004), situation has changed and there are voices which support the views in favour of Article 371 (A) or the so called **'Shared Sovereignty'**. Recently Naga Senior Citizen's Association (NSCA) expressed:

> "Even if Article 371 (A) of the Indian Constitution may be contentious in Nagaland yet it is considered the only reliable guarantee that grudgingly provides even a bit of confidence for Nagaland to moderate its troubled link with India under the present indefinite circumstance".[370]

The Final Peace Accord: Subject of Serious Scrutiny

The final peace accord whenever it is signed, it will be viewed with suspicion by other NSCN factions because there are differences of opinion between the NSCN(IM) and (K) or (KK) or Reformation group. It is certain that the signing of the accord in August 2015 may be a 'rush job' keeping in view the NSCN(IM) leadership's concern over the deteriorating health of outfit Chairman Isaac Chisi Swu, who later passed away on June 28, 2016. It is believed that Swu was insisting that he signs the document with NSCN(IM) General Secretary Thuingaleng Muivah.[371] It is evident that NSCN(IM) leadership also know the secession or absolute sovereignty is ruled out but they are bargaining hard to extract maximum from the Government. It is a matter of speculation for the time being as to how much freedom or what kind of freedom they would achieve.

There are other groups which debate that if the sovereignty is not attainable then it is better to join Indian mainstream. **Z. Kaitry** opined that enough of time has passed and there is a requirement to change the Naga mindset on this issue. He said that:

> "In the wisdom of the Nagas, if freedom is unattainable, then will it not be a wise decision for the Nagas to give up our

---

[370]*The Nagaland Post*, 26 December 2016.

[371]**Namrata Goswami**, 'Naga Peace Accord: Why Now?', *IDSA Magazine*, Delhi, 07 August 2015.

struggle and join the mainstream, instead of bringing more bloodshed, suffering and miseries to our people? History is full of such glaring examples and Nagas are not going to be an exception."[372]

Even majority of Indian politicians, ideologues and scholars feel that 'the most difficult problem will be deciding the degree of autonomy that is short of independence, the Nagas should enjoy'.[373] Thus, there are moderates as well as hardliners on both the sides, whose voice will be important for arriving at a final agreement. Hence, negotiators will have to tread the path carefully and cautiously.

Naga Territorial Integration

Naga territorial integration is another vexed and highly emotive issue on which very little progress has been made. It has been already brought out that Nagas are deeply attached to the land but not with the neighbour, especially when the neighbour belongs to a different tribe. Earlier, there had been not much of problem so far as territory was concerned but since the day NSCN (IM) has come to the helm of affairs, territorial integration has become very important issue. It is because of the fact that Muivah and his lieutenants in powerful appointments in group hierarchy are Thangkuls, the Manipuri Nagas. Thus, Muivah and his followers do not have a constituency in existing Nagaland and in Manipur, they are poor cousins of Meiteis. The idea of integration of all Naga inhabited areas has been another 'non-negotiable' clause and certainly would prove to be a stumbling block in reaching an acceptable solution as it involves various stakeholders viz. Assam, Arunachal Pradesh, Nagaland, Manipur (Indian states) and Myanmar.

It is noteworthy that integration of all Naga areas is a political necessity for Muivah group to sustain and survive in power else they would be reduced to non-entity in Naga

---

[372]**Z Katiry**, Time for Nagas to be Realistic, *The Nagaland Post*, Dimapur, 14 November, 2003.

[373]Barun Das Gupta, 'Difficult Tasks Ahead', *Frontline*, July 25, 1997.

politics. Though, integration of all Naga areas into one geo-political entity has many pitfalls for the centre and all the states that border Nagaland. The integration of Naga areas means further disintegration of Assam and other states and almost extinction of Manipur as a state. Since Manipur is a state with a history of four thousand years and they would not like to see it disintegrating and thus, entire Manipur goes into frenzy whenever any step is taken by the government that could be remotely viewed against Manipur. On the other hand, recent creation of seven new districts specially in Naga dominated areas (Senapati, Chandel, Ukhrul and Tamenglong) of Manipur is seriously being opposed by the Nagas of Manipur under the umbrella organization United Naga Council(UNC) alongwith economic blockade established on National Highways (NH-39 and NH-2).[374]

None in the Government in Delhi or for that matter in any other state capitals can even think of redrawing of state boundaries today for a greater Nagaland (say Nagalim). It requires lot of political 'will' and wholehearted support of all the political parties and administrative preparation given the sensitive nature and volatility of the people of the area. The world has witnessed the Manipur state assembly house going up in flames in June, 2001 when ceasefire with NSCN (IM) was extended beyond territorial limits of Nagaland. **Okenjeet Sandham** writes:

> "...Within the days of declaration of ceasefire, lakhs of people in Manipur Valley took to the streets protesting against the centre's declaration of the truce pact with the Naga militant group. The main apprehension of the people of Manipur especially majority Meitei tribes is that most of Manipur will be sliced off..."[375]

Therefore, to deal with the issue, sensitivity of Manipur and other states have to be taken care of, and that cannot be achieved without political consensus and that does not seem to be a possibility even in a foreseeable future.

---

[374]*The Nagaland Post*, 29 December 2016

[375]**Oken Jeet Sandham**, 'Vajpayee Misses Finest Opportunity', *The Nagaland Post*, Dimapur, 30 October 2003.

In fact, none in the Nagaland state could afford to air their views against the integration. All the state politicians have voted for integration thrice knowing well that this is almost an impossible and unattainable demand but political expediency has compelled them to vote for the proposals as this was also agreed in 16 Point Agreement (Point 13, Appendix 'F'). The problem arises for the Central Government that if Naga areas are given the so called greater Nagaland/Nagalim, 92 percent of hill areas of Manipur will be sliced off leaving only Imphal valley of 700 square km area as Manipur, which is neither desirable nor viable to survive as a state. Politically volatile and aggressive mobilization of opinion will catapult Manipur to volcanic state which may lead to civil war. It is also noteworthy to mention here that post state assembly elections in February 2017 and change of guard in Manipur led by N Biren Singh, followed by bonhomie created by goodwill visit by the Chief Minister of Nagaland, Surozhelie Liezietsu to Imphal, capital of Manipur, coincided with the release of press note by NSCN(IM) on '**Shared Sovereignty**' is possibly a signal to the common Nagas and other stake holders on the territorial integration issue.

Socio-political Integration of Nagas

To avoid political embarrassment and find an amicable solution to the problem **Mr. Hokishe Sema**, Ex Chief Minister of Nagaland and veteran Bharatiya Janata Party leader of Nagaland had suggested another way of socio-political integration of Nagas without redrawing the boundaries. The proposal was badly shot down by the overground workers and thus NSCN(IM) had to express similar kind of views as they have been saying 'Integration of Naga areas is non-negotiable'. With the hard stand on non-negotiable clauses e.g. sovereignty and integration, acceptance of 'unique history' and 'culture', the talks have progressed very little in the past. **Capt Hekiye Sema** (Retd), BJP leader and a progressive minded leader had following to say about the stance of NSCN (IM) on integration:

"The government accepts the unique history of Naga People. Practically it may be meaning nothing (to India). But they could strike a deal on that account and talks can move. Muivah says that Naga integration is not-negotiable and his friends cannot put him wise. Talks are likely to face rough weather on integration issue."[376]

It is apparent that till date (August, 2017) talks have not concluded because of these issues. **Capt Sema's** solution for integration appears to be pragmatic and has a merit. Reiterating the methods of integration, Capt Sema said:

"You can not integrate all the five territories (Tirap, Changlang of Arunachal Pradesh, Naga areas in Assam (DAB), Hill areas of Manipur) in Nagaland and Myanmar overnight. Time is required to interact with one another socially, culturally, economically (read development). They should be given time to arrive at consensus, say about 5-10 or even 20 years and let them amalgamate, create an atmosphere for greater Nagaland. For the time being, they can be connected loosely through apex body of all Naga tribes like Hoho established through constitutional statute..."[377]

As the Nagas are highly emotional and volatile on any suggestion less than total geographical integration but the proposal of outright rejection is also fraught with dangerous consequences and that will not be in the interest of the nation. Moreover, Assam and Arunachal Pradesh people have expressed their sentiments against redrawing of boundaries. Even if geographical integration of Naga areas in India is done, still it will not meet the demand fully as Naga areas in Myanmar will not be integrated. Thus, fractured Nagalim will never satisfy the Naga groups, hence, answer has to be found in a different manner.

---

[376]**Capt (Retd) Hekiye Sema**, Interview with the author, Dimapur, Nagaland on 14 March 2004. (The entire script of the interview is given at Appendix 'J').

[377]Capt Sema's interview.

Naga Unity and Reconciliation

Another major stumbling block in the peace process is lack of Naga unity being a non-homogeneous group. They have problem of a common identity except the tribal identity of Nagas which has been given by the plains people (or Indians) from whom they seek independence. So much so, political leaders, social activists and common man cry out for social as well as political unity, but it is difficult to achieve today and probably will remain so in near future. Well, it should not be out rightly rejected either, given the progress they have made in less than 70 years in developing a common Naga identity. This endeavour will get a boost for socio-political expediency and various factions will be under pressure from the society at large to shun the bitterness away that exists today.

Many enlightened people like individual politicians, Church, NGO's, Naga Hoho etc. cry their heart out for reconciliation. The Church had been making relentless efforts for Naga national reconciliation in the name of God. Also Naga Senior Citizens Forum/Association (NSCA) drawn from all the Naga areas are working towards this goal.

In one of the latest communiqué from NSCN (IM) calls for Naga Unity and Reconciliation among the Nagas specially to Khaplang and Reformation groups in the following manner:

> "The Govt of India and the NSCN in their political negotiations have now reached the most crucial and concluding stage. It will therefore be unwise, rather absurd on the part of the Nagas to prolong or wait indefinitely. The world is racing and how can the Nagas think of nineteen (19) years of negotiation as not long enough? ... the Covenant of Naga Reconciliation on July 13, 2009 was signed by SS Khaplang, Singya and Isak Chishi Swu who are the highest authorities of the three Naga political (underground) groups. ...But unfortunately SS Khaplang backed out from this historic Agreement..."[378]

It is also noteworthy that **Kitovi** had parted ways with **SS Khaplang**, blaming it on the latter for withdrawing from

[378]*The Sangai Express*, NSCN(IM) Bats for Naga Unity, 18 May 2016.

the Naga reconciliation process, and appeared that Kitovi was seriously committed to the cause of unity and reconciliation. Later, he refused to join hands with the NSCN (IM) under the collective leadership of Isaac Chishi Swu and Th Muivah, they would rather seek separate talks and that too for the Nagas of Nagaland only and approached the Government of India to appoint a separate Interlocutor to which the Government of India refused! Singya on the other hand appears to have been facing dilemma when they confessed that their president was none other than Adinno, exposing their non commitment to the Naga Reconciliation.[379]

The situation is not very different even today. It cannot be said comprehensively that when the Nagas will reach to that kind of consensus? Till Nagas do acheive reconciliation by accepting each other among the tribes and groups; peace cannot be lasting even if an agreement is arrived.

Who Represents the Nagas Today?

Presently the negotiations based on the '**Framework Agreement**' between the Government and NSCN(IM) is in advanced stage and talks are being held regularly to hammer out a peaceful and honourable solution. But the question remains, will there be peace and tranquility in Nagaland and all the Naga inhabited areas? Reasons are obvious 'NO' till all the stakeholders are brought to the same platform and agree with NSCN(IM), as is known that they are 'NOT' the sole representative of the Naga people.

NSCN (IM) is calling the shots today does not want to share the glory which they might get, if they clinch a deal. If they succeed, they will try to compel others specially NSCN(K), NSCN(Khole-Kitovi), breakaway group from Khaplang, NSCN(Reformation) and other NNC groups to toe the line and reap the benefits, which may not be feasible as the situation exists today and Forum for Naga Reconciliation is working hard to forge a consensus. If they do not succeed, they may

---

[379]*The Sangai Express*, 18 May 2016.

blame it on the Government of India and NSCN (IM) together. In case, the NSCN(IM) clinches a deal, they may automatically wipe out opponents in the electoral politics which may follow immediately.

Thus, striking a deal under these circumstances is extremely difficult and ensuring acceptance of the same by all the groups would be even more difficult. This is a tight ropewalk by the concerned authorities as it needs very high precision to maintain a delicate balance. Tilting towards any of the sides will be fatal. Thus the dilemma lies 'whom to talk to or who represents the Nagas: NSCN (IM/K/KK/R) or NNC (all groups) or all of them?'.

Other Demands

The major issues in respect of the settlement towards the Naga problem have been discussed in this chapter. It is believed that there are approximately 32 point demands on which talks are progressing as given in Appendix 'I'. Some of these issues have not been discussed e.g. Issue of foreign relations, currency, defence, flag, taxation, communication etc. These issues can be categorised as Government of India competencies, state competencies (Naga State) and some are joint competencies. Those issues are important for running the administration and other affairs once the political solution is arrived and not a bone of contention for hammering out a solution, hence, not being discussed further.

Conclusion

Global Scenario

21st Century is expected to be the century of Asia wherein entire globe is expected to shrink for increased socio-economic interaction. The nation-states have been experimenting politico-economic union (Like European Union) which may be replicated in other parts provided that it succeeds despite exit of Britain. India has taken the lead to form BRICS, a conglomerate of Brazil, Russia, India, China and South Africa, which is more of economic grouping. Though, there is a trend of unification based on shared common economic interests globally, there is a disturbing trend fully developed and that is forces of dissociation due to politico-religious divides and are embroiled in civil war specially Middle East of Asia. Back home, India has been fighting another separatist movement in Kashmir supported by Pakistan which propagates its national agenda through export of terror indirectly promoted and funded by oil rich Islamic nations and even by mobilizing opinion within India in the name of religion.

The nation states are likely to face this kind of problem increasingly, contrary to the belief that was propagated in the second half of the last millennium that with the development and economic interactions, there will be homogeneous amalgamation of various nationalities and the staunch sub-nationalistic views will be history. But those utopian concepts appear to be farfetched dream. In fact ethnicity, sub-nationalism, regionalism, religious fundamentalism, sense of perceived inequality and exploitation would remain to be the cause of disintegration of the societies and conflict in this century too, at least for few more decades.

Issues that Will Remain Unsettled

In the context of South Asia, insurgency, terror and other forms of expression of dissent will continue to be the order of the day till such time the voice of dissent is not quelled by the forces of integration, economic development and social unity based on common socio-politico-economic interests. The globalization of economy, interdependence, shared values are welcome changes which are being facilitated by increasing interaction on multicultural, multinational platforms. The North East of India is expected to continue to face the challenges thrown upon due to increased migration of people across the borders as well as from hinterland of India for realizing better avenues. These will be resented due to the acute sub-nationalistic feelings and fear of being overrun culturally and economically till such time India as a nation finds a solution, adequately addressing the ethnic demands and allows no room for exploitation of the ethnic cleavages.

Nagaland, in particular, has been witnessing confrontation of ethnic dissent and the authorities trying to quell the ethnicity driven insurgency. An attempt was made to study the ethnicity of Nagas in historical perspective, the cause of Naga dissent, lack of socio-politico integration and political mismanagement in the early years turned a small group of dissenting voices to a mass uprising. The leadership's wrong judgment and incorrect appreciation of the situation, therefore, inept handling of the political crisis as a law and order problem gave way to an armed struggle. The insurgency which began in mid 1950s saw many ups and downs, many hot war conditions and ceasefires, endless negotiations, unaccounted number of deaths but has remained far from over. The peace processes initiated by various agencies and the government authorities, even clinched agreements and acclaimed successes of having addressed the problem squarely, proved to be failure time and again, even before the ink of the agreement could dry up, sending the population again under the grip of violence. Many solutions were suggested but all fell short of arriving at permanent peace.

'Frame Work Agreement': Can It Usher in Peace?

The talks with NSCN (IM) have been going on since 1997 and the '**Framework Agreement**' signed in August 2015, is a welcome progress and now both the sides have broken the stalemate. They need to continue to talk for comprehensive peace and reach a common meeting point. It also must be remembered that this Agreement has given much needed breather and honourable exit to the IM leadership as the cadres are neither ideologically motivated nor disciplined. In case, they fail to clinch a deal, they will leave a fractured legacy to the second and third rung leaders. It will be also a fallacy to accept and expect that by making an agreement with the NSCN(IM), the Naga issue will get resolved with certainty. The other groups are watching the progress very cautiously and Khaplang group has attacked army more than six times since signing of the Agreement, apparently to vent their ire of having been neglected by the Government of India and also to make a point that they are also one of the stakeholders to the conflict. The NNC (Accordists) and other groups like NSCN (KK), NSCN(R) may not hold that kind of clout or support from the masses but can be a potential threat to peace.

In addition, common Nagas are interested in an environment of Peace wherein they are not unduly burdened with multiple taxes (by various factions) in the name of Naga sovereignty and independence. On the other hand, elite Nagas have amassed wealth and are part of the mainstream socio-economic process of India and would not like to jeopardize their affluent life. Many Nagas have the privilege to send their children for higher studies in metropolis and admission to premier institutes in India is almost guaranteed which is a gateway to success. Many Nagas have accumulated properties not only in Guwahati but also in Kolkata, Delhi and Bangalore. For many of them who have settled in Dimapur in their respective tribal pockets, Delhi or Bangalore is nearer than their ancestral village in Mokukchung, Tuensang or Mon area. Thus, it would not be socio-economically incorrect to state that many of them desire to remain with India rather than seceding away and then keep on fighting for visa for sending their children for studies to Delhi or Bangalore.

Healthy Interactions: Need of Hour

In these intervening seven decades, there have been sweeping changes all over the globe. The globalization of economy and inter-relatedness is felt more and more and there is a need to increase the interaction which can be done by removing apprehensions about perceptions of the people in the North East in general and Nagaland in particular. Interlocutors will have to work seriously to remove the feeling of insecurity and alienation from the minds of common Nagas by ensuring their status of 'unique history' and 'Naga culture'. Although, the '**Framework Agreement**' has paved the path for ushering peace but not without uncanny thorns. On ground the '**Covenant of Reconciliation**' (COR) between the groups of NSCN i.e. IM, K, KK and Reformation, and NNC groups is in place through the **Forum for Naga Reconciliation** (FNR) platform. Now it will be the responsibility of NSCN(IM) specially Muivah to bring all other groups to the table and accept the final agreement, whenever it is signed. But in case, the agreement does not meet the aspirations of all the groups, specially Khaplang group, then what? Will there be a repeat of the history? This is a matter of great concern. So, in order to formulate the recommended solution, I shall make an endeavour to dwell upon the issues one by one.

Recommendations for Conflict-resolution

Sovereignty and Independence

This is a very sensitive issue and to which every Naga has

been obsessed with, because of 70 years old concept of fighting against occupational forces. The leaders (undergrounds and overgrounds both) know very well that in today's world no nation is sovereign and during their interviews they accept it and put it across in a different manner but openly they say 'sovereignty is non-negotiable' due to political compulsion. Now they have started using a new term explaining the sovereignty with 'Shared Sovereignty', of which nothing has been clarified to the public at large. Possibly they are trying to gauge the mood of Naga people in general and the other groups like K/KK/Reformation or NNC. They have to bring everybody on board on this issue else fate of any future agreement is a foregone conclusion.

Previously, Nagas were offered Bhutan kind of protectorate status in 1966 by Indira Gandhi, which was then rejected by the NNC. But today, it does not appear that Government of India is in a position to offer that either because of changed geo-political reality. Moreover, India neither can grant sovereignty beyond the Article 371(A) of the Constitution to a particular state/ethnic group nor will it accept secession. In fact, similar proposal had been rejected by the NSCN (IM) leadership in the past. But there is a possibility to revisit the status of 'autonomy' clause under the various provisions of the Constitution. Although, it is argued by many in the country for abrogation of Article 371 (including Article 370 for the state of Jammu and Kashmir) and implementation of Uniform Civil Code (UCC) by the present ruling dispensation. It would be prudent to say at this juncture that this is not the opportune moment to do that kind of experiment and nation needs some more time to bring homogeneity and cohesiveness among all the states/societies and sub nationalities. We need to have patience for that, when the socio-politico cum economy based divides will be blurred and no more those social identities will remain important for deciding a state or district boundary (similar to USA).

It is also prudent to say that there is no harm in accepting 'unique history and culture' of the 'Nagas. They are independent people like any other groups in India and let them live their life the way they have been doing since ages.

There should be no infringement from outside and no binding on them to join the national cultural mainstream. Has anyone forced a south Indian to follow north Indian lifestyle or vice versa? Has anyone infringed in the lifestyle of any other tribal group say *Santhals* (single largest tribe in the world), Bhils, Mundas, Lambadis, Gurjars, Banjaras or Oraons? None, so far! Indians are very proud of having diverse culture, language, traditions in the country and that makes India, a culture of acceptance and tolerance of 5000 years, still it is one nation of which Nagas as well as all other tribes are part of.

The issue of sovereignty has to be seen in this light and the government should have no problem to guarantee that there is no violation in this regard. In addition, Government of India will have the responsibility to extend all the help needed for their internal governance and administration as desired by them.

This kind of independence should be acceptable to both the parties as in no sense, Naga freedom is curtailed. A Naga is born free as Naga and will die as free citizen of Nagaland within India and they have entire country for their education, work and rest of their life activities, as they do now. This special status for Nagas will be envied by the rest of India.

Issue of Integration

This issue of integration of all Naga inhabited areas has come into the forefront since 1997, though this was definitely an issue even in 16 Point Agreement. But since the day NSCN (IM) has taken over the Naga affairs it has caught the fancy as they need to have constituency of their own as mostly Thangkuls (hill based Nagas of Manipur) are heading it. Therefore, it has become imperative to integrate the adjoining areas of Manipur else where would they go for political survival? It has been discussed that integration of all the Naga inhabited areas will have serious consequences not only within India but also in Myanmar. The proposal of integration, if accepted can only be effected in India and that will have severe backlash in adjoining states. Moreover, the so called 'Nagalim' dream will remain unfulfilled till Myanmar accedes to this demand and why would they do it? It will be wise to learn the lessons from history. In 1971, on independence of Bangladesh, there was a school of thought that both the Bengals* should be united (whether within India or as an independent nation!) for the Bengalis. Despite having linguistic, cultural and lineage relations on both the sides, Indian Bengalis realize that it was a noble proposition academically but co-existence with Islamized Bengalis is difficult and it was good that the thought process did not gain fancy. They are better off as Indian Bengalis rather than 'Bangladeshi citizen' or even independent Bengalis.

Many Bangladeshi citizens have already merged into the mainstream of India and acquired citizenship and voting rights in elections, may be it is for economic reasons but they do not want to go back.

Thus it would be prudent to integrate what India has under its control and make them as one entity but only **socio-politically and not geographically**. The Naga leadership must understand that by adopting tough line for political independence, sovereignty and integration, they may lose out to be part of a big nation with vibrant economy. **Puerto Rico** chose to be the part of giant economy USA rather than remaining as its poor neighbour. Thus, it would be in the interest of the Naga people to see the package in holistic manner rather than deal with the problem in piecemeal. I have brought here the issue of citizenship and integration with a bigger nation together with an aim to bring home the lesson that for a better life for common people one should not be sentimental on the issue of geographical integration.

Example of Sikh Community: Worth Emulation

It would also be pertinent to mention here that the Sikh community is settled all over the globe, leave aside in all the states of India from Kashmir to Kanyakumari and Morvi (Gujarat border town) to Moreh (Manipur) and beyond, but

* East and West Bengal were bifurcated in 1947 just before partition, East Bengal is now Bangladesh.

they have not lost their socio-political as well as religious identity. They are minority in India but have a major contribution in industry, economy and defence of the nation. Moreover, they have not lost out on socio-political integration. The **Shiromani Gurdwara Prabandhak Committee** (SGPC) known as '**Parliament of Sikh nation**'* under the Gurdwara Act 1925, of India which looks after all the Gurdwaras in Pakistan, Bangladesh and Afghanistan, all Islamic nations. It is an example for the world to see that all the Sikh population throughout the world is connected to the Golden Temple of Amritsar which is administered by the SGPC. In addition, the SGPC has fair amount of say in provincial politics of Punjab (India) and also in the centre when it is the era of coalition government. Thus, a Sikh settled anywhere in the world, holding Overseas Citizen of India (OCI) status with power almost equivalent to citizens residing in India, remains connected to his religion, land and society and interacting socially as well as politically with the mainstream India.

Integration through Socio-political Body

Similar analogy can be drawn from the success story of Sikhs in this case too. Why Nagas (of India and Myanmar) cannot remain united through a socio-political body like Naga Hoho, wherein all the tribes can send their representatives irrespective of their tribal sub-nationality? In the years to come, there will be large number of Nagas settled in all metropolitan cities of India (due to economic reasons) and elsewhere in the world and they would also like to be in touch with the ancestral homes in the villages of their forefathers. Thus, it would be a worthwhile idea to have an umbrella organization for the Nagas of the whole world and not limited to Nagas of Nagaland or Manipur! Members of Naga Hoho of respective countries can also be participating in their local/regional politics as well and contribute in their sphere of activity. The members of Naga Hoho can be nominated as members for Rajya Sabha

* http://sgpc.net/about-sgpc/

(the upper house in the parliament) as being done from the present assembly of Nagaland State. By sending member(s) of Naga Hoho to Indian Parliament as Member of Rajya Sabha would *de-facto* mean that all the Nagas of the world have a say in Indian politics as well. The detailed modalities can be worked out by more learned people with experience in this field.

External Affairs: Since the settlement is recommended on the lines of being an autonomous state of India with special provision of independence in respect of the uniqueness of their history, culture and tradition, the Government of India is duty bound to look after the interests of each Naga citizen. Thus, in international fora all the interests of Naga people will be collectively kept secured as that of any Indian individual citizen. Moreover, whenever any special issue which comes up with Myanmar, the central Government can have a provision of incorporating the views of Naga political assembly. As discussed earlier, the Parliament of all the tribes (Hoho) will directly or indirectly control the people and thus the Government. Hence, Nagas should feel safe so far as any external affairs is concerned.

Allow Trade, Travel with Neighbours

Though Delhi will be controlling the policies keeping in view the overall interest of the nation, the economic interest of Nagas should be given special attention. Why only Nagas, all the bordering states e.g. Assam, Mizoram, Manipur, Arunachal Pradesh, Sikkim etc should be allowed to do trade with neighbouring areas, but adequate safeguard mechanism to be put in place so that smuggling and drug cartels do not take benefit out of it. Thus, the external affairs should be the matter of Government of India, however, specific issues can be discussed as they appear. Nagas should be allowed to interact socially with other Naga tribes and forge a bond of their common heritage. This can only be possible through economic, social and cultural interaction and all the Nagas including of

Myanmar will have no restriction to visit Naga areas within India. However, entry of Nagas of Myanmar to India should be controlled by External Affairs Ministry, may grant liberalized visa on reciprocal basis, as deemed fit. Hence there would be a requirement of upgrading Dimapur and Imphal Airports to the status of international airports and should the economic viability exist there can be flights between Naga areas in India and Myanmar as well. Possibility of granting Indian visa (long term) to the Nagas of Myanmar who wish to do business (as per laws of India), work or study in Nagaland can be explored. May be the Nagas of Myanmar be allowed to invest in industry in Nagaland if the people and the Government of Nagaland agree on this aspect. In this way, Nagas will not only be integrated economically but also their social integration on the sidelines of the business will be more meaningful than geographical integration.

Defence: Government of India

It is undeniable fact that Nagaland can not defend itself in case of all out war with any other nation, hence, justifiably the external defence of the Nagas should be the responsibility of Delhi. However, internal security, law and order should be subject of the Nagas. It is noteworthy that Indian Army has already raised Naga battalions of which number can be increased.

Flag: One Nation-One Flag

The demand for having a separate flag should be a non-issue as the Nagas have almost agreed on 'shared-sovereignty'. In fact, India being such a diverse country, all the states cannot have separate flags which will be in hindrance to the idea of India and concept of one nation-one flag. Indian national flag tri-colour which is one of the most recognised and respected flag should remain as the only flag in the country and be given due respect as being practiced. The Governors of the states should continue to fly the tri-colour as in vogue.

Currency under Control of Centre

Though, there is a demand for a separate currency for the Nagas, it is not pragmatic demand in today's parlance. Since all the Naga areas are so closely linked with neighbouring states, the business will be cumbersome if Nagas wish to have a separate currency. In any case, there are other currencies in which trade is done in Indian bordering areas. These currencies of Nepal, Bhutan and Bangladesh are in vogue but it is well known fact that which currency is of value. Thus, it will be a wasteful effort to have another currency, which will increase unnecessary burden on the exchequer. In addition, a new Currency would entail establishment of another Reserve Bank/Central Bank for Nagaland and associated infrastructure which should be avoided.

Communication

It would be prudent to keep the communication so far as erstwhile P&T and now BSNL system is concerned, the responsibility of Delhi as existing. Reasons are basically commercial viability. Today the cost of development of basic infrastructure is very high and the requisite network infrastructure (Government owned and private companies) is already in place under the regulation of the Government of India, so there is no need to tweak it further and thus communication should be the responsibility of Delhi.

So far as, surface transport and Air traffic communication is concerned, the present status is adequate. National and state Highways should be the respective subject. However, if commercially found viable, Nagaland government can float a separate airline for internal services in all the Naga inhabited areas or have an arrangement with any existing airlines which will be easy but commercial feasibility has to be looked into.

Commerce

So far as trade and commerce is concerned it should be adequate if the Naga government administers the local trade under its supervision. However, the trade with neighbouring countries should be under the regulation of Government of India as the currency transaction would take place at central level. Import and export through other states of India will be as presently being followed. However, direct air cargo services can be started from Dimapur and Imphal provided that customs and visa clearance is organised.

Inner Line Permit and Sale of Land

The system of Inner Line Permit (ILP) can be continued till such time it is required. In fact, there are many non-Nagas doing yeoman service in the Nagaland state and other Naga areas specially in teaching, medical services, trade and commerce. The vibrant economy will get a boost if this 'Inner Line Permit' is removed. In fact, all the areas are being visited by anyone who desires and only limitation is the 'ILP'. Should the Inner Line Permit be abolished, the tourism in Naga areas will get a boost. But to safeguard the interest of land rights, culture etc, it is felt that the people from outside should not be allowed to settle there permanently. But this clause is detrimental to trade, commerce and industry. If the ILP is removed, Nagaland can become Netherlands of the orient wherein exotic flower industry can flourish.

It is also noticeable that in the bordering areas, many small scale industries can be established by any Indian or international company but due to these two restrictions Nagaland and Jammu and Kashmir state are showing poor economic growth. Thus, clause for Inner Line Permit and restriction on sale of land (specially for industry purposes) should be suitably modified. Thus, ILP issue is to be reviewed with pragmatic approach with some effective checks and balances.

Minerals

The right over the minerals under the surface is one of the major demands, but it has been the property of the Government of

India as per the law. In case, this clause is not acceptable to the Nagas, the right of ownership can be given to the Naga people. But there will be problem to decide the actual ownership of the land under the surface. Thus, the propriety right of all the minerals can be given to the government of the Nagas as per demand. However, sale and purchase of minerals within India or export should be governed as per the Indian rules for trade and commerce. It is also possible that let the status quo be maintained and a royalty to the local government of Nagas be paid as price of the material to be distributed to the villagers under whose land the minerals are being extracted.

Other Demands to be Sanctioned

There are other minor demands e.g. railway network, location of new capital, surface communication and extension of national highways to the areas inhabited by Nagas specially in Manipur and other states, economic policy and the central aid for the proposed Naga state, foreign development aid (collection and use for development in Naga areas), Naga tourism offices abroad, transportation regulations and policies, trade and commerce with foreign countries and other Indian states, customs and excise duties, sales tax exemption, own civil service, land rights, official language (proposed - English), education and culture (for maintenance of their own without any external infringement), stamps, status of minorities in the Naga areas (in business or job), rights over natural resources including minerals, Naga commission on human rights, judiciary (separate High Court bench) and forest including those in Disputed Area Belt (DAB), for which an amicable solution will not be difficult to achieve. Once the major issues such as sovereignty and integration are resolved, all other issues would not be an impediment for hammering out an workable solution.

Final Words

The major question still remains; will there be peace at the end of the day after signing an agreement with the NSCN (IM)?

Since there are many parties in this conflict which are at the logger heads, the success of any agreement depends on the participation of all the groups in the talks. Since, NSCN(IM) has been the major player and signed the Framework Agreement, it will be the responsibility of Muivah the sole leader of NSCN (IM) to place the proposed agreement on the table at Forum for Naga Reconciliation (FNR) and get a consensus of all the parties i.e. NSCN(K, KK and Reformation), NNC (Accordists/ Non Accordists) along-with their political wings, before signing of the final agreement. It will also be important that Naga society at large arrive at a consensus in the 'Journey of Common Hope' and ensure bringing in permanent peace. Also the Government of India will equally be responsible to implement the Agreement in letter and spirit.

The responsibility of the Government of India at this juncture would be to take all the groups (undergrounds) together, may not be in the same meeting with NSCN (IM), to arrive at a consensus. It would be prudent to take the Khaplang group as well (after the death of S S Khaplang on 09 June 2017) but it is easier said than done, thus possibility of track two or backdoor channel should also be explored to get them around. In addition, other parties of the FNR should also be interacted with e.g. NSCN(K) now being led by Khango Konyak, NNC groups, the Church (CNBC & NBCC), mainstream politicians and the NGOs. Once the agreement is signed, these are the people who are going to go to the masses to build public opinion in favour of the Peace Agreement. Since, the transparency at this moment is totally lacking and as the issues are very sensitive, thus, it is imperative that the government takes adequate measures before announcing the final outcome of the negotiation.

Naga insurgency has been an emotional issue for both the sides and the world has changed so much that no nation is truly independent today and simultaneously no state controls everything of their own country. It would be prudent if a particular ethnic group wishes to live their life in their own way and genius, it should be allowed within the national framework or accepted norms and a time will come when these ethnic overtones will get automatically blurred in the light of development and shrinking geographical barriers. If not done by this present generation of leaders, future generations would be deprived of the opportunity to grow in the context of globalization. If the ethnic groups wish to go back to the primitive communes, well it will be at the cost of the future of their progenies.

The young generation should move forward and claim the rightful place in the truly globalised society where competence is the only criteria for success. Thus, an amicable and honourable solution must be found despite the **'Road to Peace is Thorny'**.

Appendix A

Naga Memorandum to Simon Commission

Memorandum on the Naga Hills dated 10 January, 1929

Sir,

We the undersigned Nagas of the Naga Club at Kohima who are the only persons at present who can voice (the opinions) for our people have heard with great regret that our Hills (have been) included within the Reformed Scheme of India without our Knowledge, but as the administration of our Hills continued to be in the hands of the British Officers we learn that you have come to India as representatives to the British Government to enquire into the working to the system of Government and the growth of education and we beg to submit below our view with the prayer that our Hills may be withdrawn from the Reformed Scheme and placed outside Reforms but directly under British Government. We never asked for any reforms and we do not wish for any reforms.

Before the British Government conquered our country in 1879-1880, we were living in a state of intermittent warfare with the Assamese of the Assam valley to the North and West of our country and the Manipur is to the South. They never conquered us, nor were we ever subjected to their rule. On the other hand, we were always a terror to these people. Our country within the administered area consists of more than eight tribes quite different from one another with quite different language which cannot be understood by each other, and there are more tribes outside the administered area which are not known at present. We have no unity among us and it is only the British Government that is holding us together now.

Our education at present is poor. The occupation of our country by the British Government being so recent as 1880, we have had no chance or opportunity to improve in education and though we can boast of two or three graduates of an Indian University in our country, we have not got one yet who is able to represent all our different tribes or master our languages much less one to represent us in any council of a province. Moreover, our population numbering 102000 is very small in comparison with the population of the plains districts in the province, and any representation that may be allotted to us in the council will be negligible and will have no weight whatever our language is quite different from those of the plains and we have no social affinities with Hindus or Musalmans. We are looked down upon by the one for our 'beef' and the other for our 'pork' and by both for our want in education which is not due to any fault of ours.

Our country is poor and it does not pay for its administration. Therefore, if it is continued to be placed under the Reformed Scheme, we are afraid that new and heavy taxes will have to be imposed on us and when we cannot pay them all our lands will have to be sold and in the long run we shall have no share in the land of our birth and life will not be worth living then. Though our land at present is within the British territory, Government has always recognized our private rights in it, but if we are forced to enter the council of the majority, all these rights may be extinguished by unsympathetic council the majority of whose number is sure to belong to the plain districts. We also have much fear of the introduction of foreign laws and customs to supersede our customary laws which we now enjoy.

For the above reasons, we pray that the British Government will continue to safeguard our rights against all encroachment from other people who are more advanced than us by withdrawing our country from the Reformed Scheme and placing it directly under its own protection. If the British Government however, wants to throw us away, we pray that we should not be thrust to the mercy of the people who could never subjugate us, but to leave us alone to determine for ourselves as in ancient times. We claim (Not only the members of the Naga Club) to represent all these tribes to which we belong Angamis, Kacha Nagas, Kukis, Semas, Loths and Rengmas.

Signed by

1. Nihu, Head Interpreter Angami
2. Nisale, Peshkar, Angami
3. Nisher, Master, Angami
4. Khosa, Doctor, Angami
5. Gepo Interpreter, Kacha Naga
6. Vipunyu, Potdar, Angami
7. Goyiepra, Treasurer, Angami
8. Rushukhrie, Master, Angami
9. Dikhrie, Sub-Overseer, Angami
10. Zupulhoulie, Master, Angami
11. Zepulie, Interpreter, Angami
12. Katshumo,Interpreter,Angami
13. Nuolhoukielie,Clerk, Angami
14. Luzevi, Sema, Interpreter
15. Apamo, Interpreter, Lotha
16. Resuki,Interpreter, Rengma
17. Lengjang, Interpreter, Kuki
18. Nikhriehu.,Interpreter, Angami
19. Miakrao, Chaprasi Angami
20. Levi, Clerk, Kacha Naga

Appendix B

Part of Nehru's Letter to Sakhrie on 01 August, 1946

"...It is obvious that the Naga territory in Eastern Assam is much too small to stand by itself politically or economically. It lies between two huge countries, India and China, and part of it consists of rather backward people who require considerable help. Inevitably, therefore, this Naga territory must form part of India and of Assam with which it has developed such close association. At the same time, it is our policy that tribal areas should have as much freedom and autonomy as possible so that they can live their own lives according to their own customs and desires. Thus the solution would be that the Naga territory should be an integral part of Assam province and yet should have a certain measure of autonomy for its own purposes. I am glad that the Naga National Council stands for the solidarity of all the Naga tribes including those who live in the so called unadministered territory.

I agree entirely with your decision that the Naga Hills should constitutionally be included in an autonomous Assam in a free India with local autonomy and due safeguards for the interests of the Nagas. As for separate electorate for the Nagas,generally speaking, we are against keeping it separated from the rest of the nation. But if the Naga territory is given a measure of autonomy, some arrangement will have to be made for their proper representation. As I have said above, the Excluded Areas should be incorporated with other areas. It may be that certain provisions for their protection and development will be made.

I should like them to be treated as part of the entire Naga territory. I see no reason whatever, why an extraneous judicial system should be enforced upon the Naga Hills. They should have perfect freedom to continue their village panchayats, tribal courts, etc according to their wishes. The question of common language must also be finally decided by the Nagas themselves. The only two possible languages which would be helpful to them are Assamese or Hindustani. Assam is still largely undeveloped and there is plenty of room for agricultural, horticultural and industrial development. This development should be organized as to benefit the people of the soil. Certainly, the people of the Naga Hills should not be exploited by them. We should be entirely against the development of large estates owned by outsiders there. I might add that I am specially interested in these tribal areas not only in the North-East of India but in the North-West as well as the centre.

They represent different problems. I do not want them to be swamped by people from other parts of the country who might go there to exploit them to their own advantage…"

Appendix C

The Hydari Agreement, 1947

The Nine Points Agreement arrived at between the Naga National Council and the Governor of Assam, Sir Akbar Hydari in June 27-29, 1947

In right of the Naga to develop themselves according to their freely expressed wishes is recognized.

1. **Judicials**: All cases whether Civil or Criminalising between Nagas in the Naga Hills will be disposed off by duly constituted Naga courts according to Naga customary law, or such law as may be introduced with the consent of duly recognized Naga representative organization; save that where a transportation or death has been passed there will be right of appeal to the Governor.

   In cases arising between Nagas and Non-Nagas in (a) Kohima and Mokokchung Town areas and (b) in the neighbouring district, the Judge, if not a Naga, will be assisted by a Naga assessor.

2. **Executive**: The general principle is accepted that what the Naga National Council will control. This principle will apply equally to the work done as well as the staff employed. While the District Officer will be appointed at the discretion of the Governor, Sub-Division of the Naga Hills should be administered by a Sub-Divisional Council, who would be responsible to the District Officer for all matters falling within their responsibility in regard to:

Appendix H

Major Human Rights Violation Against Army Personnel by Naga Insurgents

1. February 1982, the insurgents killed twenty-four personnel of the Indian Army (21st Sikh Light Infantry) and captured twenty-seven arms and thousand rounds of ammunition at Mathilok in the Wung (Thangkul) region.
2. July 1987, the entire company of (3rd Assam Rifles) was overrun by the insurgents at Oinam village. The full armoury of the company (about ninety SLRs, twenty three Sten Carbine, ten LMGs, two 2″ Mortars, three hundred hand grenades, and twenty-four thousand live ammunition) was looted. Apart from the ten killed who were on sentry duty; the rest rank and file surrendered and was, thus, left unharmed.
3. On April 9, 1988, the insurgents killed ten CRPF personnels and injured several others at Selungphug in the Zelinag Region.
4. June 1988, the insurgents killed three Jawans including two Majors at Ukhrul in the Wung (Thangkul) Region.
5. February 6, 1989 the insurgents seriously injured three Jawans (20th Assam Rifles) at Lungshangkong in the Wung (Thangkul) Region.
6. September 1989, insurgents killed twenty nine BSF personnel at Lainy village in the Wung (Thangkul) region.
7. On September 1, 1990 insurgents killed four Indian paramilitary force personnels (Manipur Rifles)

and injured two others at Makhang village in the Shepoumaram region.

8. On October 20, 1990, insurgents liquidated a section of BSF at Khudengthabi and 4 SLRs, 1 Sten Carbine and 1 Automatic Pistol along with a huge quantity of ammunition.
9. On Aprl 10, 1991, insurgents killed four Jawans and injured two others at Kachai village in the Wung (Thangkul) region and 4 SLRs and 2 Sten Carbines, one with a silencer was taken away.
10. On June 11, 1991, insurgents killed four Army personnel including intelligence officer at Jessami village in the Wung (Thangkul region) and took away Rs 73,00,000/- (Rupees seventy three lakhs only).
11. On August 14, 1991, insurgents attacked the flying squad of Nagaland Police in Dimapur and captured 3 AK-47 assaults Rifles. There were12 casualties.
12. On December 9, 1991, insurgents killed 9 CRPF personnel and a police sub-inspector at Lokchao village in the Khurmi Region and tookaway 1 LMG, 11 SLRs and 3 Sten Carbines. A sum of Rs 52,00,000/- (Rupees fifty two lakhs only) was also collected.
13. On February 14, 1992, insurgents attacked the treasure convoy at Aghunato in the Sumi Region and captured 1 LMG and 9 service rifles along with 45,00,000/- (Rupees forty five lakhs only).
14. On Jun 12, 1992, insurgents killed fourteen Jawans (GR) personal including one Second Lieutenant between Chezami and Lainy villages in the Chakesang Region and took away one x two inch Mortar, one LMG, two carbines, seven SLRs and a huge quantity of ammunition.
15. On August 5, 1992, the insurgents killed seven BSF personnel at Mahur village in the Zeliang region.
16. On September 6, 1992 insurgents killed seven Jawans of 3rd Assam Rifles and seriously injured eighteen others at Tamei village in the Zeliang region.

Appendix D

Interview with Mr. S.C. Jamir, Ex Chief Minister of Nagaland at Kohima: 17 August, 2003

Q.1. *Since you being the veteran ....?*

Ans. 1946! When there was tension in the country, the British was likely to leave India, at that time, educated Naga people, Naga elders had consultation to decide the future of Naga' People. In 1946, officially the representatives met and then they changed the name of the Naga Club after first resolution to the NNC, the objective of the NNC was to train our people in the art of administration. That the...

Q.2. *You are Right, Sir...*

Ans. But the process when this movement continued, Phizo took the leadership...

Q.3. *That is again a long story, Phizo was miniscule ..., he was supported by 5/6 people out of 29 (in the NNC)...*

Ans. Only when he took over as the President, then approach of the NNC completely changed. That time there was no division as such, he said that we should only have a demand of sovereignty. He said 'Nagas are not Indians. Therefore, we have to have separate homeland for ours'. Accordingly to assess the views of the Naga people an official plebiscite was conducted in 1951. There was a big form in which there were two columns, you have to write or say 'Yes' or 'No'. We did it openly during the day then we took that form to the villages and actually, it was done correctly.

Q.4. *Don't you think, that canvassing done by Phizo in the name of 'Independenti' at Kohima? .... There was a serious question that the plebiscite was a sham!*

Ans. No, No! It was correct, actually done! We did it. I am a witness. People did not know the real meaning of plebiscite and so they were asked that whether you would like to be independent or dependent. At that time, our people were not educated and naturally so we were told that the Nagas are Not Indians and so we will have a separate homeland of ours and on that basis plebiscite was conducted.

Q.5. *If you recall that, there was SP Kanwar (Randeep Singh) a Prince of Rajput family, he says when he visited villages, Gaonburhas, used to say that 'I am for independent and I am for India' in the same breath!*

Ans. I don't think that is correct. That kind of consciousness was not there. All we told that the Nagas are not Indians and they knew it.

Q.6. *Later on Hydari Agreement. Before the Hydari Agreement could be put on test on ground or implementation...*

Ans. Actually, Hydari agreement was prior to plebiscite.

Q.7. *That's right Sir, it is in 1947! It was 14 July if I am not wrong Sir, and after one month UDI (Unilateral Declaration of Independence) was done by Phizo...*

Ans. According to the agreement, after 10 years it should be reviewed. As to whether the same would continue or stop (Whatever best suited). That was the point of contention. Nagas interpreted that after the expiry of 10 Years, Nagas will decide what they want. Whereas the interpretation of the government was that it will be reviewed and action will be taken which is most suited at that point of time, so that was the divergence of views. So it became a deadlock.

Q.8. *How the non-violent movement started initially became violent after 1952?*

Ans. It was peaceful movement! It was overground movement! It was a political movement. When Pandit

inclusion of the Reserve Forests and of contiguous areas inhabited by the Nagas. They were referred to the provisions in Articles 3 and 4 of the Constitution, prescribing the procedure for the transfer of areas from one state to another.

13. **Consolidation of Contiguous Naga Areas:** The delegation wished the following to be placed on record:

    The Naga leaders expressed the wish for the contiguous areas to join the new state, It was pointed out to them on behalf of the Government of India that Articles 3 and 4 of the Constitution provided for increasing the areas of any state, but that it was not possible for the Government of India to make any commitment in this regard at this stage.

14. **Formation of Separate Naga Regiment:** In order that the Naga people can fulfill their desire of planning a full role in the defence of India the question of raising a separate Naga Regiment should be duly examined for action.

15. **Transitional Period:**

    (a) On reaching the political settlement with the Government of India, the Government of India will prepare a Bill for such amendment of the Constitution as may be necessary, in order to implement the decision. The Draft Bill, before presentation to Parliament, will be shown to the delegates of the NPC.

    (b) There shall be constituted an 'Interim Body' with elected representatives form every tribe, to assist and advise the Government in the demonstration of the Nagaland during the transitional period. The tenure of office of the Interim Body will be 3 (three) years subject to re-election.

16. **Inner-Line Regulation:** Rules embodied in the Bengal Eastern Frontier Regulation, 1873 shall remain in force in Nagaland.

Appendix G

The Armed Forces (Special Powers) Act, 1958 (Act 28 of 1959)

An act to enable certain special powers to be conferred up on members of the armed forces in disturbed areas in the States of Assam, Manipur, Meghalaya, Nagaland and Tripura and the Union Territories of Arunachal Pradesh and Mizoram.

Be it enacted by Parliament in the Ninth Year of the Republic of India as follows:

1. **Short title and extent:**
   (a) This Act may be called the Armed Forces (Special Powers) Act, 1958.
   (b) It extends to the whole of the State of Assam, Manipur, Meghalaya, Nagaland and Tripura and the Union Territories of Arunachal Pradesh and Mizoram.
2. **Definitions**: In this Act, unless the context otherwise requires,
   (a) "armed forces" means the military forces and the air forces operating as land forces, and includes any other armed forces of the Union so operating;
   (b) "disturbed area" means an area which is for the time being declared by notification under S. 3 to be a disturbed area;
   (c) All other words and expressions used herein, but not defined in the Air Force Act, 1950 or the Army Act 1950, shall have the meanings respectively attached to them in those Acts.
3. **Power to declare areas to be Disturbed Areas:** If, in relation to any State or Union Territory to which this Act

Sukhato was the president. They declared President Rule and dissolved the cabinet …then reacting to that again Sukhato group formed the Revolutionary group… Actually that started the split within the federal government. That was the beginning of the crack in the Naga political movement…

Q.17. *Then Finally Shillong Accord was Signed?*

Ans. No! No! After that bulk of the Naga Army surrendered and they formed into BSF 111 and 112... Even now it is there.

Q.18. *It is there, Sir…*

Ans. But Naga federal groups continued. Then in the process, after I think one or two years, it was Nagaland Government decided to put pressure on the villagers …'if you do not bring out the villagers who are underground, we will not allow you to harvest'... That kind of pressure was mounted on the villagers and Army was brought in and almost all the districts were cleaned up barring Chekhesang and Kohima… So they told the remnants that instead of surrendering you are made to sign the Shillong Accord.

Q.19. *It was made to!*

Ans. Actually, it was made to! Other wise, there was no…

Q.20. *It was not a genuine accord?*

Ans. It was only a capitulationary.

Q.21. *Now the history is very clear. After 1975 NSCN was formed. But surprisingly there was a vacuum (in information) between 1975 and 1997 that there was nothing published articles etc in the Newspapers/national or any media?*

Ans. You see! After the Shillong, reacting to that NSCN was formed by Issac, Muivah and Khaplang in the eastern part of Nagaland. So at the… strong, it was the national... They did not have much activity for quite some time. But they only challenged Shillong Accord. Then Phizo also kept mum. These people … Accordist… they went to London to meet Phizo and Vizol also went that time. He (Phizo) could not give the reply and that was another 'watershed' in the Naga movement and there was split…in two... One was Shillong Accordist and other was NSCN.

Q.22. *Then later they split (again)?*

Ans. So that time… I became the Chief Minister in 1983-85… So that time there was lots of effort on the part the Shillong Accordists to solve the problem. There was the vertical split of the Federal Group… NNC and other side was NSCN… So there was a vacuum and there was nothing written that time... When I went to Rajya Sabha, Hokishe Sema was the Chief Minister. At that time I think there was certain arrangement to have dialogue between the Government of India and NSCN... That agenda was not discussed and strong suspicion arose between Issac Muivah and Khaplang group and lot of infighting in NSCN and exploded openly …again NSCN split up in two groups NSCN … Issac Muivah group, NSCN Khaplang-Konyak Group.

Q.23. *Meanwhile there was one development (that) took place, your Government (Congress) passed three Resolutions in 1964, 1970 and 1994 for integration of contiguous areas. How can it be done in this context?*

Ans. If you go through the 16 Point Agreement… point (was there for)… integration of Naga areas in Manipur, Assam and Arunachal Pradesh, we said that integration of areas… not by force… by choice.

Q.24. *It has already been seen in Manipur… the back lash in last year!*

Ans. Consequent to 16 Point Agreement …Nagaland Assembly also when formed the popular government… that assembly passed three resolutions.

Q.25. *Present Peace Talks which is undergoing… in any conflict (there are) three parties… Government, Undergrounds and fence seaters (common people)… at the moment they are ignorant in which direction the talks are going?*

Ans. I have been making my position very clear. Naga issue is a Naga issue …and not a factional issue. If Naga

Sema : Yeah, Then these people started working towards resolving the deadlock met Manmohan Singh, Manishankar Aiyer, Mr Gujral, Mr Chandrashekar and the people who were in the government. That's how visit of Issac and Muivah took place in January 2003, this also fructified in terms of visit of Mr Vajpayee to Nagaland in October 2003. This was a historic event.

Sen : *Issue of Greater Nagaland?*

Sema : You see, the government has accepted the unique history of Naga people, practically it may be meaning nothing, but they could strike a deal on that account and talks moved. Muivah says that Naga Integration is not negotiable and his friends can not put him wise. Talks are likely to face rough weather on integration issue.

Sen : *Sir, if you have seen the proceedings of Bangkok wherein the body language and expression of Issac was to find out a via media between sovereignty and the Constitution of India!*

Sema : Government of India and leaders of Nagaland are working on practical aspects of independence, sovereignty and integration.

Sen : *But integration of all the Naga inhabited area specially Manipur and Burma!*

Sema : Integration of these areas (within India) is not impossible. You have to bridge the economic gap, allow them to interact socially, culturally and let them amalgamate, create an atmosphere for Greater Nagalim.

Sen : *How about Eastern Nagas?*

Sema : With Burma, its international problem. You see within India, boundaries are redundant so the currency. As a big brother, specially in relation to Naga identity. Practical aspect has to be understood in its correct perspective.

Sen : *How to do the conflict Resolution?*

Sema : I will give couple of Mantras:

1. You can get independence but people may not be sovereign.
2. You can not integrate all the five territories (Tirap Changlang in Arunachal, Naga areas in Assam, Manipur, Nagaland and Myanmar) overnight, time is required to interact with one another socially, culturally, economically (read development). They should be given time to arrive at consensus, say about 5-10 or even 20 years.
3. Inter tribal rivalry may not make peace suitable. It may undermine this integration. So we may think to give autonomy to all these five areas instead of one greater Nagaland, whose Headquarters is based at Kohima (you know Tizit/Khonsa is nearer to Delhi than Kohima).
4. Economic aid to these areas to develop, almost 99 percent of the expenditure will have to be from Delhi.
5. Economic exploitation of Nagas by the business community (Marwaris, Bengalis, Assamese, Biharis etc) will have to be stopped and then see.

Sen : *What is the present state now?*

Sema : Nothing more I can say. These things have been conveyed to all big leaders, you can interpret these mantras for integration and coin your terms accordingly.

Q.33. *That is not happening…*

Ans. Nothing is happening actually...

Q.34. *What is the IM people going to speak their constituency i.e. people that 'Look' what we have got for you?*

Ans. Unless there is a settlement and that should be transparent…

Q.35. *That is not happening? That means that Peace Talks are heading ...*

Ans. … nowhere … They have hit the wall with no exit for last six years we are talking about issues are;-

1. Should be in foreign land.
2. Should be at Prime Minister level.
3. They also said Third Country observer should also be there.

And this issue be it in Bengal, Amsterdam and Delhi etc. except that I think they have been talking on substantive issues. How can you talk on substantive issues? Unless they consult Naga people…

Q.36. *That means in the present context peace will remain elusively away!*

Ans. We may not say 'peace', but political issue will be elusive as ever. Government of India should be very definite... They should have played diplomacy which won people. I think sharing of our mind, ideas and this is more important than trying to appease… because appeasement policy won't work. That is my thinking...

Q.37. *What would be your role in future if that kind of reconciliation is achieved?*

Ans. As far as we are concerned we shall continue to contribute whatever… within our power, as layman or political leader, in any capacity our services will be available.

Appendix E

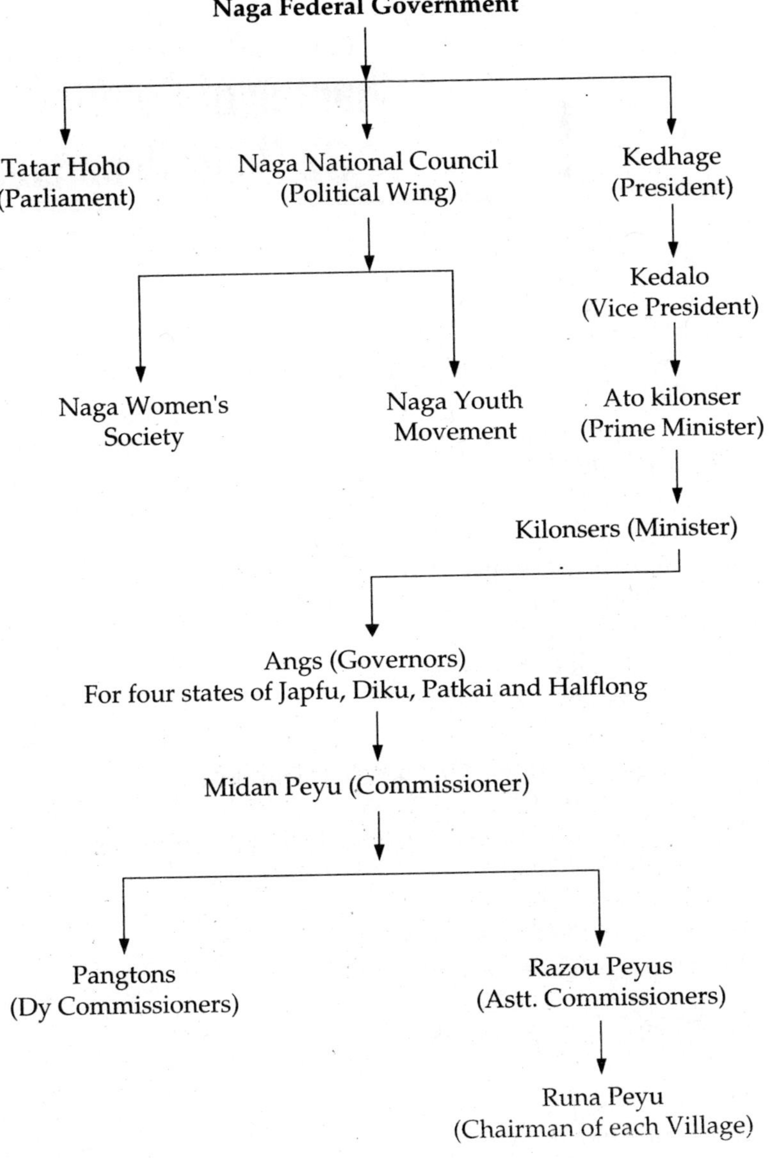

Naga Federal Government
Tatar Hoho
(Parliament)
Naga National Council
(Political Wing)
Kedhage
(President)
Kedalo
(Vice President)
Naga Women's
Society
Naga Youth
Movement
Ato kilonser
(Prime Minister)
Kilonsers (Minister)
Angs (Governors)
For four states of Japfu, Diku, Patkai and Halflong
Midan Peyu (Commissioner)
Pangtons
(Dy Commissioners)
Razou Peyus
(Astt. Commissioners)
Runa Peyu
(Chairman of each Village)

Appendix I

Charter of Demands: 32 Point Proposal

1. Sovereignty.
2. Integration of Contiguous Naga Areas.
3. Defence.
4. Foreign Affairs.
5. Separate Flag.
6. Currency.
7. Naga Army.
8. Naga Constitution.
9. Assembly-Tatar Hoho.
10. Entry Regulations.
11. Trade and Commerce.
12. International Air Port.
13. Railways.
14. Communication - Postal and Telegraph.
15. New Capital.
16. Surface Communication and National Highways.
17. Economic Policy.
18. Foreign Development Aid.
19. Tourism Offices Abroad.
20. Transportation Policy.
21. Trade and Commerce.
22. Customs, Excise, Sales Tax Exemption.
23. Own Civil Service.
24. Land Rights.
25. Education and Culture.
26. Official Language-English.

27. Stamps.
28. Minorities.
29. Naga Commission on Human Rights.
30. Judiciary.
31. Forest.
32. Natural Resources.

bodies with matters concerning the respective tribes and areas:

(1) The Village Council.

(2) The Range Council; and

(3) The Tribal Council.

These Councils will also deal with disputes and cases involving breaches of customary laws and usages.

9. **Administration of Justice:** The existing system of administration of civil and criminal justice shall continue.

(a) Appellate Courts:

(1) The District Court-cum-Sessions Court (for each district), High Court and Supreme Court of India.

(2) The Naga Tribunal (for the whole of the Nagaland) in respect of cases decided according to Customary Law.

10. **Administration of Tuensang District:**

(1) The Governor shall carry on the administration of the Tuensang District for a period of 10 (ten) years until such time when the tribes in the Tuensang District are capable of shouldering more responsibility of the advanced system of administration. The commencement of the ten-year period of administration will start simultaneously with the enforcement of detailed workings of the constitution in other parts of the Nagaland.

(2) Provided further that a Regional Council shall be formed for Tuensang District by elected representatives from all the tribes in Tuensang district, and the Governor may nominate representatives to the Regional Council as well, The Deputy Commissioner will be the Ex-officio Chairman of the Council. The Regional Council will elect members to the Naga Legislative Assembly to represent Tuensang District.

(3) Provided further that on the advice of the Regional Council, steps will be taken to start various councils and courts, in those areas where the people feel themselves capable of establishing such institutions.

(4) Provided further that no Act or Law passed by the Naga Legislative Assembly shall be applicable to Tuensang district unless specifically recommended by the Regional Council.

(5) Provided further that the Regional Council shall supervise and guide the working of the various councils and Tribal courts within Tuensang district and whenever necessary depute the local officers to act as chairman thereof.

(6) Provided further that council of such areas inhabited by a mixed population or which have not as yet decided to which specific tribal council to be affiliated to shall be directly under the Regional Council for the time being. And at the end of ten years the situation will be reviewed and if the people so desire the period will be further extended.

11. Financial Assistance from the Government of India

To supplement the revenues of Nagaland, there will be fund for the Government of India to pay out of the consolidated fund of India:

(1) A lump sum each year for the development programme in the Nagaland; and

(2) A grant-in-aid towards meeting the cost of administration.

Proposals for the above grants shall be prepared and submitted by the Government of Nagaland to the Government of India for their approval. The Governor will have general responsibility for ensuring that the funds made available by the Government of India are spent for purposes for which they have been approved.

12. Consolidation of Forest Areas

The delegation wished the following to be placed on record:

The Naga delegation discussed the question of the

Nehru visited Kohima with U Nu, Nagas wanted to submit a memorandum to Pandit Nehru, because he was with U Nu.

Q.9. *That Deputy Commissioner bungled it up...*

Ans. The Deputy Commissioner here knowing the sentiments of Naga people, he prevented them to submit the memorandum. Therefore, there was the order already, except the boycott which happened. After that they (Government authorities) issued arrest warrant, so they went underground. That was the beginning of our underground movement.

Q. 10. *That is right Sir?*

Ans. They started arresting those Naga National Council workers. They started beating them, torturing them and putting them in Jail. So after having seen those atrocities of Assam Police, then Nagas also decided to organize into 'Safeguards'. They had collected the second World War weapons which were left over and also started safeguarding themselves. They called themselves *safeguards*. Naturally when you are arrested, the condition between...Assam Police and safeguards... that was the beginning of violence in Nagaland.

Q. 11. *That was the beginning of deployment of Army also?*

Ans. That was the beginning ... when 75 Battalion of Assam Battalion in Satakha ... was armed, then situation became out of control and we had to deploy Army in 1955.

Q. 12. *After that there was three conventions of NPC-Kohima, Ungma ...*

Ans. In 1957 Kohima, 1958 in my village (Ungma), I was Chairman of the Reception Committee and then 1959 in Mokukchung.

Q.13. *By then you had graduated from Allahabad University and you became political worker since then...*

Ans. That I was elected as a Joint Secretary of Naga People's Convention (NPC). Since then I am deeply involved in the political matters.

Q.14. *So in 1960, NPC convention culminated in 16 Point Term Agreement, Sir!*

Ans. That is in 1959! We passed resolution and we got 16 Point Memorandum, on the basis of which we had to negotiate with the Government. So this was the point. Accordingly, we went to Shillong to meet the then Governor of Assam ...Shri Nagesh... But as a Governor he could not decide political lines... and therefore, he referred it to the Prime Minister. So accordingly we went to Delhi in the month of July 1960... by a delegation... We met the Prime Minister... two days (of) discussion. He agreed to grant statehood to Nagaland and on that basis we came back and three years interim period was arranged prior to the general election... so after completion of three years in 1964... first general election was held in Nagaland we formed the government in Nagaland.

Q.15. *Now in between Peace Talks (held) in Khensa/Chumkdeima wherein Jaiprakash Narayan took the lead...*

Ans. Actually the first Peace Talk started in Chedema and that time only Gundevia came. He was the Foreign Secretary... and I was Parliamentary Secretary to the Prime Minister.

Q.16. *Y.D. Gundevia!*

Ans. Yes! We came together, so that was the first Naga Peace Talk with Naga Federal... Issac Swu was Foreign Secretary that time (of the federal government). So that was the beginning of Peace Talks and then second Peace Talk was held at Khensa. Then after that they came to Delhi two times and the last round of talks in 1968, when we were about to conclude an agreement. But some how there was some misunderstanding... so they said that talks ended in a deadlock and that was the end of the Peace process which started in 1964. When they came back (to) Assam there was difference of opinion between our Sema group and the other group and they declared President Rule. Because that time Kughato Sukhai was the prime minister and extends , the Governor of that State or the Administrator of that Union Territory of the Central Government in either case, is of the opinion that the whole or any part of such State or Union territory, as the case may be, in such a disturbed or dangerous condition that the use of armed forces in aid of the civil power is necessary, the Governor of that State or the Administrator of that Union Territory or the Central Government, as the case may be, may, by notification in the Official Gazette, declare the whole or such part of such State or Union Territory to be a disturbed area.

4. **Special Powers of the Armed Forces**. Any commissioned officer, warrant officer, non commissioned officer or any other of equivalent rank in the armed forces may, in a disturbed area :-
   (a) if he is of the opinion that it is necessary to do so for the maintenance of public order, after giving such due warning as he may consider necessary, fire upon or otherwise use force, even to the causing of death, against any person who is acting in contravention of any law or order for the time being in force in the disturbed area prohibiting the assembly of five or more persons or the carrying of weapons or of things capable of being used as weapons or of fire-arms, ammunition or explosive substances;
   (b) if he is of opinion that it is necessary so to do, destroy any arms dump, prepared or fortified position or shelter from which armed attacks are made or are likely to be made or are attempted to be made or any structure used as training camp for armed volunteers or utilised as a hideout by armed gangs or absconders wanted for any office;
   (a) arrest without warrant, any person who has committed a cognizable offence or against whom a reasonable suspicion exists that he has committed or is about to commit a cognizable offence and may use such force as may be necessary to effect the arrest;

(b) Enter and search without warrant any premises to make any such arrest as aforesaid or to recover any person believed to be wrongfully restrained and confined or any property reasonably suspected to be stolen property or any arms, ammunition or explosive substances believed to be unlawfully kept in such premises, and may for that purpose use such force as may be necessary.

5. **Arrested Persons to be made over to the Police:** Any person arrested and taken into custody under this Act shall be made over to the officer in charge of the nearest police station with the least possible delay, together with a report of the circumstances occasioning the arrest.

6. **Protection to Persons Acting under Act:** No prosecution, suit or other legal proceedings shall be instituted, except with the previous sanction of the Central Government, against any person in respect of anything done or purported to be done in exercise of the powers conferred by this Act.

7. **Repeal and Saving**
   (1) The Armed Forces (Assam and Manipur) Special Powers Ordinance, 1958, is hereby repealed
   (2) Not withstanding such repeal anything done or any action taken under the said ordinance shall be deemed to have been or taken under this Act, as if this had commenced on the 22nd day of May, 1958.

(a) **Agriculture:** The Naga National Council will exercise all the powers now vested in the District Officer.

(b) **C.W.D:** The Naga National Council will take over full control.

(c) **Education & Forest:** The Naga National Council is prepared to pay for all service and staff.

3. **Legislative**: That no laws passed by the provincial or Central Legislatures which would materially affect the terms of this agreement or the religious practices of the Nagas shall have legal force in the Naga Hills without the consent of the Naga National Council.

   In case of dispute as to whether law did so affect this agreement the matter would be referred by the Naga National Council to the Governor who would then direct that the law in question should not have legal force in the Naga Hills pending the decision of the Central Government.
4. **Land:** That land with its resources in the Naga Hills should not be alienated to a Non-Naga without the consent of the Naga National Council.
5. **Taxation:** That the Naga National Council will be responsible for the imposition, collection and expenditure of land revenue and house tax and of such other taxes as may be imposed by the Naga National Council.
6. **Boundaries:** That the present administrative divisions should be modified so as (1) to bring back into the Naga Hills Districts in the past and (2) to bring under one unified administrative unit as far as possible all Nagas.

   All the areas so included will be within the scope of the present proposed agreement.

   No areas should be transferred out of the Naga Hills without the consent of the Naga National Council.
7. **Arms Act:** The District Officer will act on the advice of the Naga National Council in accordance with the provisions of the Arms Act.

8. **Regulations:** The Chin Hills Regulation and the Bengal Eastern Frontier Regulation will remain in force.
9. **Period of Agreement:** The Governor of Assam as to the Agent of the Government of the Indian Union will have a special responsibility for a period of ten years to ensure the due observance to this agreement. At the end of this period, the Naga National Council will be asked whether they require the above agreement to be extended for a further period, or a new agreement regarding the future of the Naga people arrived at.

17. On February 1, 1993 insurgents killed six CRPF personnel and seriously injured five others at Taphou village in the Shepoumaramth region.
18. On march 2, 1992, three Central Industrial Security Force personnel were killed by insurgents at Aurupathar in Golaghat district of Assam and took away one sten carbine and two SLRs.
19. On May 6, 1993, five Jawans of 8th Assam Rifles were killed at a place 5 kms away from Ungma village in the Ao region.
20. On July 19, 1993, insurgents killed twenty-six Army personnel including two officers and injured for others at Khudei Lamkhei village in the Khurmi region.
21. On November 28, 1993, insurgents killed forty personnel of the 15 KUMAON at a place in between Phesami and Shotumi village in the Chakesang region.
22. On December 7, 1993, the insurgents killed twenty-one Army (16th Maratha Light Infantry) personnel including the Commandant Col KK Nair and critically injured fourteen others at Chungtia village in the Ao region and decamped with 34 SLRs, three LMGs, nine sten carbines, two 9 mm pistols, one compass set, one wireless set, one 7.82 mm MMG, and thousands of ammunition rounds.
23. On May 8, 1994, the insurgents killed Major Sunil K Bakshi and Captain Labh Singh of the (20th Assam Rifles) at Ukhrul town in the Wung (Thangkul) region.
24. On August 16, 1994, six Jawans of the Assam Rifles were killed and four others were injured by insurgents at Chaddad area in the Wung (Thangkul) region.
25. On August 18, 1994, insurgents killed twenty-nine personnel and seriously injured twelve others at Yangkhullen village in the Shepoumaramth region.
26. On September 5, 1994, insurgents killed about seven Army personnel near Angprusu village in the Khurmi region and decamped with five arms including an LMG and thousands of ammunition rounds.

27. On December 9, 1994, insurgents killed eleven CRPF personnel, injured another ten near Tamei village in the Zeliangrong region.
28. On May 3, 1995, insurgents killed six personnel of (Rashtriya Rifles) including a Major at Muojung about 60 km from the Maibung town of the North Cachhar (NC) Hills.
29. On August 30, 1995, insurgents killed six Jawans of the 20 JAT at Unger village and captured six rifles.
30. On December 18, 1995, insurgents killed five personnel including its Company Commander Major Pathak of 4 Assam Rifles at Seigang village.
31. On February 07, 1996, insurgents killed five personnel of the 66th Bn CRPF including the Assistant Commandant Mr Rohit Srivastava and injured five others at a place about twenty km away from Lailing Forest Gate in the NC Hills.
32. On May 22, 1996 insurgents killed Lt Col Sharma, the Officiating Commandant of the 16th Rashtriya Rifles Battalion and injured nine others near Bhandari town.
33. On June, 30, 1997, insurgents killed seven personnel of (3rd Assam Rifles) and seriously injured two others.

Appendix F

The Sixteen Point Agreement

The Sixteen Point Agreement Arrived at Between the Naga People's Convention and the Government of India in July 1960

The point placed by the delegates of the Naga People's Convention before the Prime Minister on 26 July 1960, as finally recast by the Delegation in the light of discussion on 27 and 28 July, 1960 with the Foreign Secretary.

1. **The Name:** The territories that were heretofore known as the Naga Hills Tuensang Area under the Naga Hills-Tuensang Area Act 1957, shall form state within the Indian union and be hereafter known as Nagaland.
2. **The Ministry Incharge:** The Nagaland shall be under the Ministry of External Affairs of the Government of India.
3. **The Governor of Nagaland**
   (1) The President of India shall appoint a Governor for Nagaland and he will be vested with the executive powers of the Government of Nagaland. He will have his headquarters in Nagaland.
   (2) His administrative secretariat will be headed by a Chief Secretary stationed at the Headquarters with other Secretariat Staff as necessary.
   (3) The Governor shall have special responsibility with regard to law and order during the transitional period and for so long as the law and order situation

continues to remain disturbed on account of hostile activities. In exercising this special responsibility, the Governor shall, after consultation with the Ministry, act in his individual judgment. This special responsibility of the Governor will cease when normalcy returns.

4. **Council of Ministers**
   (1) There shall be a Council of Ministers with a Chief Minister at the head to assist and advise the Governor in the exercise of his functions.
   (2) The Council of Ministers shall be responsible to the Naga Legislative Assembly.
5. **The Legislature:** There shall be constituted a Legislative Assembly consisting of elected and nominated members as may be deemed necessary representing different Tribes. (Further a duly constituted body of experts may be formed to examine and determine the principles of representation on democratic basis).
6. **Representation in Parliament:** Two elected members shall represent Nagaland in the Union Parliament, that is to say one for the Lok Sabha and the other for the Rajya Sabha.
7. **Act of Parliament:** No act or law passed by the union parliament affecting the following provisions shall have legal force in the Nagaland unless specifically applied to it by a majority vote of the Nagaland Legislative Assembly.
   (1) The Religious or Social Practices of the Nagas.
   (2) Naga Customary Law and procedure.
   (3) Civil and Criminal Justice so far as these concern decisions according to Naga Customary Law.
   The existing laws relating to administration of civil and criminal justice as provided in the Rules for the Administration of Justice and Police in the Naga Hills District shall continue to be in force.
   (4) The ownership and transfer of land and its resources.
8. **Local Self Government:** Each tribe shall have the following units or rule-making and administrative local

Appendix J

Interview of Capt Hekiye Sema (Retd)

Note: Capt Hekiye Sema (Retd) is an ex-servicemen who is engaged in politics of Nagaland. Being ex CM's son, he is a political heavy weight and his father is BJP MLA in the present Assembly. Interview was more of a monologue and he indirectly avoided to be interviewed in the presence of any crew with video camera. Reasons are obvious. But the discussion was jotted down as he proceeded.

Sen : *Sir! being the son of ex CM, who is close to the centre, you must be privy to the progress made in ongoing peace talks between Govt of India and NSCN (IM) hierarchy?*

Sema : Yeah! But I won't be able to tell you everything what I know but I will certainly share some information with you. The story of past I am not going into, you are more aware of. I shall begin the story since 1996 onwards when the process of ceasefire talks began. Because of army operation undergrounds were on the run and they were really pushed to the wall.

Sen : *It was because of Op Brutus Two?*

Sema : I am not very clear about the operation's name, but the fact remains that undergrounds were on the run. Talks began during Rao government but finally ceasefire was signed during Mr Gujral's time. This was a big respite for undergrounds. Since then they have been moving freely doing extortion in the name of tax collection. Common man is the sufferer.

Sen : *It's rampant.*

Sema : Yeah! It's rampant. They are extorting money, recruiting the cadres ex police and unemployed youth. In fact, the formulation of Cease Fire Ground Rules (CFGR) took long time. Meanwhile, Inter factional rivalry was going on. They were (K) and (IM) group killing each other. People reacted very sharply to the violence, and approach of the army is negative. In fact, they are cut off totally, confined to barracks. There is no worthwhile intelligence and whatever they get it is of third grade or of no value. Op Readiness has been linked to Assam Rifles only. Counter Insurgency philosophy and training at CIJW (Veirengte, Mizoram) is out dated. Actually all training précis and manuals be rewritten after 9/11.

Sen : *How about negotiation?*

Sema : It has taken too long period as interlocutors do not have any say of their own. They are doing merely a post office job.

Sen : *What are they talking? what is the hitch?*

Sema : You see, NSCN (IM)'s stand is clear. Sovereignty is not-negotiable. Due to this tough stand they hit the wall and talks ended in a deadlock in the year 2000. But none of the parties wanted to break away from talks.

Sen : *But sir! if you have seen Bangkok 2002 Meet, wherein all delegates who attended from Nagaland and elsewhere were funded by NSCN (IM)?*

Sema : Including me.

Sen : *But you were not seen in the proceedings.*

Sema : Yeah. I was not supposed to be seen. In fact, NSCN (IM) hierarchy contacted us in Nagaland those who have good links in Delhi, to resolve the issue. Then my father Mr Hokishe Sema, Mr Vizol, Mr JB Jasokie got together as part of 'Elder Citizen's Forum' to find out a via media to break the deadlock.

Sen : *In fact in year 2002, there were couple of meetings of this forum reported in the media.*

problem is to be resolved, those people, whose political fate is to be decided, shall have to be involved. Now we have three factions IM, Khaplang and NNC. So our stand made is ... unless you bring all the groups and get them involved in the political discussion, political decisions... factional Naga can not be solution. Secondly, common... they are majority because in a population of two million... hardly 10,000... and we don't want any more Shillong Accord. Suppose any Agreement with one faction... naturally it has to be within the parameters of the constitution of India... because the Government of India will not compromise on sovereignty ...Suppose if that kind of arrangement is made without consulting the (common) Nagas, those people who have been fighting all the time for sovereignty and many of them still hoping that they will get sovereignty... and they are promised that 'you will be sent as Ambassadors to this/that country'... so educated people also does hope that independence also in the back of mind... So that kind of promises have been made over the years... Suppose Agreement is made, defence will naturally be Government of India; foreign affairs will definitely be central subject... so how many you can send as ambassadors?

Q.26. *Sovereignty without defence or foreign affairs is meaningless... is no sovereignty!*

Ans. So at that point of time their own cadres will tell them why have you betrayed us? if we have to be part and parcel of Indian Union... why should you allow us to suffer for so long?... Why you kept us in dark?

Q.27. *And in the present context, sovereignty is out...*

Ans. That's why... If that kind of arrangement is made... there are two options for them either join the undergrounds wholesale or they will surrender... so it will come to square one. So I have been telling the Government of India unless you involve all others and since the settlement will have to be minus sovereignty...

Q.28. *Everybody has to be brought in …*

Ans. Don't make any exit point… once all the members are involved whether small, medium… that will be a common decision and they can not make excuses at that time… That is why we said, if you are aiming at durable, permanent solution… invoked without which there can't be any permanent solution.

Q.29. *Presently the Reconciliation process…*

Ans. What is reconciliation?

Q.30. *Nagas, per se are divided in two types of division… firstly politically they are divided… undergrounds in three parts, over grounds …Indian Nagas or nationalised Nagas who are say BJP, Congress … then second kind of division is tribal division that is very acute …ethnic relations run deep…*

Ans. Our main problem is politics… If political settlement could be worked out honourably which can be acceptable to all sections… The core is political issue … once you resolve… all this unity etc… lets not expect...

Q.31. *So lets now to have a leader… with whom Government of India ....(talking about) collective leadership, how do you see yourself or Mr Vero or any body for that matter?*

Ans. It is like this…suppose Government of India says 'yes' …unless all the groups are involved, it will be extremely difficult for us to tell you the final word. They have to say like that, because we are interested in peace… welfare of Naga people… and this will be possible when there is peace, unity and final … of the leadership. And we don't want to neglect any section of Naga community. Therefore, Government can tell them that we want final result…till all of you come together. We also love you equally, because we maintain equidistance with all our groups. If this can be spelt out loudly…

Q.32. *That is not being done!*

Ans. That is why… I say if you want to solve the Naga problem, be frank, be open. If this is possible... don't hang up.

Bibliography

A. PRIMARY SOURCES

Millennium Issue – *Statistical Handbook of Nagaland – 2001* (Directorate of Economics & Statistics, Government of Nagaland, Kohima).

Budget of NSCN (IM) – 2002-2003.

NNC, NSCN (IM) and NSCN (K) Circulations.

White Paper on Nagalim, NSCN (IM).

Speech by Shri SC Jamir, CM, Nagaland on 01 Dec,2002 at Kohima.

NSCN (IM) Souvenir: 50 Years of Resistance.

Voices of Peace, DIPR, Government of Nagaland, 2002.

Bedrock of Naga Society, NPCC (I), 2002.

Rev L Sushie Mhasi: What Are the Nagas Undergoing?

L Panger Imchen: Working Paper of Naga Scholars Society, Vol 2, No 3,1992..

Naga Student's Federation Papers, New Delhi.

The Mahabharat, Shri Ved Vyas, Geeta Press, Gorakhpur.

Naga Vigil Human Rights Group Circulations.

Naga People's Movement for Human Rights (NPMHR)

Souvenir: Embracing Hopes and Dreams, Kohima, 2003.

Captured documents of the underground factions (GPRN/NNC).

B. SECONDARY SOURCES

Ahmed, Istiaq: *State, Nation and Ethnicity in Contemporary South Asia*, Pinter, London, 1996.

Allen, B.C.: *Gazetteer of Bengal & North East India,* Mittal Publications, New Delhi, 2001.

Anand, V.K.: *Nagaland in Transition,* Associate Publishing House, New Delhi, 1968.

Anderson, Benedict: *Imagined Countries: Reflection on the Origin and Spiral of Nationalisation,* Verso, London, 1983

Ao A.L.: *From Phizo to Muivah,* Mittal Publications, New Delhi,2002.

Ao. M. Alemchiba: *A Brief Historical Account of Nagaland,* Private Publication, Kohima, 1970.

Ao, Tajenyuba: *British Occupation of Naga Country,* Naga Literature Society, Mokukchung, Nagaland, 1993.

Aosenba: *The Naga Resistance Movement, Prospects of Peace and Armed Conflict,* Regency Publications, New Delhi, 2001.

Aram, Dr. M.: *Peace in Nagaland: Eight Years Story (1964-72),* Arnold Heineman Publishers (India) Private Limited, New Delhi-1974.

Bachler, Gunther: *Federalism Against Ethnicity, Institutional, Legal and Democratic Instruments to Prevent Violent Minority Conflicts,* Verla Rugger, Zurich, 1997.

Bantas, M.P.: *Ethnicity: Ethnic Groups, Michael MM's Encyclopedia of Sociology,* London, 1983.

Bendangangshi: *Glimpses of Naga History,* Sopungwati Ao, Mokokchung Town, Nagaland, Revised Edition, 2000.

Barua, (Rai Sahab) Golap Chandra: *Ahom Buranji: From the Earliest Time to the End of Ahom Rule,* Spectrum Publications, Guwahati, 1930. (Reprint 1985).

Bhaskar, Colonel (Retd) Sarkar: *Tackling Insurgency and Terror: Blue Print of Action,* Vision Books, New Delhi, 2001.

Bhatnagar, S.S. and Kumar. P.: *Regional Political Parties in India,* ESS & ESS, New Delhi, 1994.

Calvin, Goldscheider: *Population, Ethnicity and Nation Building,* West View Press, Colorado, USA, 1995.

Charles, Chasie: *The Naga Imbroglio: A Personal Perspective,* Standred Printers and Publications, Kohima.

Changkiri, Dr. Atola. L.: *The Angami Nagas and The British (1830-1947)*, Spectrum Publication, Guwahati, 1999.

Chaube S.K.: *Hill Politics in North East India*, Orient Longman, Reprinted Edition, 1999.

Chaudhary Prosenjit & Mehtabuddin Ahmed: *The Turbulent North East*, Aksher Publications, New Delhi, 1996.

Das. S.K.: *ULFA: A Political Analysis*, Ajanta, New Delhi, 1994.

Dev S.C.: *Nagaland, The Untold Story*, Kolkata, 1988.

Easton, David: *A System of Primitive Life*, John Wiley & Son, 1965.

Elwin, Verrier: *Nagaland*, Spectrum Publications, Guwahati, 1997.

Elwin, Verrier: *The Nagas in the Nineteenth Century*, Oxford University Press, 1969.

Erikson, T.H.: *Ethnicity and Nationalism, Anthropological Responsibilities*, London & Sterling, Pluto Press, 1993.

Gangte, T.S.: *Nehru & North East India*, S Chand & Company, New Delhi, 1991.

Ganguly, Milada: *A Pilgrimage to the Nagas*, Oxford & IBH Publishing Company, New Delhi, 1984.

Ghosh, B.B.: *History of Nagaland*, S Chand & Company, New Delhi, 1982.

Ghosh, P.S.: *Co-operation and Conflict in South Asia*, Manohar Publications, New Delhi, 1989.

Ghosh, Subir: *Frontier Travails*, Macmillan India Ltd, New Delhi 2001.

Gundevia, Y.D.: *War and Peace in Nagaland*, Palit & Palit, Dehradun and Delhi, 1975.

Hazarika, S.: *Strangers in the Mist*, Viking, New Delhi, 1994.

Hazarika, S.: *Bangladesh and Assam: Land Pressure, Migration and Ethnic Conflict*, Cambridge MA, 1993.

Hazarika, S.: *Rites to Passage*, Penguin (India), 2001.

Heimendorf, Fuerer Von Christopher: *Return to the Naked Nagas*, John Murray, London, 1976.

Horam, Dr. M.: *Naga Insurgency: The Last Thirty Years*, Cosmo Publications, New Delhi, 1988.

Horam, Dr. M.: *Naga Polity*, Low Price Publication, New Delhi, 1992.

Iralu. D. Kaka: *Nagaland and India, The Blood and the Tears*, Pvt Publication, 2000.

James, Sir Johnstone: *Manipur and The Naga Hills*, Manas Publications, New Delhi, 1987.

Jamir S.C.: *Speeches of SC Jamir, Chief Minister Nagaland, 1997 & 1999*, The Directorate Info and Public Relation, Govt of Nagaland, Kohima.

Joseph Athickal: *Maram Nagas: A Socio Cultural Study*, Mittal Publication, New Delhi, 1992.

Joshi Hargovind: *Nagaland: Past and Present*, Akanksha Publishing House, New Delhi, 2001.

Kanwar, Randip Singh: *The Nagas of Nagaland: Desperadoes and Heroes of Peace*, Deep & Deep Publications, New Delhi, 1987.

Kaviraj, Sudipla: *Crisis of the Nation-States in India: Political Studies*, Vol XLII, 1994.

Krishnan, Gopal R.: *Insurgent North Eastern Region of India*, Vikas Publishing Hose, New Delhi , 1995.

Krishna Rao, General K.V. (Retd): *Prepare or Perish: A Study of National Security*, Lancer Publishers, New Delhi, 1991.

Kumar, Narayan Ram & Murthy Laxmi: *Four Years of the Ceasefire*, Civil Society Initiative on the Naga Peace Process, B-14 (2nd Floor), Gulmohar Park, New Delhi, 2002.

Kupiainen, Jari et al. (ed): *Cultural Identity in Transition*, Atlantic Publishers, New Delhi, 2004.

Lampe, R. John: *Yugoslavia as History*, Cambridge University Press, 1996.

Lithui, Luingam & Nandita Haksar: *Nagaland File, A Question of Human Rights*, Lancer International, 1984.

Longchar, Dr. Purtongzuk: *Historical Development of the Ao Nagas in Nagaland*, Print House, Dimapur, 2002.

Mackenzie, Alexander: *The North East Frontier of India*, Reproduced Book from 1884 edition (History of the Relations of The Government with the Hills Tribes of the

North East Frontier of Bengal), Mittal Publications, New Delhi, 2001.

Maitra, K.S.: *The Rebel and Insurgency in the North East*, Vikas Publishing House, New Delhi, 1998.

Mankekar, D.R.: *On the Slippery Slopes in Nagaland*, PC Manektala & Sons, Mumbai, 1967.

Mao, Dr Daili Ashiko: *Nagas: Problems and Politics*, Ashish Publishing House, New Delhi, 1992.

Mar, Atsongcher: *Unforgettable Memories from Nagaland*, Tribal Communication and Research Centre, Mokukchung, Nagaland, 1994.

Martin, Von Creveld: *On Future War*, Brasseys, London, 1991.

Marwah, Ved: *Uncivil Wars: Pathology of Terrorism in India*, Harper Collins, New Delhi, 1995.

Mills, J.P.: *The Ao Nagas*, OUP Publications, 1973.

Mukherjee, Lt Gen (Retd) J.R.: *Insurgency in India's North East*, Anthem South Asian Studies, London, 2005.

Narhari, Lt Gen (Retd) N.S.: *Security Threat to North East India*, Manas Publications, New Delhi, 2002.

Nayar, Lt Gen (Retd) V.K.: *Threat From Within: India's Internal Security Environment*, Lancer Publications, New Delhi, 1992.

Nepram, Lakshmi Bina: *South Asian Fractured Frontiers*, Mittal Publications, New Delhi, 2002.

Nibedon, Nirmal: *North East India: The Ethnic Explosion*, Lancer Publications, New Delhi, 1981.

Nibedon, Nirmal: *Nights of the Guerillas*, Lancer Publications, New Delhi, 1992.

NNC Publications: *The Naga National Rights and Movement*, Kohima Nagaland 1st ed, 1993.

Nuh, V.K.: *Struggle for Identity in North East India: A Theological Response*, Spectrum Publications, Guwahati, 2001.

Nuh, V.K. (Compiler) & Wetshokhrolo Lasuh (ed): *The Naga Chronicle*, Regency Publication, New Delhi, 2002.

Pakem, B.: *Insurgency in North East India*, Lancer Publications, New Delhi, 1998.

Palit, Maj Gen (Retd) D.K., VrC: *Sentinels of North East: The Assam Rifles*, Palit & Palit Publications, New Delhi, 1984.

Phadnis, Urmila: *Ethnicity and Nation Building in South Asia*, Sage Publications, New Delhi 1989.

Phukan, Girin: *Politics of Regionalism in North East India*, Spectrum Publication, Guwahati, 1996.

Ram, Maj Gen (Retd) Samay: *Tackling Insurgency and Terrorism*, Manas Publications, New Delhi, 2002.

Ramunny, Murkot: *The World of Nagas*, Northern Book Centre, New Delhi, 1993.

Raza, Maroof: *Low Intensity Conflicts: The New Dimension to India's Military Commitments*, Kartikeya Publication, Meerut, India, 1995.

Roy, Shivani and Rizvi SHM: *Ethnic Diversities in India: In Search of Roots*, BR Publishing Corporation, 2003.

Sanyu, Visier: *A History of Nagas and Nagaland*, Common-Wealth Publications, New Delhi, 1996.

Sanajaoba, N.: *Human Rights in the New Millennium*, Manas Publications, New Delhi, 2000.

Scott, Michael Rev: *Nagas Problem, India's or World?* London, 1967.

Sema, Hokishe: *Emergence of Nagaland: Socio Economic and Political Transformation and Future*, Vikas Publishing House, New Delhi, 1986.

Sema, Dr. Piketo: *British Policy & Administration in Nagaland (1881-1947)*, Scholar Publishing House, New Delhi, 1992.

Sen, Sipra: *Tribes of Nagaland*, Mittal Publications, New Delhi, 1987.

Sengupta, Dipankar and Sudhir K. Singh (ed) *Insurgency in North East India*, Authors Press, New Delhi, 2004.

Sharma, Gokulesh: *Human Rights and Legal Remedies*, Deep & Deep Publications, New Delhi, 2003.

Singh, Chandrika: *Political Valuation of Nagaland*, Lancer Publications, New Delhi, 1981.

Singh, G.P.: *The Kiratas in Ancient India*, Gian Publishing House, New Delhi, 1990.

Smith, A.D.: *The Ethnic Revival,* Cambridge University Press, 1981.

Sonal, Capt Ashish, VrC: *Terrorism and Insurgency in India,* Lancer Publications, New Delhi, 1994.

Stack, John F. Jr (ed): *The Primordial Challenge: Ethnicity and Contemporary World,* Green Wood Press, London, 1986.

Symonides, J. (ed): *Human Rights: International Protection, Monitoring, Enforcement,* Ashgate Publishers, UNESCO, Hants, England, 2003.

Tarapot, Phanjoubam: *Insurgency Movement in North Eastern India,* Vikas Publishing House, New Delhi, 1993.

Tinoo, Ratna: *Indo Pakistan Relations: Politics of Divergence and Convergence,* National Publishing House, New Delhi, 1987.

Vashum, R.: *Indo Naga Conflict: Problem and Resolution,* Indian Social Institute, New Delhi, 2001.

Vashum, R.: *Nagas, Right to Self Determination,* Mittal Publications, New Delhi, 2000.

Varghese, B.G.: *India's North East Resurgent,* Konark Publication, 1996.

Index